The Public and the Schools

The Public and the Schools

Shaping the St. Louis System, 1838-1920

Selwyn K. Troen

University of Missouri Press
Columbia, 1975

Copyright © 1975 by
The Curators of the University of Missouri
Library of Congress Catalog Card Number 74–30075
Printed and bound in the United States of America
University of Missouri Press, Columbia, Missouri 65201

Library of Congress Cataloging in Publication Data

Troen, Selwyn K   1940–
     The public and the schools.

     Bibliography: p.
     Includes index.
     1. St. Louis—Schools—History. I. Title.
LA 318.S3T76   371'.009778'66   74–30075
ISBN 0–8262–0177–6

For Carol

Acknowledgments

Among the many satisfactions occasioned by the completion of this study is the opportunity to acknowledge publicly the assistance I have received from numerous individuals and institutions. Richard J. Storr aroused my interest in the history of education and by example and through instruction conveyed the excitement of the good question and the pleasure of scholarship. Richard C. Wade led me into urban history, directed the first stage of the study, found the means for its support, and gave continuing encouragement.

Thomas B. Alexander, a generous colleague and teacher, guided me into the mysteries of quantitative techniques. Stephan Thernstrom provided valuable counsel in the preparation of the occupational code. Carmel Mazzocco ensured that the computer produced intelligible results from my raw data. A year as a Visiting Fellow at the Shelby Cullom Davis Center for Historical Studies at Princeton University provided the freedom and resources necessary for completing the manuscript and a forum for testing my ideas. I am particularly grateful for the criticisms of Lawrence Stone, director of the Davis Center, and of Davis Seminar members David Allmendinger, Arthur Zilversmit, Howard Miller, James McLachlan, James McPherson, and Dorothy Ross. At various stages, I benefited from David Tyack's insights and critical advice.

Support for research came from the Center for Urban Studies at the University of Chicago, a Ford Foundation Dissertation Fellowship, and the University of Missouri Research Council. I received patient assistance from the staffs of the Mercantile Library, Central Verein, Municipal Reference Library and Missouri Historical Society in St. Louis, the St. Louis Public Library, the State Historical Society of Missouri in Columbia, and the libraries of Washington

University, St. Louis University, Notre Dame University, and the University of Missouri. Deborah Wahl, Peggy Lodes, James Worstell, Deborah Rothstein, Walter Kamphoefner, and Sandra Imhoff aided in research and the collection of data. Blanche Stashower not only assisted in the typing but was a source of encouragement and support.

My greatest debt is owed to my wife, Carol Rosenberg Troen. In addition to managing a happy and ever-expanding household and pursuing her own interests, she generously shared her energy, intelligence, and considerable talents. The dedication is offered her in gratitude and in recognition of the role she played in writing this book.

S.K.T.
Columbia, Missouri
January, 1975

Contents

List of Tables

x

The Public and the Schools

Introduction

The development of systems of public education was one of the great accomplishments of nineteenth century urban society. At the beginning of the century few cities supported public schools; by 1900 they were an accepted feature of urban life. Initially, they competed for the young with a number of other institutions. By midcentury public schools had become the chief educator of youth, demanding increasing commitments of time and money and generating hopes for social reform and individual betterment. Despite the enormity of this achievement and the significance that has been attached to it, much is still not known about how it was accomplished. Because of a traditional focus on the ideas of educators and of social philosophers, historians so far have neglected to analyse how ideas about education were translated into the building of schools. The result is an abundant superstructure of rhetoric without the support of a foundation in the social and political forces that shaped individual systems.

Case studies provide the best means of correcting this imbalance. Since the United States, unlike other western or modernizing nations, has never had a coherent national educational policy, the implementation of ideology and the management of schools have always been a local endeavor with prime responsibility in the hands of municipal and other local officials. Nevertheless, there has been widespread imitation because of a considerable interchange of personnel and ideas and because of similarities in problems and expectations. The reconstruction of the history of the St. Louis system, which commanded much national attention, not only informs us about schooling in a particular city but can illuminate developments and issues in the history of urban education.

Beginning with the superintendency of William Torrey

1

Harris (1868–1880), one of the most influential nineteenth-century educators, St. Louis schools attracted national interest and provided a model for other cities. Harris and his successor superintendents, as well as Susan Blow, an architect of the public school kindergarten, and Calvin Woodward, a founder of the manual training and comprehensive high school movements, were important innovators and highly articulate commentators on the promise and problems of urban education. The ideas and perceptions of these individuals are an important source for this study. Their writings are placed within the framework of social change and municipal politics, however, for these delimited the direction and boundaries of the system's work.

Two fundamental factors affected public education in St. Louis. First, St. Louis was one of the great boom towns of the nineteenth century. Founded by French merchant–explorers in 1764 just below the confluence of the Mississippi and Missouri rivers at the center of more than 5,000 miles of navigable waters, St. Louis was favored to play a major role in the development of the West and of the Mississippi Valley. Already a major frontier trading center in 1800, its greater destiny was fulfilled when the tide of western migration reached midcontinent and the technology of the steamboat was developed. For uncounted thousands St. Louis was the "gateway city" to the promise of the American West. For other thousands, it became a place to settle down and build a future. Large numbers of Virginians, Kentuckians, and New Englanders commingled in the bustling metropolis. They were joined by the Irish and especially Germans who gave a special ethnic cast to so many other midwestern cities. After the Civil War, St. Louis, which already had a significant black population, became a major beneficiary of the black exodus from the South. The flood of immigration was so great that by 1870 St. Louis was the nation's fourth largest city with a population of 310,864.

The economic development of the city is the second factor affecting the course of public education. The first settlers came because of the opportunities presented by geography.

Early fortunes were naturally based on the city's emergence as a fur-trading center; as a major outfitter for the military, trappers, and transient pioneers; and as the distributor of the rich lead deposits of southeast Missouri and upriver in Illinois and Wisconsin. By midcentury, entrepreneurs added an industrial base to this commercial activity providing the possibility of new wealth and a wide variety of employments for a multitude of workers. Access by inexpensive river transportation to cheap coal across the river in Illinois and to mineral resources throughout the vast hinterland resulted in the growth of foundries and machine shops that produced a host of articles from river boats to stoves. The same access to a rich agricultural hinterland led to the development of vast processing industries that made the city a major center for leather goods, especially shoes, beer, all manner of foods, chemicals, and clothing. Even with the passing of the steamboat St. Louis managed the transition to rails well enough to remain a major transportation nexus, superseded only by Chicago in the interior of the continent. Strength in commerce, manufacturing, transportation, and banking enabled the city to become the focal point for the wealth of a large area ranging from the middle Mississippi valley through the Southwest. In 1900, only New York, Chicago, and Philadelphia produced or earned more than St. Louis.

The heterogeneity of the population and the maturation of a successful commercial–industrial economy required the constant modification of the role and substance of education and of the way in which it was institutionalized. Between the opening of the first schools in 1838 and the beginning of the twentieth century when the familiar modern system emerged, there was not a static continuum but a dynamic period of reformulation and redefinition. In charting this transformation of the schools there are two broad categories of issues: analysing the composition of the student body and defining the nature of the curriculum. These are interrelated, for adjustments in the curriculum were usually connected with the incorporation or exclusion of a class or group. It is for this reason that the basic principle used in organizing this study has been the analysis of shifts in the composition of the student body.

By focusing on the different constituencies that the schools sought to serve, it becomes apparent that there were two distinct phases in the history of the system. Between the 1830s and the 1880s the major challenge was reconciling contending class, ethnic, sectarian, and racial interests within a system of publicly supported schools. By the end of the century, after the public schools had become the prime agent for mass instruction, the critical challenge was the extension of formal education to teenagers whose failure to attend became, for the first time, a major concern. Substantial alterations in educational politics, in the bureaucratic structure of the schools, and in the value the public placed on schooling accompanied this orientation. That these changes should have occurred was not foreordained in the schools' original mandate. Rather, they were consequences that flowed from the system's responses to changes in urban life, political pressures, educational theory, and the decisions of students and parents. When viewed in this context, the history of the school system becomes not only a study of an institution but a window through which to observe the society that shaped it.

1

The Importance of Free Schools: Reconciling the Claims of the Poor and the Rich

With the opening of two schools for 288 pupils in 1838, St. Louis joined the common school movement. From this modest beginning the system grew insistently until it comprehended about 80,000 pupils in elementary schools by 1900 and thousands more in high, evening, and normal schools. By mid-nineteenth century, public schools had become the educator of the majority of children, not only in St. Louis but throughout the country. While a sense of triumph filled both the builders of the system and the historians who witnessed this movement, their self-congratulations should not obscure the difficulties inherent in this undertaking. Many obstacles, some of which never have been successfully resolved, frustrated the effort to bring all children together for a common education in publicly supported institutions. The goal of implanting one system for all of the city's children was necessarily limited by the social tensions that aggravated urban life in general.[1]

1. The celebrationist character of the historiography of American education is analysed in Lawrence A. Cremin, *The Wonderful World of Ellwood Patterson Cubberley; An Essay on the Historiography of American Education* (New York: Bureau of Publications, Teachers College, Columbia University, 1965). Basic studies on the common schools include Lawrence A. Cremin, *The American Common School: An Historic Conception* (New York: Bureau of Publications, Teachers College, Columbia University, 1951); and Ruth Welter, *Popular Education and Democratic Thought in America* (New York: Columbia University Press, 1962). Recent studies offer a more critical and detailed analysis of individual urban school systems: Carl F. Kaestle, *The Evolution of an Urban School System: New York City, 1750–1850* (Cambridge: Harvard University Press, 1973); Michael B. Katz, *Class, Bureaucracy and Schools; The Illusion of Educational Change in America* (New York: Praeger, 1972); and Stanley K. Schultz, *The Culture Factory: Boston Public Schools, 1789–1860* (New York: Oxford University Press, 1973).

The issue that seemed most critical to the first generation of school supporters and which they first sought to resolve was the question of bringing together children of different classes for a common education.[2] Operating under a set of imperatives that were held by other antebellum reformers, they wished to democratize American society and safeguard republican institutions. Indeed, from Horace Mann to John Dewey through the present there is a persistent stream of thought arguing that schools can and should be a main support of a society that is envisaged in egalitarian terms. Mixing the children of different classes, however, was complicated by the reluctance of both the middle class and the poor to participate in so novel an undertaking. On the one hand, the middle class had to be persuaded to accept the innovation of public education and induced to depart from their tradition of patronizing private institutions. The poor, on the other hand, had to be reassured that free instruction was not being offered as charity. Achieving the participation of the poor was simpler because they had less choice. Incorporating the middle class was not only more difficult but more necessary, since only they could provide the political and financial support essential to the success of the system.[3] Compounding the difficulties facing educators was a limited amount of funds, which required making decisions that favored the interests of one group over the other. In St. Louis, these problems were exposed twice during the years from 1838 to 1865, as educators sought to make common schooling attractive and available to all: first, in the controversy over tuition charges and the introduction of the high school during the antebellum period; and second,

2. The significance of class has been explored best in Michael B. Katz, *The Irony of Early School Reform: Educational Innovation in Mid-Nineteenth Century Massachusetts* (Cambridge: Harvard University Press, 1969); Katz, *Class, Bureaucracy and Schools*; Kaestle, *The Evolution of an Urban School System*; and Schultz, *The Culture Factory*.

3. The subject of inequalities based on wealth is developing a significant literature. Two good studies are James B. Conant, *Slums and Suburbs* (New York: Signet Books, 1961), and Arthur Wise, *Rich Schools, Poor Schools: The Promise of Equal Educational Opportunity* (Chicago: University of Chicago Press, 1967).

in the debate over the reimposition of tuition during a financial crisis caused by the disruption of the Civil War. By the end of the war, one system for all classes was an established fact, but the public system had to pay a price to gain the involvement of the wealthy.

I

The public schools could have opened a quarter of a century earlier on an adequate basis of support. In the winter of 1812, Thomas Riddick, a clerk in the land claims office, traveled to Washington to appeal to the territorial delegate to Congress for legislation that would establish free education in the frontier community. Modeling his proposal on the Northwest Ordinance that applied to the more eastern and northern areas of the trans-Allegheny West, he succeeded in obtaining an act of Congress that set aside one-twentieth of the vacant lands of St. Louis "for the support of the schools." Riddick apparently acted on his own and without popular backing, for attempts to implement the law were greeted with indifference and even antagonism.[4]

Problems appeared soon after passage of the act. In 1813, attempts were made to survey the lands, a necessary first step in gaining control. This survey was frustrated by the efforts of speculators and opposing claimants.[5] In 1817, the Missouri territorial legislature granted a charter to a group of successful St. Louisans to manage the land grant. Auguste Chouteau, a founder of St. Louis; Alexander McNair, the future governor of Missouri; Thomas Hart Benton, the future senator from the state of Missouri; and four other accomplished men were incorporated into the Board of Trustees. However, these men, so successful in other endeavors, failed to manage and preserve the lands under

4. "Sketch of Edward Hempstead," *Steven Hempstead Papers* (Missouri Historical Society), p. 203.

5. *First Annual Report of the Superintendent of the St. Louis Public Schools for the Year Ending July 1, 1854* (St. Louis: George Knapp and Co., 1854), pp. 38 ff. Hereafter these volumes shall be called *Annual Reports*.

their trust. They also failed to heed the call of the city's first mayor, William Carr Lane, who in his 1823 message claimed "that a free school is more needed here than in any town of the same magnitude in the union."[6] They responded by resolving to make a plat of school lands. Whether or not they carried out their resolution is not known, for such a plat, if it ever existed, disappeared with any records the Board of Trustees may have generated.[7]

By 1833, the trustees' failures were so conspicuous that the state legislature established a new agency to manage the lands and oversee public education. In April they incorporated the "Board of President and Directors of the St. Louis Public Schools." Instead of a closed board of a few trustees, the entire white male population comprised the corporation. Within a year, elections were held and the first leases of school lands were made. With this revenue the board was able to open the first schools five years later. Twenty-six years had passed before the children of St. Louis had received any benefit from the land grant.[8]

The failure to introduce schools earlier was not peculiar to St. Louis. Even more established eastern cities like Boston, New York, and Philadelphia began building school systems only during the 1820s and 1830s. It was during this period that Americans responded to the imperatives of a new ideology, collectively forming the common school movement. Such currents reached Missouri on a state-wide level in 1832 with the election of Governor Daniel Dunklin, who restated the popular faith in education, proclaiming it "the best safeguard to our republican institutions, and the only rampart capable of resisting the approach of aristocracy." He initiated a series of commissions and bills that resulted in the Geyer Act of 1839, which became the state's fundamental educational law providing for schools from the local level to the university. The decision to exploit the generous patrimony that was established through Riddick's foresight was made in the context of a widespread enthusi-

6. *Missouri Republican*, January 5, 1878.
7. *Annual Report, 1854*, pp. 42–44.
8. *Annual Report, 1854*, pp. 46 ff.

asm for public schooling that extended from Massachusetts to Missouri and which found its most immediate expression in urban centers.[9]

Such belated action did not mean that cities lacked the means to educate children. From their beginnings, American cities had a wide variety of instructional institutions. For example, in 1642 the fundamental educational legislation of Massachusetts stipulated that the colony's towns must establish schools to counteract "the great neglect of many parents and masters in training their children in learning and labor." By the end of the century, scholarship and literacy were so widespread that Boston emerged, after London, as the second-largest publishing center in the British Empire, producing great quantities of religious and practical literature. By mid-eighteenth century, American cities had extensive and varied educational establishments. Philadelphia had perhaps the largest selection: sectarian elementary schools organized by Baptists, Moravians, Lutherans, German Reformed, and Quakers; academies and private institutions that taught mathematics, foreign languages, scientific subjects, and clerical skills; charity schools that instructed the children of the poor in basic literacy; evening schools for working girls offering a wide variety of subjects from arithmetic to psalmody; colleges that conducted courses in medicine, law, and higher learning; and numerous societies that offered lectures and provided a forum for discussion and popular education. Historian Carl Bridenbaugh has characterized colonial Philadelphia as "a literary republic," pointing to the wide diffusion of formal instruction if only on an elementary level.[10]

Although its programs were not so extensive or diverse as Philadelphia's, St. Louis also offered a variety of educational opportunities since its beginnings under the French and the Spanish. The first French classes were offered in the 1770s by Maria Josepha Rigauche for girls and John

9. David D. March, *The History of Missouri*, 1 (New York: Lewis Historical Publishing Company, 1967), 722–23.

10. Carl Bridenbaugh, *Rebels and Gentlemen: Philadelphia in the Age of Franklin* (New York: Oxford University Press, 1965), pp. 26–28.

Trudeau for boys. In 1808, George Tompkins, a young Virginian who later became the Chief Justice of the Supreme Court of Missouri, opened the first English school. Among the most popular sources of instruction were the schools opened by various orders of nuns and priests who taught the rich in academies and convents and the poor in mission schools. The most important effort was the first college in the trans-Mississippi West, Saint Louis University, which was founded by the Jesuits in 1819. There were also very successful private entrepreneurs who catered to the sons of the well-to-do. Among these, the most notable were Elihu Shepherd and Wayman Crow, who became active supporters of public education, serving for long periods on the school board even as they managed their own flowering institutions. As a measure of the importance of private schools, several of the public system's superintendents, including William T. Harris, John Tice, Louis Soldan, and Benjamin Blewett, as well as numerous principals and teachers, found employment in these institutions before joining the public system. In addition there were music, dancing, and fencing masters, with the latter of special importance for many of the city's young men who through the 1830s frequently duelled on Bloody Island, a small strip of land across from the city near the Illinois side of the Mississippi.[11]

Wealthy children were sometimes privately educated at home or sent outside the city. Bryan Mullanphy, one of the richest men in the antebellum period, sent most of his twelve children to Europe to complete their education after arranging for lessons at home. Similarly, Susan Blow, who opened the city's first kindergartens in 1873 and who was the daughter of a wealthy St. Louis family with a fortune in drugs and lead, was educated by imported tutors before finishing her studies on the continent. Others, such as the

11. Walter B. Stevens, *St. Louis: The Fourth City, 1764–1909,* 1 (St. Louis: Clarke Publishing Co., 1909), 879–915. Thomas J. Scharf, *History of St. Louis City and County,* 1 (Philadelphia: Lewis H. Everts, 1883), 823 ff.

sons of Charles Gratiot, an important urban landowner, went to western colleges such as Bardstown and Transylvania in Kentucky. In addition, West Point, Harvard, and Yale received a small if steady influx of St. Louis students.[12]

In this context, the introduction of municipally supported schools, especially those that would mix children of different classes, was a revolutionary idea. This was equally true for members of the middle class, who had been accustomed to educate their children either at home or in private schools but always at their own expense. Only the poor were traditionally dependent on public provisions or on acts of personal charity. In 1838, for example, several Catholic orphan asylums, a school in the basement of the Methodist Episcopal Church, and Unitarian-sponsored classes held in the Church of the Messiah were among the institutions that catered to the needs of the poor.[13] There existed therefore a tradition of education and a substantial establishment that challenged and hindered the introduction and development of common schools. The significance of these traditions is reflected in the decisions parents made in choosing schools. The census of 1840 records that only one in five or 266 out of about 1,200 scholars belonged to the public schools,[14] although it is probable that if more common schools had been available more children would have attended them. It is also probable that the students who would have attended the new institutions would have been drawn largely from the poor. Only during the mid-1850s, after much discussion and a redefinition of public schooling, did the balance turn in favor of the city system and did the middle class enter.

The primary problem was the popular identification of

12. Scharf, pp. 961–73, 1034–47.

13. The nature and size of early schools can be determined from city directories and newspaper accounts or advertisements. See Charles Keemle, *The St. Louis Directory for the Year 1840–41* (St. Louis: C. Keemle, 1840), p. 4. *Missouri Argus*, April 27, 1837. *Daily Evening Gazette*, January 3, 1839; January 15, 1840; December 11, 1840; July 30, 1840.

14. United States Census Office, *The Sixth Census: 1840*, 6, pp. 203–11.

public schooling with charity education. This connection was inscribed in Article VI of the Missouri Constitution of 1820, which spoke of encouraging education through the establishment of schools "where the poor shall be taught gratis."[15] Such attitudes were not peculiar to Missouri but were common throughout the country well into the nineteenth century. Neighboring Illinois, for example, did not remove the stigma of charity from its public schools until the mid-1850s. This was also true of St. Louis.[16]

In reviewing these early years, Superintendent John Tice explained in 1854 the difficulties caused by class attitudes:

> The Board commenced its labors with the prejudices of the community against the system of public education, who regarded it as the synonyme [sic] of pauper education, because in the middle, southern and western States, twenty-five years ago, public money was only paid for the education of those who were unable to pay; a system which is still retained in some of the southern States. The Board, therefore, had little or no sympathy to aid it or to cheer it onward.[17]

Tice also observed that even if people supported public education through contributions of money or land, or by advocating favorable legislation, they hesitated to send their own children to these schools. Many considered it "as revolting as a proposition would be of sending them to the country poor houses."[18] For example, one critic of a bill to establish a property tax to support the system argued that sufficient funds were already available, since the schools were only intended for "the poor children, who are recipi-

15. Claude A. Phillips, *A History of Education in Missouri: The Essential Facts Concerning the History and Organization of Missouri Schools* (Jefferson City: Hugh Stephens Printing Co., 1911), p. 26.

16. John Pulliam, "Changing Attitudes Toward the Public Schools in Illinois, 1825–1860," *History of Education Quarterly*, 7 (Summer 1967), 191–208. For a general discussion, see Paul Monroe, *Founding of the American Public School System: A History of Education in the United States from the Early Settlements to the Close of the Civil War Period*, 1 (New York: Macmillan Company, 1940), 295 ff.

17. *Annual Report, 1855*, pp. 68–69.

18. John Tice, "Education in Missouri," *Teachers and Western Educational Magazine*, 1 (May 1853), 130.

ents of this charity, granted to them by the citizens of St. Louis."[19]

The board's handling of tuition exposes the difficulties of dissociating schools from the stigma of charity. When the system opened in 1838, the board was so embarrassed by a lack of funds that it was forced to assess a charge on admission. Initially, $2.50 per quarter or $10.00 per annum was levied on each child who did not claim poverty. During the next ten years, this charge was progressively reduced to $1.50, $1.00, and $0.50 per quarter. In 1847, fees were finally abolished although students were expected to provide their own books and stationery, a practice that continued until 1893. The progressive abolition of fees was opposed by those who felt that this would confirm the charity characterization of the system. It was argued that such schools would "not be more respectable than the 'ragged schools' of European cities." In defense of such action, Superintendent Tice wrote that maintaining tuition was a mischievous policy that led to ambiguity and dissension. He saw that "invidious distinctions, bickerings and heartburnings" were created between paying and nonpaying students. This was intolerable, for in the minds of both parents and students two institutions, one charitable and the other private, shared the same space. Tice therefore believed that charging tuition was "a fatal error."[20]

The abolition of fees did not end the problem, and considerable propagandizing was necessary. In 1853, John Low, who became the first principal of the high school, tried to meet the issue in an essay, "Public Schools vs. Charity Schools," in St. Louis's short-lived educational review, *Teachers and Western Educational Magazine*. He believed that both rich and poor continued to withhold their children from public school because of the fear of injuring their pride through association with a charity institution. Typical of other advocates of common schools, he appealed to high sentiments, claiming that public schools "are the lifeblood of the nation; they are supported from a common treasury,

19. *Missouri Republican*, May 17, 1849.
20. *Annual Report, 1854*, pp. 60–61.

because the common welfare demands it, and each individual has a right to it."[21]

Taking a more practical approach, Tice recognized that the greater problem lay in allaying the fears of the more affluent than in assuaging the pride of the poor. He advised that "it is a mistake to suppose that the poor will press in and monopolize all the privileges of them [the schools]." He argued first, that the poor did not appreciate sufficiently the benefits of a free education and would not take advantage of them; second, that the economic situation of the poor militated against their spending much time in schools, even if they did desire to do so:

> The little mite that the child can earn, is of more importance to their poor families than fifty times the amount of tuition fees at select schools would be to the wealthy. The attendance at schools, though free of charge, therefore, is a heavy tax upon the poor, which they cannot bear; and therefore, there is no danger that our schools would ever be pauperized.

Tice tried to show that the abolition of fees was without "danger" since the poor did not inundate the schools and thereby compromise their respectability. This willingness to see the common school ideal compromised through acceptance of limited participation by the poor would find its institutional expression in the building of expensive and elaborate facilities for middle-class children, even though this clearly resulted in a lack of accommodations for others.[22]

Whatever the cost, Tice felt that he had no choice; he believed that no system at all was possible without participation by the rich. There were two fundamental reasons for this. First, Tice pointed out, the mere presence of the sons and daughters of the wealthy would finally end the system's taint of a charitable institution and would prove a powerful force in mitigating any sense of shame, not only among the poor but among the large class of people that

21. John D. Low, "Public Schools vs. Charity Schools," *Teachers and Western Educational Magazine*, 1 (October 1853), 253–56.
22. John Tice, p. 130.

lay between. This large intermediate group subsequently would increase their patronage, for they are people of "great pretensions" and tend to imitate the mores and fashions of their "betters." In addition, if the rich and the not-so-rich were so committed to this system that they were willing to send their own children and not merely provide lip service to a noble cause or abstract idea, the power and influence of these groups would ensure a high standard for schools as well as adequate financial resources.[23]

In order to attract this clientele, Tice judged that he first had to provide good instruction and attractive facilities. Addressing itself to the problem of teachers, the board made every effort to secure highly qualified individuals and at one point even sent Wayman Crow, one of the members of the board and head of the city's leading boys' academy, to Massachusetts to import the best possible personnel. Since this was not an efficient solution, the board acted on suggestions calling for a teacher-training course operated by and for the system, and in 1857 it established a normal school. Moreover, the construction of better buildings provided a visible sign of progress and respectability. During the 1840s and 1850s, the board was forced to locate classes in converted bars, basements, stores, and residences. Tice understood that parents who had a choice would prefer other alternatives even if the quality of instruction was acceptable. He accurately predicted, for example, that if "a good substantial school house" would supplant one that was in "wretched condition" then the citizens of the Second Ward, "who are heavy taxpayers," would send their children in far greater numbers.[24]

The single most important effort went into the erection of a high school in 1855, two years after this department was added to the system. This building, which cost $50,000 and was more extravagant than any of its kind outside of Boston and New York, provided the kind of instrument the board needed to establish firmly a common school system.

23. Ibid.
24. *Annual Report, 1855,* 63–64.

Tice claimed that the promise of this building was sufficient to bring about "a complete revolution in these Wards (Third, Fourth and Fifth) and have increased the demands for accommodations much beyond the means of the Board to supply them." These wards, "embracing as they do the wealthiest portions of the city," flooded the board with applications for admittance. Students from this area doubled their enrollment the following year, and even then 1,000 students could not be accommodated.[25] It is possible that a large influx would have occurred even without a high school, as the population of the city doubled during the 1850s from more than 75,000 to about 160,000. What is significant, however, is that Tice interpreted the acceptance of the wealthy as a result of the board's decision to introduce high school courses and house them in lavish quarters. He demonstrated the success of this strategy in the *Annual Reports'* tables on parental occupations, an indicator that was introduced in 1854 to measure the appeal of the system. During these years each superintendent and the president of the board took delight in showing that the St. Louis schools instructed the children of both laborers and lawyers, and mechanics and merchants. Typically, Samuel Bailey, the president in 1859, asked the readers of the *Annual Report* to see that "the supporters and patrons of the Public Schools are confined to no particular class or condition in society, but that all contribute to swell the number that are constantly pressing their claims to participate in the privileges."[26] By the outbreak of the Civil War, the taint of charity had been removed and the system had been made common.

The establishment of the high school, however, placed unbearable burdens on elementary education programs. It cost about twice as much to operate as any other school in the system.[27] The board spent $12,000 both on the high school, which had 380 students, and on the Franklin School,

25. *Annual Report, 1855,* pp. 62–63; *Annual Report, 1854,* p. 3.
26. *Annual Report, 1859,* p. 13.
27. *Missouri Republican,* August 15, 1857.

a large district school that accommodated 1,585. The Mound School, which had the same enrollment as the high school, cost $9,000 less, or one-fourth as much to sustain.[28] The discrepancies were so glaring that on occasion Tice felt compelled to defend board policy. For example, in defense of the $50,000 spent on the high school building Tice wrote that although "plainer houses will answer the purpose just as well," St. Louis should emulate such centers of civilization as Athens, which subordinated economy to the quest of the aesthetic perfection of the human spirit. Magnificent structures, Tice continued, are "an expression of the refinement, public spirit, and taste of the community."[29] Considering the hundreds and, in some years, the thousands who were literally turned away from the schoolhouse door in all portions of the city, the board was spending a great deal of money on relatively few students. It knowingly accepted a reduction in the total number enrolled in order to encourage the middle class to participate in the system.

As the board reached out for a broadly representative system in its aim to fulfill one aspect of the common school ideal, they were transforming another dimension of it. The district school curriculum was largely dedicated to teaching the three Rs, singing, and some geography during the eight-year course. This was consistent with the concept understood by most people of what constituted "common schooling," a notion that prevailed during the first years of the system and persisted well into midcentury. In the controversies that were to follow in the 1870s over the introduction of German, kindergarten teaching, and continued support of the high school, a significant body of opinion both in the newspapers and in court cases sought to affirm this basic curriculum as the only legitimate one for free, municipally supported schools.[30] Nevertheless, the board,

28. *Annual Report, 1860,* p. 60.
29. *Annual Report, 1855,* pp. 60–62.
30. The discussion of the appropriate curriculum for common schools forms a substantial portion of chapters 3 and 5. The major legal case was Roach v. The Board of President and Directors of the St. Louis Public Schools. *Missouri Reports,* 77, pp. 484–89.

apparently without legal challenge and popular opposition, decided in the 1850s that it could and must depart from this definition.

It lavished funds on a very different curriculum for a few hundred scholars who studied at its high school, offering diverse courses ranging from the ancient and modern languages, and from history to the natural sciences.[31] The board even considered establishing "Chairs of Chemistry and Natural Philosophy."[32] This nomenclature reflected both what was expected of the faculty and their backgrounds. They came from academies and leading eastern and midwestern universities. Moreover, when they left St. Louis it was often for positions in genuine universities. The special standing of high school teachers was also reflected in the pay schedules that made them, together with principals of the large district schools, the best-compensated members of the teaching corps. The quality of the high school was such that in its 1860 survey, "Schools of St. Louis," the *Missouri Republican* proclaimed that its curriculum was "equal to that pursued in many *colleges* in the Western country."[33]

The success of this collegiate institution—indeed, it was sometimes called the "People's College"—represents a fundamental alteration in the aim of public education.[34] By 1860, one could no longer identify public with charity education, not only in terms of students but with respect to subject matter. Free public schools were now committed to train a limited number of students in some sophisticated areas of knowledge. This transformation, however, would be tested during the Civil War, when financial pressures

31. *Annual Report, 1859*, p. xxxix.

32. "Proceedings of the Board of Public Schools, June 14, 1855," *Missouri Republican*, June 19, 1855. The proceedings of board meetings, hereafter referred to as PBPS, were not bound until 1871 and are located in newspapers previous to that time.

33. "PBPS, June 30, 1857," *Missouri Republican*, July 3, 1857; "Schools of St. Louis," July 5, 1858.

34. Scharf, p. 852. Charles D. Drake, *Address Delivered March 24, 1856 at the Dedication of the First Public High School Building Erected in the City of St. Louis* (St. Louis, 1856).

forced St. Louisans to reassess the changes of the 1850s and redefine the basic purposes of their schools.

II

The 1850s were boom years for St. Louis and its schools. The city more than doubled its population, becoming the eighth largest city in the country, and its schools grew from 1,800 places to more than 9,000. The most spectacular part of this growth took place in the latter half of the decade, when between 1,000 and 2,500 seats were added annually. In surveying the achievements of this period, the *Missouri Republican* editorialized that the "Free Public Schools of our city, now for the first time in their history, afford ample and suitable accommodations for the children of the people, that is to say, for as many of them as will be likely to apply for admission." Similarly, Superintendent Ira Divoll, who replaced John Tice in 1859, was so confident of the prosperity of the system that he predicted that if the expansion continued at the same rate, the schools should have more than 17,500 students in another five years, and 45,000 in ten.[35]

The outbreak of the Civil War on April 12, 1861, had an immediate impact on the schools. The war, which wrought havoc with the city's economy, induced social and political divisions, and even brought military conflict to the streets of St. Louis, abruptly destroyed the capacity of the schools to meet their obligations, let alone continue their expansion.[36] On April 9, seven days before the first shots were

35. "PBPS, May 15, 1858," *Missouri Republican*, May 19, 1858; January 30, 1860. *Annual Report, 1860*, p. 63; *Annual Report, 1867*, p. 128.

36. For the impact of the war on St. Louis see, Galusha Anderson, *The Story of a Border City During the Civil War* (Boston: Little, Brown and Co., 1908); William E. Parrish, *Turbulent Partnership: Missouri and the Union, 1861–1865* (Columbia: University of Missouri Press, 1963); Sceva B. Laughlin, "Missouri Politics During the War," *Missouri Historical Review*, 24 (October 1929), 87–113; Charles Harvey, "Missouri from 1849–1861," *Missouri Historical Review*, 2 (October 1907), 23–40.

fired on Fort Sumter, Superintendent Divoll had pointed with pride to the most recent quarter when the total enrollment of the day and evening classes approached 13,000 students, the highest mark in the system's history. At a special meeting on the day after the outbreak of war, the board announced that the schools would have to shut down within a week. This decision was precipitated by the state legislature's decision to divert monies from the State School Fund to purchase arms. Without this revenue, the board explained, they could not pay the teachers' salaries or operate the schools.[37]

The closing did not pass without protest. Critics claimed that the board's decision was an attempt to exaggerate the weakness of its financial condition and thereby reverse the legislature's planned diversion of funds. Furthermore, it was argued that even if the situation were as bad as alleged, the teachers would have been willing to work without compensation. Whatever the merit of this position, the schools did close when the flow of state money was terminated. Probably nothing the board could have said would have swayed the legislature. The pressures under which it operated were so great that the state panicked into taking money from everywhere to prepare for war. The urgency of the moment was captured in the title of the bill that forced the closing of the schools: "An Act to Raise Money to Arm the State, Repeal Invasion, and Protect the Life and Property of the People of Missouri."[38] Preparations for war necessarily took precedence over the education of children. Guns were more important than books.

The suspension of classes six weeks before the normal closing date was only a prelude to the greater difficulties that lay ahead. The war seriously disrupted the city's economy, which depended on river traffic and relied heavily on trade with the South, so that only about half of the rents due to the board were being collected. The loss of this income, together with the absence of state funding, meant

37. *Missouri Republican*, April 10, 1861; April 15, 1861.
38. *Missouri Republican*, May 19, 1861; May 21, 1861; May 22, 1861.

that some parts of the system would have to be curtailed. The question was what to eliminate. To explore this problem the board established the Special Committee on the Organization and Support of the Schools, which reported in mid-August a few weeks before the normal resumption of classes.[39]

The majority's position, which was adopted by the full board, advised that since there would be a large deficit, "special regulations" would have to be in effect for the coming year. They recommended that all administrators and teachers accept a pay reduction of 27 per cent and that tuition be reimposed at the rate of $1.50 per quarter in the district schools and $7.00 in the high school and Normal School. Through these reductions and the generation of new revenue, the report argued, two major goals could be accomplished: keeping the system intact and maintaining classes for the usual forty weeks.

The minority appreciated the board's financial difficulties but recommended a different allocation of money. Fundamentally, the minority asked the board to discriminate in favor of the poor. Recognizing that some sort of tuition would be necessary, they wanted it low enough that it would not keep children of indigent families from attending school. In addition, they feared that if faced with the prospect of paying a fee many of the "foreign population" would be encouraged to send their children to places where the parents' native language was taught, referring to private German schools, and that other parents would choose to send their children to church-related institutions. Therefore, they proposed that the high and normal schools be made self-supporting and that all other monies be allocated to district schools. In effect, there was little difference between the two positions when these objectives were translated into specific tuition charges. Rather than the $1.50 per quarter that the majority proposed, the minority suggested $1.25. The difference for the high school and normal school was somewhat more substantial as the minority advised raising the charge from $7.00 to $10.00 per quarter.

39. *Missouri Republican*, August 17, 1861.

The significance of the minority report was its realistic appreciation of the class nature of school attendance. It assumed that high school students, who were generally from comfortable backgrounds, could bear tuition charges better than district school students who were from all classes. Understanding that the board's financial embarrassment chiefly threatened the poor, it concluded with the proposal that each school director be permitted to admit, free of charge, any child whom he judged unable to pay. This practice was partially accepted but offered only limited relief in the difficult times ahead.

The majority of the board and much of the community dismissed the minority's dark warnings. The *Missouri Republican* simply denied that the tuition arrangements would be a burden, claiming that the $1.50 was "but a trifle." Continuing in the vein of blind optimism, the paper editorialized that because of the difficulties of the times, large numbers of children would be withdrawn from private schools and placed in public institutions, since they were cheaper and superior.[40] Superintendent Divoll also prophesied that the general financial difficulties of the community would work to the district school's advantage, since their tuition was from one-fourth to one-third that of private institutions.[41] In sum, there were expectations that the present difficulties would work to the system's advantage by completing the process of bringing middle-class children into the schools to swell enrollment.

That these hopes failed to materialize is indicated by comparing the attendance figures of 1860–1861 with those of 1861–1862. In the earlier year 12,166 were enrolled, with 8,098 the average daily attendance. One year later this high dipped to 5,787 enrolled, and 3,654 attending. Not since 1857 had so few students made use of the public schools.[42] It was as if the reforms, expenditures, and efforts of the past five years had been wiped out at a single blow. The magnitude of the reversal was revealed immediately at the

40. Ibid.
41. *Missouri Republican*, August 28, 1861.
42. *Annual Report, 1865*, p. 47.

beginning of the 1861–1862 term. Only 3,000 students had registered by the end of the first week, as compared with 8,000 in the previous year. The newspapers tried to forestall a debacle by advertising the superior advantages of the public system. One promotional piece trumpeted the district schools as "the best appointed schools in the country. They are the pride and ornament of our city."[43]

Despite such appeals, registration improved only slowly and unsatisfactorily. As a result, many district schools were closed or put to other purposes. For example, the Madison, Clark, and Carr schools shut their doors and their pupils were transferred. The Mound School, one of the city's oldest, was converted into a church. The Carroll School became a private institution until the number of paying pupils reached forty, when it was readmitted into the system. In the Jackson School, which was used as a headquarters for a gang, twenty pikes were discovered during cleaning operations the following summer. While some schools became churches, private institutions, or gang armories, many others remained empty or only partially used, resulting in 5,500 empty places in 1861–1862, and 3,500 the following year. Thus, between 1861 and 1863, for the first and only time, the number of seats declined and additional thousands remained unused.[44]

In the face of these difficulties the board rejected several suggestions that might have boosted enrollment. In one instance, it turned down the petition of a group of citizens who requested monthly payments, or $0.50 installments, rather than quarterly payments.[45] The board did resolve that "orphans who are unable to pay, the children of indigent widows, and the children of indigent parents who are invalids, be admitted to the Public Schools free of charge." The resolution, however, was amended to provide that the children admitted under this new rule "shall, in no case, so far increase the number of pupils in any school as to cause

43. *Missouri Republican*, September 10, 1861.
44. *Missouri Republican*, October 12, 1861; May 16, 1862; April 11, 1862; July 12, 1862. *Annual Report, 1865*, p. 47.
45. *Missouri Republican*, August 17, 1861.

additional expense to its maintenance." Moreover, the board advised that children with one living parent would not be considered "orphans."[46] Consequently, its new regulations had very little impact. Only 384 "free permits" were issued during the year.[47] The plight of the thousands of children who were half-orphans or who had poor but healthy parents was not relieved, as the board remained steadfast in its commitment to financial integrity and efficient management.

Table 1. Changes in School Attendance in District Schools, 1860–1861, 1861–1862, by Percentage and Number of Students*

Occupations	Unskilled labor	Skilled labor	Clerk & minor white collar	Businessmen & managers	Professionals	Unclassified	Total number
1860–1861 (Number)	24 (2,807)	31 (3,662)	8 (899)	22 (2,608)	3 (401)	12 (1,391)	(11,?
1861–1862	17 (941)	22 (1,197)	11 (612)	27 (1,472)	5 (262)	19 (1,036)	(5,?
Students lost 1860–1862	−66 (−1,866)	−67 (−2,465)	−32 (−287)	−42 (−1,136)	−35 (−139)	−26 (−355)	(−6,?
Percentage of total number lost (−6,248)	30	39	5	18	2	6	

* See Appendix A for source of data.

At the end of the first year of crisis, the board was forced to admit that its policies had resulted in the exclusion of

46. *Annual Report, 1862*, p. 56.
47. *Missouri Republican*, May 15, 1862. An alternate explanation for the decline in enrollments during this year might be that St. Louis lost population and that the number of possible students declined. There is no evidence to support this. On the contrary, it is possible that people came to the city for safety, and the population may have actually increased. Moreover, here the board saw the problem in terms of tuition, and in the sections that follow it is clear that the board never viewed the attendance problem in any other terms. In this same report, for example, the board estimated that 5,000 children could not afford tuition.

thousands of children, amounting to a 47 per cent reduction in enrollment in but one year.[48] An analysis of its records gives definition to the extent that different segments of the community suffered. Table 1 shows that children of blue-collar workers, unskilled and skilled laborers, were affected the most, losing about two-thirds of the number they sent to the district schools in the year previous and accounting for 69 per cent of the total decrease in the school population. Tuition was also important for white-collar workers—clerks, businessmen, and professionals—because they suffered a 40 per cent decline but accounted for only 25 per cent of the decrease. Thus, tuition was a burden for all groups, not just the lower classes, although it was significantly heavier for them. Moreover, it was the special hardship imposed on working-class children on whom critics of the board's policy focused. Given the fact that only about 3 per cent of the enrollment in a normal year consisted of high school students and that many thousands of children were left out, it is no wonder that critics demanded the total concentration of the system's resources on the district schools.[49]

While the district schools were weakened, the high school continued relatively unchanged. Although its enrollment dropped from 301 in 1859–1860 to 230 during the first year of crisis, it nearly regained these losses the following year with 297 students. Nevertheless, Charles Childs, the principal of the high school, felt compelled to explain why the early expectations of a dramatic rise in enrollment had proved to be false. He pointed out that many potential students were drawn into the labor market because of an increased demand for manpower caused by army recruiting. Neither he nor anyone else complained that charging tuition caused the lack of expansion. On the contrary, he was quite content with the condition of the school and attributed its stability to "the public confidence which its long course of efficiency has inspired, and on the ability, diligence and

48. Ibid.
49. See Appendix A for the data and assumptions underlying this analysis.

perseverance of the corps of assistants upon whom the burden of its teaching now rests." Superintendent Divoll was so confident that it would operate at capacity that he warned the public not to expect any relaxation of standards. He concluded a special advertisement before the opening of schools in 1862 with the advice "that the meritorious only need apply." Both Childs and Divoll recognized that there was a sizable segment of the community that sought quality education and would pay for it. They were surprised, however, that the public schools did not receive a greater share. The competition was keen, as evidenced by the fact that on the same day the *Missouri Republican* discussed the reopening of schools, it carried twenty-seven advertisements from private schools and academies from Missouri and as distant as Indiana and Ohio.[50]

While the financial crisis did not significantly affect the high school, it had immediately harmful effects on the normal school. Newly established in 1857 to provide teachers for a rapidly expanding system, this school suffered a loss of more than 50 per cent or a decrease from eighty to thirty-eight students in the first year of the war. Not until 1866 would the number attain prewar levels.[51] Divoll expected tuition to bring about a decline, since those "who avail themselves of the privileges afforded by this school are principally drawn from the humbler walks of life."[52] Another, and perhaps more important, reason that he apparently did not appreciate was the undesirability of a teaching career during these years. Fewer students decreased the demand for teachers. In 1860–1861 there were 181 teachers but only 76, 111, and 162 were employed in the following three years. For the first time in the history of the system there was an oversupply of teachers.[53]

Insecurity was still another factor that must have entered into the thinking of anyone who considered entering the

50. *Annual Report, 1866,* p. 24; *Annual Report, 1864,* p. 28. *Missouri Republican,* August 28, 1862.

51. Statistics on the normal school are located in *Annual Report, 1863,* p. 49; *Annual Report, 1865,* p. 42; *Annual Report, 1866,* p. 27.

52. *Annual Report, 1862,* p. 46.

53. *Annual Report, 1867,* p. 128.

normal school. Between 1861 and 1863 the board was notoriously irregular in the payment of salaries. William T. Harris, the future superintendent but at this period principal of a district school, wrote his uncle that the board's difficulties required that he wait more than three months before receiving his salary. In June, 1862, when the board made assignments for the following year, it warned that if there were not enough pupils, it would not be responsible for maintaining the appointment. Furthermore, even if the pupils did enroll, teachers were advised that they would be paid only if the board had enough money. At least in one case, when it could not pay, a principal took matters into his own hands by retaining a portion of the tuition money he had collected. Finally, even when salaries were paid, they were at their lowest level since 1857. In view of the diminished demand for teachers and the precariousness of the profession, it is not surprising that the normal school suffered a temporary decline. Its prosperity was directly connected to the condition of the system as a whole.[54]

After the severe losses of 1861–1862, the board established another special committee to evaluate its actions and suggest procedures for the coming year. This time it clearly understood the impact of tuition, and its decisions would be made on the basis of knowledge, not surmise. The result was a move to end tuition so that the schools might regain the lost students. This recommendation was, in effect, overruled by the Ways and Means Committee, which felt that the system was still financially unsound. The committee, moreover, rejected suggestions that the board borrow money to fulfill its obligations to the city's children on the basis that this was too adventurous a course to take in uncertain times.[55]

The dilemma was one to which there was no completely satisfying solution. On the one hand, the directors were responsible for maintaining the financial integrity of the

54. William Torrey Harris to Dr. Peckham, June 26, 1861, *William T. Harris MSS*, folder 1, Missouri Historical Society. *Missouri Republican*, June 27, 1862; January 12, 1863; August 15, 1862.

55. *Missouri Republican*, July 11, 1862; August 15, 1862.

schools, and, on the other hand, they felt compelled to provide free education for the public. Even though these goals seemed mutually exclusive, a wide latitude of choice still existed in deciding how to effect a compromise. The majority considered that their primary obligation was to preserve the institutional framework of the system. This meant that the district school system, the high school, and the normal school must all be kept operational. They knew that if they reverted to free education, the district schools would be inundated with children. Since supporting these would compromise the existence of the upper schools, the majority reluctantly decided to continue tuition for the lower schools, although at a reduced rate. A minority on the board continued to oppose this decision, arguing that "the spirit of the charter demands support of our common schools, and all our revenue in the present embarrassed state of our finances should most certainly be devoted to that object alone." They viewed the high and normal schools as extravagances that could be dispensed with. Insisting that elementary education was their authentic and sole concern, the minority demanded that the board return to original purposes.[56]

These factions were in effect contesting the definition of the basic character and mission of public education. Was the school system essentially a publicly supported, supercharity school for teaching the three Rs as it had been in the early years of its history? Or had the inclusion of the middle class and the extension of responsibilities undertaken in the prosperous and expansive 1850s permanently transformed public education? Over the objections of a minority, the board chose to maintain the structure of the 1850s with the full understanding of what this would mean to the city's children, particularly the poor. While waiting for the financial crisis to pass, they took solace in asserting: "The system has been preserved."

By the summer of 1863, the worst was over. At a meeting in July, the directors voted to reinstitute free education for

56. Ibid.

the district schools while maintaining the $7 per quarter rate for the high and normal schools. The usually cautious board took this action on the expectation that the State School Fund would be reactivated, and income from rents would rise substantially. They even restored a small part of the reduction that had been made in teachers' salaries. In the end of August and the beginning of September, newspapers carried notices advertising the opening of twenty-two large schoolhouses with places for 9,000 children. Announcement was made also of the reintroduction of the special courses in drawing and music that had been curtailed in the district schools during the period of financial stringency. Optimism about finances increased to such an extent that free permits were extended to the high and normal schools, just as their usefulness for the lower grades was ended.[57]

The restoration of free elementary education was greeted with enthusiasm. The *Missouri Republican,* which two years earlier had called $1.50 per quarter a "trifle," recanted by editorializing on the significance of the occasion. The newspaper observed that "the announcement of no tuition in the district schools will give great satisfaction to the community; for it is undeniable that the tuition fee, small as it was, which the board felt obligated to charge during the past two years, kept many children away from the schools." The editorial went on to say that "under the present arrangement there will be no excuse for any [child] to stay away at least not until the public schools are filled."[58]

This time the *Missouri Republican* was correct. The children came, and they filled the schools. On the first day of classes, 2,000 more young scholars presented themselves than on any other opening day in previous history. Some schools were even filled by the end of the first hour. For the first time in several years, students had so exceeded the seating capacity of the schools that the directors discussed renting rooms and building new schoolhouses. Because of

57. Ibid., July 21, 1863; August 27, 1863.
58. *Missouri Republican,* August 27, 1863.

the "extraordinary filling up of the schools" new appointments were made. The drought was beginning to end for the teachers as well.[59]

By the fall of 1864, when the income of the board had sufficiently increased, tuition was eliminated in the upper schools. With the reestablishment of a totally free system, the pre-Civil War problem of matching the supply of accommodations with the demand for free schooling became a dominant concern. Once financial integrity had been restored, the board confronted these pressures and rededicated itself to the principle that became the legend on many official publications: "Schools should be free and ample for all who wish to attend them."[60]

59. *Missouri Republican*, September 12, 1863; October 16, 1863.

60. *Annual Report, 1865*, pp. 30–31. There is a subtle change in emphasis in this statement from one made three years earlier. In 1862, the board declared: "The great American doctrine on the subject of public instruction is this: *The Public schools shall be made good, and ample and free for all.*" The emphasis in 1865 is solely on having enough places for those who want a free education. See, *Annual Report, 1862*, p. 64.

2

A Conflict of Purposes: Parochial Needs versus a Public Vision

A substantial number of St. Louisans never shared the vision of a common schooling for the city's children. Irreconcilable differences between public and parochial educators inevitably led to the development of competing school systems. Common school advocates were concerned about the disintegration of a relatively stable and homogeneous society through the influx of millions of non-Protestant and non-English immigrants. Witnessing the appearance of the divisive politics of nativism and the outbreak of municipal rioting that produced the most violent epoch in the history of urban America, not excepting the present, they sought through assimilation in common schools to reassert public order and encourage mutual trust. Moreover, by training the masses in such virtues as honesty and self-discipline, supporters of common schools hoped to generate the moral renewal of society. This social and moral vision was unacceptable to many newcomers who were proud of their traditions and reluctant to abandon them in an alien and often hostile culture and to those who objected to transferring the responsibility for moral instruction from organized religion to a secular agency.[1] In St. Louis, both

1. My understanding of this topic has been influenced by recent writings that emphasize the anti-Catholic bias of public educators and their use of schools as instruments of social control. See David B. Tyack, "Onward Christian Soldiers; Religion in the American Common School," in Paul Nash, ed., *History and Education: The Educational Uses of the Past* (New York: Random House, 1970), pp. 212–15; Lloyd P. Jorgenson, "The Birth of a Tradition; Historical Origins of Non-Sectarian Schools," *Phi Delta Kappan*, 44 (June 1963), 407–14; Charles Bidwell, "The Moral Significance of the Common School: A Sociological Study of Common Patterns of Social Control and Moral Education in Massachusetts and New York, 1837–1840," *History of Education Quarterly*, 6 (Fall 1966), 50–91; and Timothy Smith, "Protestant Schooling and American Nationality, 1800–1850," *Journal of American History*, 53 (March 1967), 679–95.

ethnic and religious factors combined to cause German-speaking Catholics and Lutherans, who came in large numbers beginning in the 1830s, to build educational institutions independent of the public schools, thereby foreclosing the possibility of establishing a genuine common school system.[2]

Public educators, however, distinguished the problems of ethnicity from those of religion and devised different strategies for dealing with each. In the case of the Germans, who were the largest non-English-speaking group, assimilation into public schools was accomplished by special provisions for language instruction from the 1860s to the 1880s. The question of sectarianism was not so easily resolved, however, and concerns us here.[3]

Until the purchase of the Louisiana Territory by the United States in 1803, French and Spanish Catholics governed St. Louis and made the city into a commercial and religious outpost. It was therefore natural that St. Louis became the missionary and educational center for much of the American West, earning the title of "the Baltimore of the West."[4] In the three decades before the opening of

2. General accounts of Catholic and Lutheran schools in St. Louis include John Rothensteiner, *History of the Archdiocese of St. Louis in its Various Stages of Development from A.D. 1763 to A.D. 1928* (St. Louis: Blackwell Wielandy Co., 1928); J. A. Burns, *The Catholic School System in the United States: Its Principles, Origin, and Establishment* (New York: Benziger, 1908); Walter Bek, *Lutheran Elementary Schools in the United States: A History of the Development of Parochial Schools and Synodical Educational Practices and Programs* (St. Louis: Concordia Publishing House, 1939); Walter O. Forster, *Zion on the Mississippi: The Settlement of the Saxon Lutherans in Missouri 1839–1841* (St. Louis: Concordia Publishing, 1953); August R. Suelflow, *The Heart of Missouri: A History of the Western District of the Lutheran Church—Missouri Synod 1854–1954* (St. Louis: Concordia Publishing, 1954); and August C. Stellhorn, *Schools of the Lutheran Church—Missouri Synod* (St. Louis: Concordia Publishing, 1963).

3. Ethnic issues and the language question are discussed in Chapter 3.

4. Floyd Calvin Shoemaker, *Missouri and Missourians: Land of Contrasts and People of Achievements* (Chicago: Lewis Publishing Co., 1943), p. 322. J. A. Burns, E. J. Kohlbrenner, and J. D. Peterson, *A History of Catholic Education in the United States* (New York: Benziger, 1937), pp. 91 ff.

public schools, the archdiocese had already founded orphan asylums, parochial schools, seminaries, and Saint Louis University, the first college west of the Mississippi. Although there are no attendance records on a regular basis, it is clear that Catholic schools were educating more children than the city system until 1850, when both instructed about 2,500 pupils.[5]

German Lutherans also established their own schools although on a far smaller scale. From the late 1830s, many of the Lutherans who left Germany for the United States settled in the middle West, particularly in and around St. Louis. Among them was Carl Friedrich Walther, a leading figure in nineteenth-century Lutheranism, who came from Saxony in 1840. Within a few days of his arrival, Walther reaffirmed a practice that began in Germany and was even maintained on board ships carrying Lutheran communities across the Atlantic. He reestablished the rule that *Schulamt* (teaching office) and *Predigtamt* (preaching office) be founded concurrently. With this emphasis on church-sponsored education, the Missouri Synod, which included several midwestern states, counted 55 congregations, 50 schools, and 1,734 pupils in 1850. By 1860, there were 125 congregations, 179 schools, and 11,653 students. While it is difficult to obtain figures for St. Louis alone, a sense of the presence of their schools is indicated by a parade of the Lutheran community through the city streets in 1855 that included pupils of five parish schools marching in honor of the three hundredth anniversary of the Treaty of Augsburg. Growing steadily if slowly, there were about 2,000 students in St. Louis parish schools around the turn of the century. Apparently, the majority of Lutherans opted for a combination of Sunday School instruction and public education.[6] The same was true of Jews, who only intermittently supported a Hebrew day school.[7]

5. *Missouri Republican*, January 26, 1852.

6. Bek, pp. 104–5, 117. *Missouri Republican*, September 27, 1855. Thomas Graebner, *The Lutheran Church Guide of St. Louis, Missouri* (St. Louis: Concordia Seminary, 1916), pp. 166–67.

7. A survey of city directories from the 1830s through 1900 shows that only occasionally was there even one Hebrew day school. Jewish

Parochial education was primarily a Catholic enterprise. In 1860, for example, with the exception of four Evangelical Lutheran and one Hebrew school, the remaining forty-eight parochial schools listed in the city directory were Catholic. These institutions enrolled about 7,000 students or almost three times as many as in 1850, when public and Catholic schools were approximately equal. By 1860, however, there were 5,000 more students in the city system. Beginning in the 1850s, Catholic schools grew more slowly, and their share of the total student population found in both systems declined steadily until 1880, when only about 20 per cent chose parish schools. This proportion remained stable for the next forty years as both systems enjoyed the same rates of growth.

Table 2. Enrollments in Public and Catholic Parochial Schools, 1850–1920*

	Parochial schools	Public schools	Total, parochial & public	Percentage of total in parochial
1850	2,488	2,570	5,058	49.1
1860	6,972	12,166	19,138	36.5
1870	9,362	24,347	33,709	27.7
1880	12,341	51,241	63,582	19.4
1890	14,772	58,316	73,088	20.3
1900	17,179	78,263	95,442	18.0
1910	21,296	87,931	109,227	19.4
1920	26,753	106,991	133,743	20.0

* Source: For the public schools, see *Annual Report, 1859*, p. lxix; *Annual Report, 1870*, p. 32; and *Annual Report, 1920*, p. 249. For Catholic parochial schools, see the *Catholic Directory* for each year.

The continued expansion of Catholic schools cannot be attributed solely to the desire of the clergy to maintain the traditional interests and prerogatives of the Church. It also stemmed from the needs and initiative of the immigrants themselves. At an 1860 meeting of the *Central Verein*, a

---

education was apparently conducted in conjunction with synagogues and was supplementary to public schooling.

benevolent association of lay German–Catholics, its officers described the conditions that prompted them to work for independent charitable, religious, and educational institutions:

> Transplanted from our native soil to a foreign country, most of us experienced hardships. Although America offered for many of us better living conditions and better opportunities than the poor homeland, we found ourselves in a strange land with a different language and different customs, and homesickness and uncertainty were our companions. In the old environment we had been living in a world familiar to us and which, in turn, knew us; our surroundings, in fact, were part of our very existence. . . . Here, everything was different. . . . [8]

In addition to the subtler threats of strangeness and isolation, there were more direct and even physical dangers that came from nativists, including the Know Nothingism of the antebellum period, the American Protective Association of the turn of the century, and the resurgence of the Ku Klux Klan after World War I. It was natural for them, therefore, to turn inward. As Oscar Handlin has written of Boston's Irish in the nineteenth century, the St. Louis German community strengthened ethnic and religious traditions and became even more conservative perhaps than coreligionists in the old world. Thus, schools as well as clubs, societies, and churches enabled the immigrants to protect and reaffirm a cherished culture that sustained them in an alien land.[9]

The history of Saint Boniface Parish in Carondelet, an independent suburb incorporated into St. Louis in 1871, typi-

---

8. *Official Program: Centennial Convention of the Catholic Central Verein of America* (Rochester, N.Y.: 1955), pp. 44–45. Also see *62te General-Versammlung des Deutschen Romisch-Katholischen Central-Verein* (St. Louis: n.d.). Histories of the Central Verein are found in official programs located in the libraries of the Central Verein (St. Louis) and the University of Notre Dame.

9. Oscar Handlin, *Boston's Immigrants 1790–1880* (New York: Atheneum, 1968), pp. 151–77. This theme is also emphasized by the official historians of the Catholic and Lutheran schools. See, Burns, Kohlbrenner, and Peterson, pp. 115 ff. Bek, p. 2.

fies the way in which immigrants organized. In the late 1850s, a small group of German-Catholic newcomers joined with Irish and French Catholics who had settled the area earlier. Although they worshipped together for a time, the Germans grew restive. As the parish historian explained: "Strangers to the land and alien to its people, they did not feel at home in a church in which their language was not spoken or even understood." In 1860, the Germans decided to separate and successfully appealed to the city's Catholics, especially the Germans, for support in building another congregation that became Saint Boniface Parish. By means of the participation of outsiders in suppers, parties, and other social events, the small community managed to raise the funds to purchase land and initiate the construction of a church. The dedication of the church was a popular event witnessed by thousands of visitors, including a band and a contingent of marchers from a Catholic temperance society.[10]

The congregation had established its parish school even before the building was completed. Originally it served eighty children, though with very primitive facilities and inferior instructors. The teaching was so poor and lack of discipline so rampant that in 1861 the first directive of the new parish priest was to discharge the teachers and declare a school vacation until new instructors could be located. He solved this problem in the traditional manner—by inviting an order of nuns who had recently arrived from Germany and temporarily located in Milwaukee to reside in the parish and teach the young. With the staff organized, they set about raising money for a proper building since the classes had to meet in various locations in the church, usually the basement and kitchen. In addition to social events and lotteries, Saint Boniface's congregation adopted the novel technique of issuing shares of $25 each for the "School Building Fund of St. Boniface School Congregation." Over $5,000 was raised through these shares, which

10. *Saint Boniface Parish: The Record of the Growth of a Mustard Seed* (St. Louis: 1935), pp. 5, 33–40.

were redeemable over a ten-year period. Significantly, they were printed in German, the business as well as the social and religious language of the community. Social events and lotteries supplemented what was raised by tuition.[11]

The basic features of Saint Boniface's establishment and development characterized many other parishes: A small group of immigrants formed a congregation, often splitting off from a larger community for ethnic reasons; added to their own meager resources the contributions of sympathetic parties; imported professional help from newly established seminaries or even from the homeland; and established a school either concurrent with the erection of a church or, quite often, preceding it. The motto of more than one parish was: "The School first, then the Church."[12]

The recruitment of teachers bears some elaboration for it reveals the close connection between these schools and the homeland. Just as the public schools were forced to send a representative back to Massachusetts to obtain teachers from the birthplace and spiritual homeland of many of the founders, these communities imported many of their teachers from Europe.[13] In 1848, a year before the board dispatched one of its members to Massachusetts, Archbishop Peter Kenrick sent his Vicar General, Father Joseph Melcher, to search in Europe for priests and colonies of teaching sisters to assist in educating St. Louis's Catholics. The trip was successful and a group of Ursuline nuns came to engage in parish work and to establish a boarding school and a convent. In support of their work, King Louis of Bavaria donated $4,000, demonstrating the strong ties that existed between the Fatherland and the new Germanic colonies across the ocean. Within ten years, the Ursulines were so successful that, using St. Louis as a base, they estab-

11. Ibid.
12. These form the consistent themes in about forty parish histories, usually written to celebrate the fiftieth, seventy-fifth or hundredth anniversary of parish foundings. These histories are found in the libraries of the Central Verein (St. Louis), Saint Louis University, and the University of Notre Dame.
13. *Annual Report, 1854*, pp. 62, 73.

lished other communities throughout the Midwest and even in New York.[14]

While the Ursulines were among the first of a wave of teaching orders that arrived during midcentury, even larger numbers arrived during the 1860s and 1870s as a result of the *Kulturkampf* that raged in the Germanic states. In 1871, Saint Agatha's parish invited several Sisters of Adoration of the Precious Blood who were anxious to find refuge from anticlerical discrimination. The May Laws of 1872, which expropriated their property and threatened the order with dissolution, forced the remainder to flee to St. Louis. Similarly, 107 Franciscan fathers, clerics, candidates, and lay brothers came to St. Louis in 1857 to join others of their order who had also come the previous decade to escape German liberalism. In addition, probably an equal number of Irish came to work in the city's English-language parishes.[15]

The following table, which is based on a sampling of teachers found in the manuscript census of 1880, indicates how different were the origins of the staffs of public and parochial schools. A child in public school was almost certain to have a native-born teacher who had completed the city's normal school course. Moreover, half of the few foreign-born teachers taught only optional German-language courses for which the rules of teacher certification were relaxed. Students in parochial schools, on the other hand, were very likely to have foreign-born teachers, a circumstance dictated both by parental preference and by the fact

14. *Ursuline Centennial: Saint Louis–Kirkwood, 1848–1948* (St. Louis: 1948), pp. 1–3. *The Ursulines in St. Louis* (Kirkwood, Mo.: 1948), chapters 1–5. *100 Years of St. Mary of Victories Parish, 1843–1943* (St. Louis: 1943), p. 23.

15. *Commemorating A Hundred Years of Service to the Eternal High Priest, 1845–1945* (O'Fallon, Mo.: 1945). *The Friars Minor in the United States: With a Brief History of the Orders of St. Francis in General* (Chicago: n.d.), pp. 39–44. *History of the Franciscan Sisters (from Salzkotten Germany) of the Province of St. Clara in the United States of North America* (St. Louis: Herald Press, 1915), pp. 7–30. *Mississippi Vista: The Brothers of the Christian Schools in the Mid-West 1849–1949* (Winona, Minn.: Saint Mary's College Press, 1948), pp. 53–269.

that these were the only jobs open to teachers who had not been trained in American normal schools and therefore lacked the certification necessary for the public system. This fundamental difference between the experience of a child in the public school system with an entirely secular and mostly native-born corps of teachers, as opposed to Catholic schools with large numbers of clerics and foreign-born instructors, suggests how distinct was the choice between the two.

Table 3. Birthplaces of Teachers in Public and Parochial Schools, 1880, by Percentage*

Birthplace	Parochial schools	Total	Public schools	Total
United States		53.5		88.0
Missouri	10.4		48.1	
U.S. outside Missouri	43.1		39.9	
Foreign		45.4		10.5
Germany	16.0		6.2	
Western Europe	2.6		0.5	
Ireland	20.4		1.1	
Great Britain	1.9		1.8	
Other Foreign	4.5		0.9	
Unknown	1.1	1.1	1.6	1.6
Total number	269		439	

* Source: Manuscript Census of 1880. See Appendix B.

There were differences not only in the sociology of the communities that built the schools and the teachers who staffed them but in the content of instruction. While both public and parochial educators claimed that an important objective of their schools was the moral education of the young, there was an irreconcilable disagreement over how to achieve that end. Since the Bible was the traditional text employed for moral education, controversies centered on which version to use and whether it were possible to teach morality without it.

Henry Miller, a traveller from Pennsylvania who visited St. Louis a few months after the first common schools opened, described in his journal a public debate on the major question: "Is it expedient to admit the Bible as a reading Book in the common Schools of our City." The issue was "warmly debated" amidst "considerable excitement" as people expressed their "unfortunate sectarian prejudices." Most Protestants were in favor of teaching the Bible, suggesting, as was usually the case, that the King James version should be used. Catholics objected, insisting on the Douay or Catholic Bible. As occurred in New York, Philadelphia, and wherever this issue was raised, there was no satisfactory resolution. William G. Eliot, a Unitarian minister, finally despaired of an amicable settlement and put forward a resolution "to put a stop to this exciting question" and the meeting concluded with "an indefinite postponement."[16]

The board, not insensitive to the problems of sectarianism, had ordered prior to the opening of the schools that "no priest, clergyman, preacher, or other religious teacher may be received as a teacher in either male or female schools." As a further preventive "against collision or jealousy among our fellow citizens upon the subject of sectarian influence," the board prohibited formal religious instruction "other than to enforce moral obligations under the sanction of accountability to God." Nevertheless, the common schools were continually attacked as being partial to Protestants and Protestantism, discriminating against Catholics in hiring practices, and teaching a morality that was not in accord with Catholic beliefs. Such criticism was naturally raised when Catholics were called upon to join in support of public schools.[17]

Reverend William Greenleaf Eliot, the city's leading social reformer as well as the minister of the Messiah Unitarian

16. Thomas Marshall, ed., "The Journal of Henry B. Miller," *Missouri Historical Society Collections*, 6 (1931), 223.

17. Scharf, p. 836.

Church, set in motion the controversy after his election to the presidency of the school board in 1848. Finding that the schools were in "poor condition," he determined to improve them by securing better teachers from New England and money for expansion.[18] The key funding proposal was to change Missouri laws so that the board could levy a tax on the city's real estate. Previously, Catholics had not questioned the financing of the schools since money came from leases on lands owned by the board or from tuition. An annual tax that, in effect, forced Catholics to assist in maintaining common schools was another matter. A bitter discussion ensued over the legitimacy of the tax, the appropriate method of disbursement, and the sectarian influences in the schools.

The most serious objections were raised by "A Friend of Untrammeled Education," whose identity, except for the fact that he was a Catholic, remains a mystery. He entered into an exchange of letters with Eliot that was given much attention in the city's press, raising issues that echoed similar controversies in other American cities. Basically he argued that if money were to be raised, Catholic schools must receive a substantial share. He pointed out that they were educating more children than public schools and that those "Catholic children attending the public schools, at present, are obliged to do so from necessity, and not from choice, and are therefore trammeled in their religious beliefs." While he felt that any distribution of public funds should make provisions for parish schools since they did so much work that was valuable to the community, he was most indignant with the injury to Catholic students within the system. As a result of exposure to Protestant teachers the "consciences of Catholic children" were at stake because false prejudices and ideas were inculcated. Underlying his position was the conviction that education cannot be separated from religion. Discrimination, he claimed, would end only when Catholics were given "their propor-

18. Charlotte C. Eliot, *William Greenleaf Eliot: Minister, Educator, Philanthropist* (Boston: Houghton, Mifflin and Co., 1904) pp. 69–70.

tionate part" of public funds, enabling them to attend their own institutions.[19]

Eliot responded with a series of lengthy letters to what he perceived as an indictment of both the impartiality of the system and the concept of common schools. He based his contention that the system is not "conducted in a manner prejudicial to the interests of the Catholic portion of our community" on the fact that about a third of the board, "several" teachers, and many children, including a majority in some schools, were Catholics. He argued that the large numbers of Catholics at all levels precluded an anti-Catholic bias. Moreover, he pointed to a vigorous nonsectarianism as evidenced by the enrollment of Mormons, Jews, Protestants, Catholics, and even unbelievers. Eliot praised the board for its neutrality in the face of conflicting demands over which version of the Bible to introduce and on its decision to employ neither. He declared that a just common school system was not only possible but that St. Louis, perhaps unlike other cities, had produced one: "They [the public schools] are now untrammeled by sect or party. I trust they will so continue."[20]

Eliot's celebration of the neutrality of the schools showed that he did not appreciate a crucial aspect of the criticism. Because he was committed to the principle that public schools should foster social amalgamation, he readily accepted the absence of any formal religious teaching. This was a plausible position for a Unitarian minister; it was impossible for parents concerned with protecting their cultural and religious traditions. Acting on their objections to common schooling, Catholics continued to send their children to their own institutions, which emphasized instruction in their faith, customs, and language. Eliot won the immediate issue of greater financial support for the system, thus creating a source of revenue that enabled it ultimately to surpass parochial education, but he failed to persuade a

19. *Missouri Republican*, May 17, 1849. A large body of clippings are located in the *William G. Eliot MSS*, Washington University Library, St. Louis. Also see Charlotte Eliot, pp. 75–77.
20. *Daily Union*, May 18, 1849.

large portion of the community to accept the principle of common education and the compromises on which its success depended.

Public and parochial school advocates continued to argue past each other although there were few occasions when their controversies became politicized. The most serious incident occurred in 1870 when St. Louis Catholics, like co-religionists in other cities, launched a campaign to obtain a portion of public funds for their own schools.[21] Except for Eliot, the protagonists were new and included Father O'Reilly of Saint Patrick's, one of the city's largest churches, and Superintendent William Harris. This incident merits examination both because of the way in which the city system was attacked and because of the sophisticated case Harris made in defense of an extraecclesiastical and secular-oriented morality.

In January, 1870, Father O'Reilly opened the campaign with a speech at Saint Patrick's. Explaining that every Catholic must receive special religious instruction, he insisted that Protestant teachings or the absence of any religious training made it impossible for him to support public schooling. His position allowed for no compromise:

> But there is religious truth, and if I find that there is also this truth, indispensible and highest of all, can I as a parent or teacher withhold such most necessary truth? Take any denomination—the Catholic, if you please; I as one, believe I have a system of truth, without which I have no worthy life here or hope hereafter. Can I withhold this truth from my child? Can I send my child to a school where it is proposed *as a system* not to give such truth?[22]

A genuine fear of damnation and an unwillingness to breach conscience impelled Father O'Reilly to advocate alternatives to the city's schools. In an issue involving absolute

21. Tyack, "Onward Christian Soldiers," p. 224.
22. "Our Public Schools," *Missouri Republican*, January 31, 1870. Father O'Reilly was reflecting the opinion of other Catholic clerics whose views appeared regularly in the archdiocesan newspaper. See, for example, "Pastoral Letter of the Fathers of the Tenth Provincial Council of Baltimore," *Western Watchman*, May 15, 1869.

truths and eternal punishment, compromise is impossible.

It is far easier for those who hold to a flexible system of beliefs or who perceive no threat to themselves and their ideas to espouse tolerance and accomodation. Thus, Eliot could respond proudly that the schools were so free of religious influence that "there is scarcely any place left in the school room, where God, or Christ, or the soul's responsibility is required to be spoken of." Eliot still failed to appreciate that what he understood to be freedom, others, like Father O'Reilly, considered immoral and a flight from responsibility.[23]

Father O'Reilly also advocated political action. Although he did not admit to the legality of the city's imposition of a school tax, he urged that, since the money was available, then Catholics should receive a portion. In this effort, he was joined by Dr. Charles Smythe, a Catholic physician, pamphleteer, and most importantly a representative to the state legislature from St. Louis. Their collaboration resulted in Smythe's introduction to the legislature in February of a bill that proposed, in effect, a voucher plan whereby each child would receive $10 from the school tax that could be applied to any school that the state approved. Smythe and O'Reilly assumed that parochial schools would qualify, since approval would be granted to any school whose teachers passed an examination. In this way they hoped to circumvent prohibitions of state aid to religious institutions. If successful, the bill would have posed a serious threat to public schools, because it would have withdrawn necessary revenues and also subsidized the opposition.[24]

The board was surprised by Smythe's bill and responded immediately by sending a delegation to the Missouri legislature. By the time the board had mustered its forces,

23. William G. Eliot, "Religion in Public Schools," *Missouri Democrat*, November 27, 1870. Also see the file of Eliot's articles in the *William G. Eliot MSS*, Washington University Library, St. Louis.

24. Charles R. Smythe, *Letters on Public Schools with Special Reference to the System as Conducted in St. Louis* (St. Louis: George Knapp, 1870). "Jefferson City," *Missouri Democrat*, February 15, 1870; "Missouri Legislature, February 15, 1870," February 16, 1870. Kurt F. Leidecker, *Yankee Teacher: The Life of William Torrey Harris* (New York: Philosophical Library, 1946), pp. 290–93.

Smythe's bill had passed a first reading, perhaps because its full intent was not appreciated. After the St. Louis delegation descended on the legislature and pointed out how the bill would destroy public education by benefiting Catholic schools, it was doomed. Under such slogans as "A State without a Bishop and a Church without a King," the legislators from the largely Protestant areas outside St. Louis joined with those city representatives sympathetic to the board in defeating Smythe's proposal.[25]

In retrospect, the bill's defeat is unexceptional, for Catholics have consistently failed, not only in St. Louis but throughout the country, in obtaining a portion of public revenues. If their political attacks were ineffective, however, their criticisms were taken very seriously and had a significant impact on the way in which public educators thought about their schools. Educators from Horace Mann through William Harris were on the defensive, for they were making a revolutionary departure from the millennia-old tradition of church-sponsored moral instruction. Persons such as Father O'Reilly believed that the new, secular ways were spurious and dangerous in their neglect of the Bible, religious–ethical literature, and the catechism. What, then, gave public educators the assurance that their novel, untraditional methods would be successful?

The most coherent answer came from Superintendent Harris who had recently begun to attract national attention through his educational writings in the schools' *Annual Reports* and the *Journal of Speculative Philosophy*, which he founded and edited. The first outline of his ideas appeared in a public exchange of letters in February, 1870, in the controversy surrounding the Smythe bill and were subsequently refined for inclusion in the *Annual Report* for 1871. As befitting one who exulted in the new industrial

25. Mr. Harper, "The Schools—Defend Them," *Missouri Democrat*, March 3, 1870. For other examples of support for the continuation of public education's monopoly on public revenues and strict separation of church and state, see, "The Schools," *Missouri Democrat*, February 23, 1870; March 5, 1870. For local reporting of similar troubles in other cities, especially Cincinnati, see, "Public Schools," *Missouri Democrat*, November 3, 1869.

society and was a manager of one of its key institutions, Harris demonstrated the moral worth of the schools by offering scientific evidence from statistics rather than engaging in philosophic disputations.

Statistics revealed that ignorance was intimately connected with crime, a prime example of immoral behavior. Quoting from the writings of Colonel Dougherty, a New York prison official, Harris reported that "In the New York city prison, in 1869, out of 47,313 only 625 were well-educated, while 33,439 could not read at all, and 12,604 could only read." Similarly, the penitentiaries of Philadelphia, Massachusetts, and Connecticut counted only a few educated inmates, the great mass being illiterates or semiliterates. Noting that these states had literacy rates of 97 to 98.5 per cent, Harris concluded that "if ignorance has no influence on crime," there would be similarly high proportions of literates among inmates. "In view of such facts," Harris deduced, "we believe that to educate the people well is to prevent crime." Thus, even without the catechism, the schools were producing literate and, therefore, moral children.[26]

Since "seventy percent of the criminals of the United States have been of intemperate habits," Harris also found that through the inculcation of "self-restraint" the schools were effectively combatting crime. After demonstrating that the great majority of convicts "owed their criminal inclinations and acts to drunkenness," he claimed that the moral discipline of the schools assisted in encouraging temperance and thereby facilitated social reform. Having exposed the role of education in producing virtuous men, Harris felt he had satisfied the criticisms of the religious separatists. "It is a favorite practice," he concluded, "of those who advance the theory of the inseparableness of religion from the culture of morality, to attribute whatever

26. *Annual Report, 1871*, pp. 78–80. Superintendent Divoll had foreshadowed Harris by offering a similar argument based on numbers. He had tried to prove that $200,000 annually over the next generation would eradicate crime. He concluded that "the people must build school houses or prisons." *Annual Report, 1865*, pp. 34–35.

laxity appears in society as its origin. These statistics above considered show that there is no just foundation for such attacks."[27]

From defense by statistics, Harris went on to challenge a central assumption of parochial education, asserting that religious teaching was by itself no guarantee of morality. It is clear, he claimed, "that a school in which morality formed the staple of instruction—even were it continually supported by appeals to religion, would be a fountain of moral corruption in the community, *unless strict discipline were maintained there*. It is the habitual practice of obedience to principle, that constitutes morality."[28] In such practice the public schools excelled and were more effective, he believed, than parish schools:

> The discipline of our Public Schools, wherein punctuality and regularity are enforced and the pupils are continually taught to *suppress mere self-will* and inclination, is the best school of morality. Self-control is the basis of all moral virtues, and industrious and studious habits are the highest qualities we can form in our children.

It was fitting that this rejoinder conclude by listing "with pride" the names of several hundred children who were neither absent nor tardy during the past year. The moral system of the public schools had replaced the Bible with the rollbook.[29]

This substitution was the consequence of a concern for discipline that developed independently of the competition with parochial schools. Immorality was as unacceptable to public educators as it was to the clergy. Harris was merely employing an argument that had already been articulated in another context to the needs of the moment. He viewed the discipline of urban public schools as a radical departure from the kind of instruction he had experienced in a small, rural community. Many of his insights concerning schooling originated from his desire to educate children to live

27. Ibid.
28. *Annual Report, 1871*, p. 81.
29. *Annual Report, 1871*, p. 84.

in an urban civilization. His was not an abstract vision; it was the result of personal observation. He witnessed the mushrooming of large numbers of cities of unprecedented size. St. Louis at least doubled in population every decade between 1830 and 1870; Chicago barely existed in 1830 but reached her first million in 1890; New York surpassed most European capitals by 1860; and spectacular urban booms occurred in virtually every portion of the country. Harris foresaw that the urban movement signalled the beginning of a new epoch in the history of society, and concluded that educators must adjust the school to the new social order.[30]

The inculcation of an urban discipline was the primary objective. It was this emphasis, Harris noted, that distinguished the emerging modern urban school from its rural counterparts, particularly the one-room schoolhouse:

> Wherever any considerable collection of educational material is got together, the broad contrast between the spirit and methods of city schools and those of the country begins to make its appearance. . . . But the most important difference between country and city schools appears in the discipline. In the small community, where individuals are comparatively isolated, discipline is of little significance. In the large community, where each individual is brought into close relation to his fellows, and has to act in combination with them, if he acts at all, discipline is quite essential, and must be carried out with great minuteness. The great lesson of civilization is to learn how to combine with one's fellow-men.[31]

Seven virtues formed the basis of the school's discipline: punctuality, regularity, perseverance, earnestness, justice, truthfulness, and industry. All were explained in terms of social conformity and the production of good and function-

30. These themes recur throughout the *Annual Reports* of Harris's superintendency (1868–1880). Harris wrote, for example, that "there is no better habit on the part of the educator than that of orienting himself from time to time by the movement of society at large." He follows this observation with an extensive analysis of contemporary urbanization. *Annual Report, 1873*, pp. 199 ff.

31. "The Centennial Exposition," *Annual Report, 1876*, p. 197.

al citizens. Of these seven, punctuality and regularity were given the most emphasis. Harris explained that such concern stemmed from a realization that the precise interaction among people was necessary for the viability of an urban–industrial society and that "in a civilization that is every year becoming more complex and more dependent upon combination of the individual with the whole of society, punctuality becomes a moral issue."[32]

Although attention to the movements of the clock had been of major concern in American culture since at least the time of Poor Richard, the discipline of time took on a new significance in the modern context. Because the uncompromising mechanics of life in the industrial society "fix the times for the minor affairs of life with absolute precision," Harris explained, "in *the age of productive industry* . . . there is one general training requisite for the generations of men who are to act as directors of machinery, and of business, that depends on it—this training is in habits of punctuality and regularity." In contemporary society machines cannot wait for men; men must conform to the movements of the machine. This concept was often illustrated by pointing out the importance of discipline to the operation of a railroad. In one such disquisition, Harris asked: "How can we trust the engineer on a train if he has not a thorough character for regularity and punctuality?" Without these habits, collisions were inevitable. Similarly, machine operation, the factory system, and commerce were impossible without them. The railroad had even changed the rhythm of rural life, as it compelled the farmer to adopt more regularized patterns of behavior in playing his role in the national combination. It was a basic force in the creation of a "modern (urban)" society. Consequently, Harris believed that punctuality was the key to successful social and economic organization in every section of the country for every productive individual. Moreover, he was certain that by making "punctuality one of the great objects of life," not only the pupil, but his family and ultimately

32. *Annual Report, 1871*, pp. 30–31; *Annual Report, 1875*, p. 157.

the entire society, would be reformed. In this fashion the schools would become agents of progress and prosperity.[33]

Emphasis on discipline not only was derived from Harris's theory of the social utility of schooling but from well-established psychological tenets. As Bernard Wishy has shown, most of the literature of child rearing emphasized control rather than freedom as conducive to the proper, moral upbringing of the young.[34] Emerson White's *The Elements of Pedagogy*, a required text in the system's normal school, reflects how this attitude permeated the pedagogical literature of the period. White, who derived much of his understanding of child psychology from Harris's writings, believed children were capable of both good and evil and that the function of education, both at home and at school, was to extirpate evil inclinations by encouraging the practice of good behavior. Both White and Harris were convinced that good habits could be developed without explicit reference to established religious teachings. In the terminology of the period, the "will" of the child was to be directed into the acquisition of good "habits." As White stated it: "The home-life and the school-life of the child should prepare him for this transition to freedom (adulthood) by effective training in self-control and self-guidance, and, to this end, the will must be disciplined by an increasing use of motives that quicken the sense of right and make the conscience regal in conduct." Significantly, White characterized the ideal method of rearing as subjecting the child to "the authoritative control of the family and the school."[35]

Such concern for discipline often led schoolmen to undesirable excesses. Harris admitted, for example, that it was "a notable fact that the American public school always lay

33. *Annual Report, 1871*, pp. 31–32, 162; *Annual Report, 1874*, p. 78; *Annual Report, 1875*, p. 21.

34. Bernard Wishy, *The Child and the Republic: The Dawn of Modern American Child Nurture* (Philadelphia: University of Pennsylvania, 1968).

35. Emerson E. White, *The Elements of Pedagogy: A Manual for Teachers, Normal Schools, Normal Institutes, Teachers' Reading Circles, and All Persons Interested in School Education* (New York: American Book Co., 1890), pp. 318–20. Compare with Harris's concept of suppressing the will in *Annual Report, 1871*, p. 81.

more stress on discipline than on the speedy acquirement of knowledge."[36] This was an echoing of Henry Barnard's belief that schools should be concerned "not so much with their [children's] intellectual culture, as the regulation of the feelings and dispositions, the extirpation of vicious propensities." Barnard foresaw terrible consequences to the child if proper discipline, particularly punctuality, were not strictly enforced: "A disgust to study and the school, follows his loss of self-respect; habits of truancy are acquired, and by and by he is turned out upon society, a pest and a burden, a prepared victim of idleness, vice and crime."[37] As a consequence of this attention to the clock, the most visible indicator of moral behavior, mid-nineteenth-century school reports included large sections of tables and statistics, which were often carried out to the second and third place after the decimal point, describing the schools' success in the war against tardiness and irregular attendance. It is not surprising, therefore, that except for one scholarship for a graduate of the high school to Washington University, excellence in punctuality was the only award a nineteenth-century student could receive.

The schools were so successful in imposing controls over children that toward the end of the century they were widely criticized for having sacrificed spontaneity and individuality.[38] Nevertheless, the dominant attitude was appreciation for the work of the public system even, on occasion, among the sectarians. Johann Friedrich Buenger, for example, a colleague of Reverend Walther and one of the founders of the city's Lutheran schools, used to visit the public schools in order to learn its methods so that he might improve the discipline of his classroom. Reverend Walther recorded that Buenger "soon learned the secret, namely, that pupils in these schools were specially exercised and drilled in discipline. He learned various other things,

---

36. *Annual Report, 1871*, p. 161.

37. John S. Brubacher, ed., *Henry Barnard on Education* (New York: McGraw–Hill, 1931), p. 254.

38. The outstanding example is Joseph Mayer Rice, *The Public School System of the United States* (New York: Century and Co., 1893).

but especially how to rule a large number of children with few words."[39] Aside from attacks by the Catholic clergy and isolated individuals, there was widespread appreciation and confidence in the methods of the schools.

The real difference between public and parochial education lay in the ultimate purposes of schooling rather than in the emphasis on discipline, for it is unlikely that parish schools were any less strict than their public counterparts. Harris defined the aim of his system as the "initiation of the child into the manners and customs, into the general forms of right doing—the conventionalities of civilization —this in its broad context is ethical education, and it is the first necessity of the child when he grows up to the capacity of self-activity."[40] Public educators sought to achieve this goal by giving training in those skills and virtues that were required for successful participation in the life of the community. This largely meant training in the three Rs and the special discipline of an urban society. Such preparation was not necessarily within the competence or purpose of parochial education. It was, however, a major justification of public education. Unlike Father O'Reilly, who was concerned with revealed truth and divine injunctions, Harris was preoccupied with understanding and responding to historical change. His values were functional, not absolute; for him, the test of morality was how well it served the community. As this concept was applied to the schools, it meant their dedication to the socialization of the child for life in a modern city. Ultimately, schools had to meet public needs. They were agents of the community and were dedicated to its service.

However worthwhile the ideal of preparing the children of the city to contribute to its harmony and development, parochial education addressed itself primarily to other ends. That it served to perpetuate the special interests of immigrant groups is testified to by the persistent connection between language instruction and religious education. St.

39. Stellhorn, p. 84.
40. *Annual Report, 1871*, p. 76.

Louis Lutherans, for example, established German as the official language of their worship services and of their schools in 1842 and departed from these practices only during World War I.[41] The same connection obtained in many German, Italian, Czech, and Polish Catholic parishes. The parish school was also the vehicle through which organized religion sought to transmit absolute verities and ethical teachings. In this objective, St. Louis's parochial schools were following a well-established American precedent. The early educational institutions of Massachusetts, after all, had been founded with the desire of holding the Puritan pioneers on the New England frontier to the beliefs of their fathers. So too, men like Father O'Reilly and the Lutheran leader, Reverend Walther, were anxious to preserve their truths. If the danger no longer stemmed from a raw wilderness peopled by pagans and primitives, these separatists nevertheless found themselves insidiously threatened by the new, polyglot metropolis that devoted so much of its energy to creating an educational system that democratically reduced orthodoxies to common denominators and taught a civic rather than a religious morality. Unlike Harris's system, parochial schools met private and personal needs. They were agents of churches and immigrant communities, and dedicated to their service.

This difference in perspective and function, so apparent by the time of Eliot's struggle for the school tax, became elaborated and further entrenched with Harris's defense in later controversies over public funds. Indeed, a century after the debates of the 1870s, St. Louis still supports a variety of educational systems. The ideal of the common school where all children of the city might meet and learn from one another was never fully realized in St. Louis, nor in any American city. Even while Harris and other educators strove to realize the building and redemption of a new, urban com-

41. Robert M. Toepper, "The Fathers' Faith—The Children's Language: The Transition of the Missouri Synod from German to English" (unpublished Master's thesis, Washington University, 1967), pp. 19–23.

munity through the public school system, there were others dedicated to preserving a personal, spiritual, and cultural heritage. Their decision to separate, made at considerable sacrifice and renewed in each generation, serves as a constant reminder of the limits of an educational ideal that is conceived in secular terms and is indifferent to private needs.

3

The Strategy and Politics
of the Melting Pot

While sectarianism and ethnicity were mutually reinforcing factors in the development of parochial schools, they
were also divisible. This was demonstrably true among
Germans, who constituted the largest foreign group in St.
Louis during the second half of the nineteenth century. In
describing the attitudes that prevailed prior to the 1890s,
Thomas Graebner, a Lutheran educator, admitted that
"even members of the irreligious majority—for at that time
the preponderance of free thinkers among the German immigrants was very large—would enter their children at the
parochial school for the sake of language." In some parishes
as many as two-thirds of the children came from homes
"indifferent to the church." He noted that only with the
ending of German immigration at the close of the century
and the growth of a generation of children with native-
born parents who were indifferent to language training did
these schools finally free themselves of the religiously un-
committed.[1] Some educators, notably Superintendent Harris, understood the validity of this distinction. When the
board experimented between 1864 and 1887 with German
instruction, which in a tangible as well as symbolic way
gave expression to the desire of many Germans for cultural
continuity, it discovered an effective means for bringing the
children of German immigrants into the public system.

The situation in St. Louis was similar to that in other
midwestern cities in the triangular area defined by Cincinnati, Milwaukee, and St. Louis. Throughout this area Germans were sufficiently numerous and well organized to
demand concessions of the community at large and, if these
were not granted, to develop and maintain independent

1. Thomas Graebner, *The Lutheran Church Guide of St. Louis
Missouri* (St. Louis: Concordia Seminary, 1916), pp. 166–67.

cultural institutions. In 1840, for example, some St. Louis Germans requested that a few columns of the *Daily Evening Gazette* be printed in their native language because "there are several thousand Germans in this city who do not understand English." Such favors were not readily granted in a society that demanded the assimilation of foreigners. On the contrary, another reader insisted, Germans should get exercise in English so that "they will learn the language, and acquire a general knowledge of the country, of their duties as citizens, and render themselves worthy citizens of the land of the great Liberator Washington."[2] Thus, if Germans wanted to read newspapers in their own tongue, they were forced to publish their own—which they did. The German community had a similar problem with schools. When they petitioned in 1843 that the board establish bilingual instruction, their request was denied on the basis that Missouri law stipulated that only English could be taught. Failing in this application, they turned in large numbers to support their own institutions.[3]

In 1837, one year before the city's first public school opened, a group of Germans formed a corporation for a "German Public School" with a nonsectarian, German–English curriculum.[4] By 1860, there were thirty-eight German schools, almost entirely parochial, with ninety-eight teachers offering instruction to 5,524 pupils. The student body and teaching staff amounted to one-half of that maintained by the public schools.[5] The ability of Germans to create and support alternatives, since public educators did not recognize and act on their demands, resulted in the emergence of parallel systems. The development of this

2. *Daily Evening Gazette*, December 2, 1840; July 13, 1840.

3. Scharf, *History of St. Louis*, p. 851.

4. William G. Bek, "The Followers of Duden: The First German Public School West of the Mississippi," *Missouri Historical Review*, 16 (October 1921), 119–45. The growth of German schools can be followed by analysis of city directories. For a historical survey that does not include all parish schools see, Max Hempel, *Geschichtliche Mitteilungen über den Deutschen Schulverein und die Freie Gemeinde von St. Louis* (St. Louis: 1900).

5. Scharf, p. 852. The total number enrolled in the public elementary schools was 10,413. *Annual Report, 1860*, p. 55.

alternative did not leave the schools *deutscherien*. By 1860, 17 per cent of the public school population, or about 1,300 children, were of German parentage. Nevertheless, the Germans preferred their own schools to the city's by four to one.[6]

The segregation of children from different backgrounds in separate educational institutions was precisely what advocates of a common school system wanted to avoid. B. Gratz Brown, a prominent local politician and later a U.S. senator from Missouri, expressed the prevailing view as well as the particular challenge facing St. Louis at the dedication of a new schoolhouse in 1853:

> We have here in this city of St. Louis a population which draws its representatives from every quarter of the globe. We have the diversities of all habits, the peculiarities of all customs, the idiom of all European tongues here concentrated in a single city. . . . They [the immigrants] have now a common country, a common destiny, and it is right they they and their descendants should have a common pervading thought —a single nationality. This can be done only in communion with education.

Brown, who was himself of German parentage, concluded the address, given in a preponderantly German district, with the hope that the school would bring together children from every national group and thereby create a "mimic republic."[7]

Demographic data culled from the manuscript census of 1880 (Table 4) demonstrate the enormity of the task facing the schools. The overwhelming proportion of white school-age children, 94 per cent, were born in the United States, but only 25 per cent of their fathers were natives. Three times as many fathers were European immigrants with the largest group, 46 per cent, from Germany, followed by 16 per cent from Ireland. Reinforcing the immigrant character

6. *Annual Report, 1860*, pp. 56–57.
7. B. Gratz Brown, "Address by B. Gratz Brown, Esq., Delivered at the Dedication of the Lafayette School House, March 28, 1853," *Teachers and Western Educational Magazine*, 1 (April 1853), 112 ff.

of the community was the small number of fathers, only 7 per cent, who were native to Missouri if not to St. Louis, while two and a half times that amount, 18 per cent, were drawn from virtually every section of the country. On the other hand, 79 per cent of the children were Missourians. St. Louis educators were trying to build a system for first-generation Americans, appealing for support from an overwhelmingly European-born community in which Germans were the dominant group, constituting nearly half of the entire adult male population. The 1880 data are not unique, for in 1860, 60 per cent of the total population was drawn from Europe, with the largest number being German, giving St. Louis the highest proportion of foreigners for any major American city at that time.[8]

Table 4. Birthplaces of Children Ages 6–16 and Their Fathers, 1880, by Percentage*

Birthplace	Children	Total	Fathers	Total
Native born		93.9		25.3
Missouri	78.6		7.4	
U.S. outside				
Missouri	15.3		17.9	
Foreign born		6.1		74.1
Germany	3.4		46.2	
Ireland	1.6		16.0	
Other Europe	1.1		11.9	
Unknown	0.0	0.0	0.5	0.5
Total	100.0		100.0	
	(6,141)		(6,141)	

* Source: Manuscript census 1880. See Appendix B.

Like so many other boom towns in the American past, St. Louis was a city with a small native population and an overwhelming majority of newcomers. The need to assemble children from different backgrounds in schools that

8. See Appendix B for information on the collection and classification of this data. United States Census Office, *The Eighth Census: 1860*, 1, xxxii.

would create a sense of community and harmonize different cultural strains with an American tradition was not a theoretical problem but a pressing reality. The difficulty of the challenge facing public educators was aggravated by the way in which they couched their appeals for support. They promised that the city's children would participate in the creation of a new culture, while their competitors held forth the comforts of religious and ethnic continuities. The need for these traditions is attested by the numerous ethnic organizations that flourished wherever there were numbers of immigrants. The Germans, for example, established many associations beginning in the 1830s, and still maintained over 300 of these as late as World War I. These included trade associations, benevolent groups, singing clubs, *Turnverein*, literary societies, military organizations, and provincial *vereine*. All this existed in addition to parish organizations.[9]

Compounding the difficulty was the fact that Germans were not a weak group at the mercy of a superior host culture. They were coming from societies with the most advanced educational systems in the world. Beginning in the 1830s, leading common school promoters such as Lyman Beecher made pilgrimages to Germany and returned urging Americans to emulate the German example.[10] From kindergartens and vocational training to university reform, Americans were learning from Germans. Indeed, in one popular book on pedagogy used in the St. Louis Normal School in the 1890s, the author voiced a common complaint that there was not yet a pedagogical vocabulary available in English and chided his countrymen for forcing him to employ foreign expressions.[11] Aside from the desirability of including their children in common schools, Germans could be valu-

9. Sister Audrey Olson, "The St. Louis Germans, 1850–1920: The Nature of an Immigrant Community and Its Reaction to the Assimilation Process," a paper delivered at the Missouri Urban History Conference, April, 1971, Columbia, Missouri, pp. 4–5.

10. Lyman Beecher, *A Plea for the West* (Cincinnati: Truman and Smith, 1853).

11. Robert H. Quick, *Essays on Educational Reformers* (N.Y.: D. Appleton and Co., 1890), p. 70.

able allies in the building of a better system. If they had continued to remain outside, not only would there be no "mimic republic," but the progress of the schools would probably have been far less vigorous.

Although the board was anxious to bring German children into the schools, it was at first unwilling to compromise the widely held notion that there must be no deviation from the common curriculum. Convinced that Germans were willing to support public schools and participate in the creation of a "mimic republic" only if their children would be given language training, Superintendent John Tice advised the board in 1855 that teaching German would be "an act of justice" and suggested that it need be offered only "in such of our schools as are situated in districts densely populated by Germans." The board turned down his proposal, and German remained out of the schools until a new political situation occasioned by the Civil War brought to power a board that was willing to disregard state statutes.[12]

The first steps to attract those Germans who had not participated in public education took place in July, 1863, at the same time that the board liberalized the tuition as necessitated by the war. Recognizing that Germans had an "appreciation for rational education," it expressed regret that "the German population of the city take comparatively so little interest in our public educational institutions." The board blamed this indifference on ignorance of the schools' character and on "prejudices intentionally nourished and promulgated by some parties for selfish purposes and impure motives." Consequently, a committee of three was established to publicize the nature and value of public schools among Germans and recruit their children. The committee failed in its mission, however, for the board still did not grant the language courses that most Germans wanted. Finally, in September, 1864, the board rescinded its policy of more than twenty years and introduced German as an "experiment." In the first year, there were only 450 students in seven classes in five schools. Within ten years German instruction spread through nearly the entire system

12. *Annual Report*, 1855, p. 81.

and involved more than 15,000 students or 47 per cent of the enrollment in elementary schools.[13]

Harris, under whose superintendency (1868–1880) the greatest expansion took place, was the most articulate apologist of this new departure. He understood that the Mississippi Valley, with St. Louis as its center, was undergoing a process of vast transformation "from the thinly settled phase of the community to the dense population of metropolitan cities." Moreover, the population was extraordinarily heterogeneous, drawing Americans from every part of the country in addition to a large European population. Within St. Louis, Harris counted at least ten distinct languages, which he feared would deepen "differences of manners and customs—of feelings, convictions and ideas." In this context of rapid urbanization and confluence of different peoples, he reiterated a central vision of common education: "Here is a great problem: to eliminate all these differences, to transcend these limits of nationality, and ascend into a new homogeneous nationality, that shall combine the inhabitants of this valley." Since Germans were the most numerous foreign group and were successfully creating an independent culture, they were potentially the greatest obstacle to realizing this ideal. Harris felt that they would not be incorporated in the dominant "Anglo–American" population unless the schools met their demands on the question of language. Only then would the children of these two major groups mix in a wholesome atmosphere and acquire a common language and culture.[14]

Although there was never any question that the common language must be English, this did not mean that it must be the exclusive language of the city or even of the schools. Harris, who was himself a master of ancient and modern tongues, believed that in certain circumstances bilingual traditions should be encouraged. Certainly this was not an

13. "PBPS, July 14, 1863," *Missouri Republican*, July 21, 1863; "PBPS, July 15, 1864," July 19, 1864. *Annual Report, 1865*, p. 26; *Annual Report, 1876*, pp. 23–24.

14. *Annual Report, 1873*, pp. 136–37. Superintendent Harris discussed this topic in every report from 1868 to 1880 in the sections entitled "German-English Instruction" or "German Instruction."

issue for the portion of St. Louis immigrants who came from more established parts of the United States, Great Britain, and Ireland. Circumstances were different for German immigrants, because if their "children learn to speak English exclusively they break the continuity of the race with an abruptness which works evil for three or four generations." Harris maintained, moreover, that the "consciousness of one's ancestry and the influence derived from communication with the oldest members of the family is very potent in giving tone to the individuality of youth and ripening age, and indeed to a community or people as a whole." Thus, the sudden departure into a new culture could lead to "calamity" not only for the generations of immigrants but for the remainder of the community. From this judgment, Harris argued that the schools must encourage the Germans to maintain ties to their history and people. Indeed, the concern that Germans demonstrated for continuity was "evidence of the advanced civilization which they represent."[15]

Although Harris respected German cultural tradition and appreciated the need to lessen the shock of immigration, he would not tolerate the indefinite continuation of separate cultural traditions within the community. He wanted to "ascend into a new homogeneous nationality" rather than create a permanently pluralistic society. He advocated a transitional ground on which each group would neither confine itself to the "narrow limits of its inherited nationality" nor "fall suddenly into cosmopolitan indifference" and thereby lose "the vital springs of energy and aspiration." Patience must be exercised and a sense of history cultivated while working toward an ultimate goal of cultural amalgamation. In this transitional period, the immigrant must not move with excessive haste toward assimilation nor become frozen into intransigent isolation. His solution lay in encouraging gradual assimilation through the German curriculum. This would bring the Germans into the public schools, where they would find a common ground

15. *Annual Report, 1870*, pp. 120–21.

with others and still preserve their personal and group integrity.[16]

Harris, who popularized and interpreted Georg Hegel's system of philosophy to America's intellectuals through his editorship of the *Journal of Speculative Philosophy*, explained assimilation in Hegelian terms:

> Perhaps it is not a pleasant thought for the German to contemplate: that he is being digested by American institutions. Nor, on the other hand, is it any more agreeable to the Anglo–American to see his peculiar ideosyncracy digested by a different national spirit. Nevertheless, a mutual process of digestion goes on, and that, very rapidly. It does not need the mind of the philosopher to perceive great mutual advantages arising therefrom. Both races are originally Teutonic, and both are renowned for industry. But there is an antithesis in their character.

He went on to explain that the German who is "theoretical, inventor of methods, scientific," and that the Anglo–Saxon who is "the creator of legal forms, the inventor of useful appliances," would eventually fuse in the inexorable fulfillment of the Hegelian synthesis. This synthesis would strengthen the community and its citizens. The schools, of course, would be the catalytic agent in the process.[17]

It must be emphasized that no such interest was lavished on non-Germanic groups. There were two reasons for this. Aside from the Irish, there were no other groups numerous enough to cause concern, or who had established their own schools. Consequently, they were not a threat to the public schools, and presumably there would be no problem in attracting and assimilating them. The Germans, on the other hand, were the largest non-Anglo–American nationality and had separate schools. Moreover, Harris valued German culture above that of any other immigrant group. He considered them to be the most "cultured and civilized immigrant that flocks to our shores." Throughout his life,

16. *Annual Report, 1873*, pp. 136–37.
17. *Annual Report, 1869*, pp. 29–31.

he studied German culture and thought and was committed to its transmission to America. This prejudice, as well as the vitality and significance of the German community, made him more sensitive to their problems and more eager for their assimilation. Thus, despite the presence of more than ten distinct foreign languages in the city, German was the only one ever seriously contemplated for inclusion into the curriculum.[18]

During the twenty-three-year "experiment" with German, the objectives expressed by Harris were accomplished. "German–Americans," as the *Annual Report* had come to call the immigrant or the child of immigrants, enrolled in large numbers. There were about 1,300 German–Americans in the system in 1860 but more than 20,000 twenty years later. Whereas in 1860 there were thirty-eight independent German schools with 5,524 pupils; in 1880, there were thirty-three such schools. Although there is no record of the number of children in 1880, there is no reason to suppose that there were any more children in a smaller number of schools. Thus, while four out of five children chose separate schools in 1860, probably four out of five attended the public schools by 1880.[19]

The signs of success were apparent soon after German was introduced. In 1870, Assistant Superintendent Francis Berg, who was responsible for the German classes, proudly pointed out that 50 per cent of the white school population was German–American, and that 75 per cent of these children had enrolled in the language classes. From these figures he concluded that such instruction was responsible for attracting large numbers of German children and added that the success of the program was more than "even the most sanguine friends of the cause could have expected." Harris

18. *Annual Report, 1877*, p. 10. Also see, *Annual Report, 1870*, pp. 121–25.

19. The national origins of public school children are in *Annual Report, 1880*, p. 126. The number of German schools is derived from examination of school and church listings in city directories. In most cases, "German" is in the title of the school; the remainder are adjuncts of "German" congregations. *Gould's St. Louis Directory for 1880* (St. Louis: David B. Gould, 1880), pp. 1382–84.

also noted that "the former tendency of German parents to send their children first to private German schools to learn German has evidently greatly diminished and seems to justify the encouragement which this Board has given to this branch of study." Even the *Missouri Republican*, which was usually hostile to German instruction, admitted in 1871 that the public schools were the greatest force for the amalgamation of the city's populations.[20]

During the 1870s, this function was continually expanded as German students and their language were incorporated into nearly all of the city's schools. In 1870 thirty-two of the thirty-eight district schools had special classes, and by 1880 German was taught in fifty-two of fifty-seven schools. Harris claimed that this diffusion prevented the tendency of Germans to settle together in one part of the city. It is impossible to be certain whether the schools were instrumental in affecting the demographic character of the city or if they merely reflected it. It is certain that they widened the choice of residence for those parents who required elements of a German education for their children.[21]

Non-Germans also benefited. Between 1867 and 1880, they comprised annually an average of 23 per cent of the students enrolled in these classes, and from 1873 to 1879 they numbered between 5,000 and 6,000. Thus, German instruction was a two-way bridge. It brought St. Louis's largest foreign group into the schools, which encouraged their social and spatial integration in the city, and it made familiarity with their culture possible for all of St. Louis's children. In this very concrete fashion the public schools fulfilled their mission as a center for cultural synthesis and interchange.[22]

Despite its success, Harris's policy was challenged on several grounds. One principal objection to German instruction was that it must necessarily interfere with the

20. Francis Berg, "Annual Report of the German-English Assistant Superintendent," *Annual Report, 1870*, p. 124. "PBPS, February 8, 1870," *Missouri Democrat*, February 10, 1870. "Nativity of the Population of St. Louis," *Missouri Republican*, March 19, 1871.
21. *Annual Report, 1878*, p. 62.
22. *Annual Report, 1880*, p. 126.

established curriculum. Considering that most children spent only three years in school and that they needed time to master the three Rs, it was argued that the child could not afford the time for a second language. Under the new curriculum pupils were either withdrawn from the classroom for special recitation, or the entire schedule was altered to accommodate the added subject. The mechanics of integrating German resulted in extensive experimentation with scheduling, teacher preparation, standardization of curriculum, and definition of subject matter. The experiments were never wholly satisfactory, as compromises had to be made. Even Harris admitted this but accepted concessions as necessary evils. If Harris was satisfied with compromise, there were always those who were not.[23]

A second objection was that German was a luxury beyond the board's resources. Especially during periods of financial crisis, it was argued that all available funds must support the more essential parts of the system. This, in effect, meant the exclusion of German. This objection, like the first, gave at least grudging acceptance to the idea of placing German in the schools but protested that cost and time made its actual inclusion impossible.

The third objection was more serious, as it denied the desirability of German even if time and money were available. This opposition was based on the fear that German would prejudice the standing and universality of the English language. Proponents of this view looked with apprehension on the diversity of peoples and tongues in St. Louis and advocated complete assimilation to Anglo–American culture. Their concern was not groundless, for German was the native tongue of nearly half the adult males. Interestingly, there were even a number of Germans who, sub-

23. As an example of Harris's judgment of this compromise, he asserted that "The problem has been solved, moreover, in such a manner as to give the German [classes] the greatest practical amount of efficiency without injuring the English [classes] more than will compensate for the advantages gained by the former." *Annual Report, 1869,* p. 30. Also see, *Annual Report, 1877,* p. 10; *Annual Report, 1870,* pp. 121–25.

scribing to this view, urged their fellows to adopt the language and culture of their new homeland. With those who demanded immediate assimilation there was no possibility of compromise. The conflict, however, was not resolved through force of argument. The German question was entwined with the larger conflicts that divided the city; ethnic prejudice and municipal politics ultimately determined its fate.[24]

In the spring of 1878, during one of the periodic crises over German, an anonymous citizen who boasted he "knew more of the ins and outs of public life in St. Louis than any other man in the city," explained the origins of German instruction. Asserting that the idea that German was introduced in order to assimilate immigrants was "moonshine—and don't amount to a row of pins," he argued that the real reason lay in the changing nature of the board and the opportunism and cowardice of Superintendent Ira Divoll. During the war, he contended, Germans had gained control over the board in the absence of the normal "American element" that was disfranchised when no longer considered "sound" because of a lack of Unionist sympathies. Divoll, who then felt insecure, was willing to accede to the wishes of the German members even though he believed that teaching any language but English was illegal. Furthermore, although the new board had called the first classes an "experiment," they firmly intended to extend them permanently throughout the system. Since Germans continued to control the board, this was accomplished. Never, this authority continued, was German willingly accepted by large numbers of Americans. Only through constant pressure and subterfuge was it implanted in the public schools.[25]

24. "Destiny of the German Nationality in the United States," *Missouri Republican*, November 17, 1867.

25. "School Matters—The True Story of the Introduction of German into the Schools," *St. Louis Daily Globe-Democrat*, March 31, 1878. For the political background to this period see Chapter 1, fn. 36; and Virgil C. Blum, "The Political and Military Activities of the German Element in St. Louis, 1859–1861," *Missouri Historical Review*, 42 (January 1948), 103–29.

This account has the ring of authenticity. Since the beginning of the war, Germans had played a major role in preserving the city for the Union and gained a prominent and perhaps dominant place in the politics of the city. As they tried to exercise their power, however, they were confronted by another important and self-conscious group, the Irish. The conflict between "John Finn and the Germans" characterized much in St. Louis politics during the Civil War, Reconstruction, and beyond. Also, since Germans were closely identified with the Republican party and Irish with the Democratic party, the question of German instruction was expressed in partisan terms.[26]

After 1867, when German was no longer an "experiment," it spread to individual schools, usually through the initiative of citizen petitions to the board. The directors' decisions closely reflected the identity and relative strength of the adversaries. Between 1867 and 1870, for example, the board usually favored these petitions by a vote of 19 to 5. Most of the majority were Radicals who enjoyed strong German support. The minority was led by John Finney, a leader of the Democrats and the Irish, and included four others of the same party and background. Radical dominance continued through much of the 1870s and provided necessary support in the face of incessant attacks.[27]

The conflict reached a peak in 1878. As was usually the case, the German question was raised before the April municipal elections. The dispute began at a board meeting in a confrontation between Irish and German members. In February Michael Glynn, an Irish member with a long record of hostility to German language classes in the public

26. "John Finn and the Germans," *Missouri Republican*, March 31, 1867. The better postwar discussions of St. Louis's ethnic politics are, Thomas S. Barclay, "The Liberal Republican Movement in Missouri," *Missouri Historical Review*, 20 (January 1926), 262–332 and 21 (October 1926), 59–108; William E. Parrish, *Missouri Under Radical Rule, 1865–1870* (Columbia: University of Missouri, 1965).

27. Nineteen of the twenty-four directors elected in 1867 were on the Radical Republican ticket. *Missouri Republican*, April 4, 1867. For sample votes see "PBPS, May 12, 1869," *Missouri Republican*, May 16, 1864; "PBPS, December 13, 1870," December 17, 1870.

schools, presented a petition to the Committee on Course of Study asking that Gaelic be added to the curriculum.[28] Two days before the committee was scheduled to report, the *Globe-Democrat* commented that the petition was offered with little expectation that it would be approved but was intended as the opening gambit of a larger struggle and foreshadowed Glynn's line of attack. In terms similar to those employed by Harris in justifying German, the editorial agreed that it would be desirable to perpetuate Gaelic. Furthermore, it argued that instruction in French and Hebrew should also be supported. Since all languages could not be taught because of the expense, the paper concluded that justice demanded that the board dispense with German and deny the petitions of the Irish and any other similarly organized group.[29]

The reaction of the German community to this conception of evenhanded justice was immediate and forceful. The *Westliche Post* not only defended the beauty of the German language and its social utility but, more to the point, threatened to arouse German voters to ensure the continuation of special language instruction. In addition, a group of sixty Germans organized a meeting at Tivoli Hall for March 11, the day before the committee was to make its report. After considerable and agitated discussion, during which several speakers criticized even Superintendent Harris, they decided to appoint Rabbi Solomon H. Sonneschein, a community activist widely known for support of workingmen's rights and public education, to present a resolution in favor of German to the board.[30]

On March 12, the committee gave a negative recommendation on the question of Gaelic. It split, however, on the reasons for denial. One group claimed that the board did not have enough money, while the other categorically denied

28. St. Louis Public Schools, *Official Proceedings*, 3, February 12, 1878, 27.

29. "German in the Schools," *Globe-Democrat*, March 10, 1878.

30. *Westliche Post*, March 10, 1878 and March 11, 1878. "PBPS, March 12, 1878," *Globe-Democrat*, March 13, 1878; "German in the Schools," March 10, 1878.

the merits of the petition. Not surprisingly, the denial generated a heated debate along ethnic lines. In the discussion, John O'Connell, a leader of the Irish faction, offered another resolution asserting that, since the board was financially pressed, it should teach only English and other basic subjects. After some parliamentary jockeying, the resolution was called and defeated by a vote of 20 to 7, with 1 abstention; all the Germans had voted against it, and O'Connell, Glynn, and the Irish for it.[31]

As the *Globe-Democrat* had predicted, the question of Irish instruction was dropped after providing a wedge for other issues. In addition to their attack on German, Democrats complained about those parts of the curriculum that went beyond the essentials of an elementary education. These included music and drawing, the high school, and kindergarten education. The kindergarten was singled out for special damning because it was closely associated with the "German position" on education. Germans had introduced the first private kindergartens in the city, were among its enthusiastic supporters, and, of course, the name itself was of German origin.[32]

The association between kindergartens and German language instruction in the public mind was reflected by many letters in the *Globe-Democrat's* special preelection section, "The School Question." Most letters either bore such legends as "Abolish German," "Against the Kindergarten," "A Plea for English," "One Nation—One Common Language for All Should Be Our Motto"; or, "Save the Kindergarten," "A Practical Plea for the Kindergarten," "Meeting in Favor of Continuing German and the Kindergarten." Whatever the merits of the kindergarten, its position was bound up with the fate of German, which had come to represent the expansion of public education beyond common schooling. Implicit in the challenge to German was a threat

31. *Official Proceedings*, 3, March 12, 1878, 35–36.
32. The controversy elicited so much popular opinion that the *Globe-Democrat* carried special sections containing letters to the editor throughout March and April, 1878. Typical of the opposition to all learning except for the three Rs is "Common School Education," *Globe-Democrat*, March 13, 1878.

to other areas of the curriculum, including the high school, music, drawing, and kindergarten.[33]

The problem of finance was raised most persistently and received the most sympathetic attention as the attack on German developed. The gist of a large number of letters and of the editorials in the *Globe-Democrat* was that public education had lost sight of its priorities. Critics estimated that German cost $100,000 per year, or the equivalent of an education for 10,000 pupils. This was intolerable considering that insufficient funds had necessitated the establishment of half-day sessions in some schools and threatened their extension to still more. One editorial described "the wild desire to accomplish impossibilities which have obtained among School Boards of the great cities during the past decade [during which] many important social conditions have been lost sight of." Since in some cities the average child attended school for only five years, and in St. Louis for merely three, the editorial maintained that it would be "the part of wisdom to teach the common and most needful branches as thoroughly as we can in that time instead of giving them a mere useless smattering of a great many." The public curriculum from the first grade through the high school was admittedly harmonious and extensive, but it was ill suited for a child who attended school for only a few years before leaving for work. "A system like the present, which only extends the benefits to 33 per cent of our children (out of the total number in the city), and only fully educates the 2 per cent that graduate from the high school, cannot be deemed successful. Is it not time," the editorial asked, "to remedy some of its defects?" The universal remedy was the suspension of German instruction and a concentration on those essential subjects that traditionally fall within the rubric of "common education." Other critics added the argument that not only was German expensive, but it produced results wholly incommensurate with the expense. Typical of such dissatisfaction was a letter from an "American" who claimed that "None [of the

33. *Globe-Democrat*, March 14, 1878; March 18, 1878; March 29, 1878.

students] could 'talk' it, few could read it intelligently, and their universal opinion was that it was a waste of time to study it as taught." Another demanded, "Either teach it thoroughly or cut it off."[34]

In the face of these widespread attacks, the German community organized to present its views and make its weight felt. The most dramatic response was a petition in favor of retention signed by 40,000 people, or about one-eighth of St. Louis's entire population. The presentation of the petition, which coincided with the election for school directors, probably caused many politicians to refrain from criticizing the teaching of German. In addition, a constant flow of letters to the editor indicated large and deep-seated support for German education. Some letters reviewed the position and justification that Harris had articulated a decade earlier. Typically, instruction was valued for furthering a useful and cherished language and ensuring that Germans would be "Americanized." One writer noted that the issue had been fully explored at the end of the 1860s and that no new facts or ideas had been offered that could change the basis for decision.[35]

Most letters did not bother to restate the old arguments. The majority of those who supported German instruction considered it a normal and irreproachable part of the system. Rather than defend it, they attacked its critics and their motives, conceiving the issue as a struggle between the enlightened supporters of public education and the "sons of darkness," "Jesuits," and "sectarians." They condemned the campaign to get rid of German as a cabal instigated by latter-day Know Nothingism. This spirit characterized a resolution adopted at another meeting at Tivoli Hall on March 10, which contended that the abolition of

34. "The School Question," *Globe-Democrat*, March 24, 1878; "Common School Education," March 13, 1878; "Half-Time Arrangement," March 14, 1878; "A Plea for Seven Up," March 15, 1878; "German in Our Public Schools," March 28, 1878; "Do Our Common Schools Instruct?" March 28, 1878.

35. *Official Proceedings*, 3, April 1878, 43, *Globe-Democrat*, April 22, 1878; "Why German Should Be Taught," March 18, 1878; "German in English Schools," March 14, 1878.

German would only give sustenance to the "enemies of the public school system" and serve no other purpose. At the same time, Rabbi Sonneschein asserted, to great applause, that "their opponents must be blinded by fanaticism." These activities culminated with a large gathering at Concordia Turner Hall on Sunday, April 7. Planned for maximum effect, it was organized by wards and held a day before the municipal elections and two days before the board was scheduled to deal with the issue again. The sense of these assemblies and of many letters was that the attack on German instruction was not only a threat to the German community of St. Louis and to German culture in general, but also to the expanding curriculum of the schools. In sum, the Germans had emerged as among the most stalwart defenders of a broadening definition of what legitimately constituted public education.[36]

The meetings, resolutions, letters, and petitions had their effect. On Tuesday, April 9, the Committee on Course of Study submitted its report, which recommended preserving German, the kindergarten, the high and normal schools, drawing, and music. Despite the objections of the minority report, the School Board upheld the established system. Again, voting was on ethnic lines with the Germans opposed by the Irish. In addition to the activity and campaigning on behalf of their program of public education, the Germans held the trump card in the contest; they continued to be the largest single group on the board.[37]

After the victory of April, 1878, the issue was perceptibly dormant for another decade, although the opponents continued to voice dissent. Irish members often took exception to those parts of committee reports that dealt with the extension of language instruction into new schools, matters of curriculum, and the training of German teachers. Director John McCann, for example, continually complained of board policies that he claimed favored German

36. "The School Question," *Globe-Democrat*, March 28, 1878; "The German Language," March 19, 1878. *Anzeiger des Westens*, April 8, 1878.
37. *Official Proceedings*, 3, April 9, 1878, 46–47.

teachers in salaries and recruitment and urged that the normal school should exclude Germans and devote its energies solely "for the training of American teachers, to teach that which was necessary for American youth to know." These activities had no real effect on board policy, but served as a constant reminder of community divisions and hostilities.[38]

Having consistently failed to alter policy through the existing board, opponents of German tried to establish a new and more favorable governing unit. In February, 1880, these opponents introduced a bill in the state legislature to repeal the board's charter. In place of the ward system of representation that had been in operation for forty-five years, they pressed for a mix of ward and at-large directors. Further breaking with the tradition of ward control, the proposed charter placed the operations of city schools under the supervision of a state board that would have included the governor, secretary of state, and attorney general. The avowed purpose of this rechartering scheme was to rid the schools of German and other "luxuries." Among the leaders of this movement was School Director Michael Glynn.[39]

The board reacted immediately by sending Superintendent Harris and a delegation of directors to Jefferson City, where they succeeded in countering the move. In September, still another effort was made, but one more mission to Jefferson City and a massive anticharter meeting at Turner Hall produced similar results. Although the strategy to reform the board and undermine German influence failed at this time, it would be successfully employed in 1887. The opponents of German had found the right tactic, but their time had not yet come.[40]

38. See, minority report of the Teachers' Committee in *Official Proceedings*, 3, December 9, 1879, 343–45. For similar incidents in which McCann tried to obstruct the German program see, *Official Proceedings*, 3, January 13, 1880, 370; February 10, 1880, 382.

39. "Another School Petition," *Globe-Democrat*, February 12, 1879; March 11, 1879.

40. "Public School Legislation," *Globe-Democrat*, February 2, 1879; "Anti-Charter," September 1, 1879. For an additional discus-

Their opportunity arrived through an alliance with a new force in St. Louis politics, reformers from the newly settled western districts who desired to rid the city of corruption. Since 1880, exposés of the leasing of board properties, the sale of books, and the construction and maintenance of buildings had made it apparent that School Board directors were badly mismanaging the system's revenues. This was particularly aggravating as the board, unable to meet the demand for new accommodations, had instituted half-day sessions in hard-pressed districts. Public indignation over the scandals and the need to change the electoral districts of school directors found a remedy in ousting ward politicians, or "boodle bosses" as Joseph Pulitzer's *Post-Dispatch* called them, by instituting nonpartisan, at-large directorships, an innovation that was commonly advocated by reformers for other municipal offices in the ensuing decades.[41] The occasion for effecting this reform came with the need to redistrict the city both because of an increase in population and its redistribution away from the river to the western suburbs. Democrats, seizing the opportunities presented by this situation, advanced their cause by embracing the program of good government and by joining in the righteous call for reform. That their moral indignation was in fact merely a disguise for usurping the positions of an entrenched Republican board was suspected by some observers. This suspicion became an acknowledged fact after the election, when members of a "reformed" board continued to abuse their positions for private gain. Paraphrasing Roscoe Conkling, reform, like patriotism, was the last refuge of the scoundrel.[42]

A bill introduced to the state legislature by Senator Drabelle, a Democratic representative from St. Louis, pro-

sion of the politics of this period, see, Elinore M. Gersman, "Progressive Reform of the St. Louis School Board, 1897," *History of Education Quarterly*, 10 (Spring 1970), 3–21. A further discussion of reform politics occurs in Chapter 10.

41. "Politics in the Schools," *Post-Dispatch*, March 2, 1887; November 9, 1887.

42. *Post-Dispatch*, November 18, 1887; "Reform Methods," September 13, 1888.

vided the means for taking over the board. The Drabelle Bill denied the board its traditional role in assigning districts by empowering a court of five judges to superintend the creation of a new board consisting of representatives from fourteen newly created districts and seven at-large members. In a clear case of gerrymandering, the Democratic majority on the court approved a plan that favored the insurgents. Republicans were quick to point out bias, for the plan lumped together as many German Republicans in one district as possible and nullified other German votes by placing them in districts with a larger Irish Democratic vote. One Republican claimed that some districts were so contrived that the Democrats "could elect a Comanche Indian if they chose." The election results testified to the skill of the court, as the Democrats won perhaps the most lopsided victory in the history of the schools, leaving only three of twenty-one directorships for Republicans. True to the mandate that the fusion party, labelled the Citizens' Ticket, considered it had won, the new board cut the salary of a few officials and announced the termination of German after the conclusion of the current school year. With the saving of $100,000 from German instruction, they also announced a new building program to relieve overcrowding in the schools. This also provided a splendid opportunity for many members of the "reformed" board to enrich themselves by allocating contracts to themselves and their friends.[43]

The new president of the board, Frederick Judson, expressed satisfaction with the ending of German, for now the system was able to reallocate funds to expand needed services and could increase the time allotted basic subjects in the curriculum. Judson was also pleased "with the acquiescence of all classes of the community" to the board's decision and credited two policies for this. First, about one hundred German teachers were retained in the system, as

43. "A Lively Row," *Post-Dispatch*, March 15, 1887; "The New Plan," October 9, 1887; "New School Districts," October 18, 1887; "A General Kick," October 19, 1887; "Looking for Gnats," June 14, 1887. Frederick Judson, "Report of the President," *Annual Report*, 1888, pp. 10–20.

was the special superintendent for German instruction who was appointed an assistant superintendent. Second, the board generously offered its facilities to any group who wished to teach German at their own expense outside of normal school hours. Moreover, Judson and other officials expressed regret over their decision but insisted on its necessity because of the need for retrenchment. Significantly and in contrast to the rhetoric of the antebellum period, there was no claim that the forces of assimilation had triumphed.[44]

Resignation rather than acquiescence is probably a better description of the feeling of the German community. They understood that the major issue was the retention of a board favorable to German instruction and organized to meet the challenge. There were mass meetings throughout the city, including one at Turner Hall, "The Cradle of Missouri Liberty." Nevertheless, they were outmaneuvered and gerrymandered into impotence at the polls. In addition, since the Drabelle Bill extended a School Board member's term of office from two to four years, any attempt to over-turn the board would have to await the 1891 election, and even then there was no guarantee that new districts could be redrawn. The problem for the Germans was complicated further by the defection of some of their number, who were persuaded by the argument that the board simply could not afford to continue to meet expanding needs and retain German in the curriculum. Finally, an internal split within the Republican party over the selection of candidates weak-ened the party organization. The result was that on election day, when there was mass confusion over the district in which a voter was able to cast his ballot, the Democrats were better organized. After the 1887 election, the issue of German, a standard feature in board elections since the Civil War, passed from school politics.[45]

Despite some predictions to the contrary, Germans did

44. Frederick Judson, "Report of the President," *Annual Report, 1889*, pp. 14–15.
45. "Here are the Seven," *Post-Dispatch*, November 15, 1887; "The School Question," November 16, 1887; "Tuesday's Tickets," Novem-ber 17, 1887; "Checking Accounts," November 24, 1887.

not withdraw their children from public schools to any noticeable degree. Apparently, after a generation of contact with public schools, the system had acquired widespread acceptance within the community. This was a vindication of the policies and vision of Harris, who was willing to accommodate the schools' avowed purpose of assimilation to the demands of perhaps the city's most politically powerful group. Certainly, the accommodation reached between 1864 and 1887 redounded to the benefit of both the schools and the immigrants, even though it temporarily exacerbated school politics. Parochial education, while not destroyed, lost its hold over many potential adherents, and the public schools gained the allegiance of a group that willingly supported expansion and innovation.

4

The Consequences of Racial Prejudice

Class, sectarian, ethnic, and racial politics were as important to the shaping of the St. Louis schools as educational theory. This was inevitable, for a pluralistic society naturally stimulated the politics of education. The apportionment of the system's resources and its attention to the special requests of particular interests depended on the capacity of an individual group to mobilize favorable community sentiment and to apply pressure on the School Board. Only rarely, as in the introduction of classes for the deaf, did an innovation meet with no resistance. Teacher education, German instruction, kindergartens, high schools, and even singing and drawing occasioned controversy. Together with German instruction, the most explosive issue of the nineteenth century was how blacks would benefit from the city's growing commitment to public education. Since blacks suffered from widespread hostility and did not command sufficient weight in community politics, they were relegated to separate and substandard facilities. The fundamental reason for this policy was a pervasive unwillingness to transcend the distinction of race while pursuing the ideal of the common school. This chapter explores the failure of St. Louis to establish a more open and equitable school system, and describes how blacks responded to discrimination in education.[1]

1. Pertinent writings on black education in St. Louis are Elinor M. Gersman, "The Development of Public Education for Blacks in Nineteenth Century St. Louis," *Journal of Negro Education*, 41 (Winter 1972), 35–47; J. W. Evans, "A Brief Sketch of the Development of Negro Education in St. Louis, Missouri," *The Journal of Negro History*, 7 (October 1938), 548–52; Henry S. Williams, "The Development of the Negro Public School System in Missouri," *Journal of Negro History*, 5 (April 1920), 137–65; Kurt F. Leidecker, "The Edu-

Prior to the 1860s most northern cities either ignored blacks or placed them in separate schools.[2] St. Louis, situated in a slave state, went beyond this and deprived the black of the right to an education. The 1833 charter, which established the school system, specified that only "free white males" could be officers or members of the school corporation. While not explicitly proscribing black children from the schools, the board forbade their entry as a matter of practice.[3] In 1846 a state law formally prohibited their inclusion, stipulating that "no person shall keep or teach any school for the instruction of negroes or mulattoes," and imposed a penalty of $500 and/or six months imprisonment. Despite instances of evasion by some nuns, a colored woman teacher, and Negro churches, blacks were denied access to formal education.[4] This condition existed despite the requirement that free Negroes support the education of white children through taxes on property that was valued at $3 million by 1860. The cataclysm of the Civil War finally created conditions in which recognition of the educational needs and rights of blacks could no longer be suppressed.[5]

The first change brought on by the war was in the size

cation of Negroes in St. Louis, Missouri, During William Torrey Harris' Administration," *Journal of Negro Education*, 10 (October 1941), 643–49; and George L. Mann, "The Development of Public Education for Negroes in St. Louis, Missouri," (unpublished Ph.D. dissertation, Indiana University, 1949).

2. Leon Litwack, *North of Slavery: The Negro in the Free States, 1790–1860* (Chicago: University of Chicago Press, 1961), pp. 113–52. Donald M. Jacobs, "The Nineteenth Century Struggle Over Segregated Education in Boston Schools," *Journal of Negro Education*, 39 (Winter 1970), 76–86.

3. *Annual Report, 1866*, pp. iii–iv.

4. Harrison A. Trexler, "Slavery in Missouri," *Johns Hopkins University Studies in Historical and Political Sciences* (Baltimore: Johns Hopkins, 1914), pp. 83–84.

5. "Colored Schools," *Annual Report, 1865*, p. 27; "Office of the Superintendent of Public Schools, St. Louis, March 20, 1866 to Editor, *Missouri Republican*," *Missouri Republican*, March 23, 1866. For a discussion of the Negro in antebellum St. Louis see, Richard C. Wade, *Slavery in the Cities: The South 1820–1860* (New York: Oxford, 1964).

of the black community. Between 1860 and 1880, St. Louis's Negro population multiplied about five times, from 3,927 to 22,256. This influx created the third-largest concentration of urban Negroes after Baltimore and Philadelphia.[6] A common expression of those who took the route up the Mississippi captures the mood and expectations of the emigrés: "I'd rather be a lamppost on Targee Street than be mayor of Dixie."[7] It was to Targee, Center, Morgan, Twelfth, and clusters of streets rarely distant from the levee that they came to find their redemption. If only because of their number, new arrangements had to be made to take care of this recently liberated population.

Sympathy engendered by the war for blacks encouraged some whites to open schools and to appeal publicly for support, despite the statutory prohibitions. The Freedman's Relief Society, a local benevolent association, responded to the Emancipation Proclamation by establishing three schools in January, 1863. Shortly thereafter, the National Freedman's Bureau offered free instruction, and several tuition institutions opened. In 1865, much of this effort was centralized by the Board of Education for Colored Schools, which supervised a system for 1,500 children. This agency, administered by Negroes, operated with the assistance of the Western Sanitary Commission, a white service agency established during the war to care for soldiers, their families, and liberated slaves.[8]

St. Louis public schools, however, remained uninvolved until the reconstructed state constitution of 1865 legally required public support for black education. The board

6. Baltimore had a Negro population of 53,716, Philadelphia 31,689, and St. Louis 22,256. If the population of New York and Brooklyn, which were separate municipalities at the time, are added, they would move ahead of St. Louis with 27,758. U. S. Census Office, *The Tenth Census, 1880; Report of the Social Statistics of Cities*, 18 pp. 469, 533, 733; 19, pp. 3, 567.

7. Quoted in Arna Bontemps and Jack Conroy, *Anyplace But Here* (New York: Hill and Wang, 1966), p. 113.

8. "Annual Report of Officers of the Freedman's Relief Society," *Missouri Republican*, February 3, 1864. *Annual Report, 1867*, p. 2; "Colored Schools," *Annual Report, 1865*, p. 26.

initially fulfilled its obligations by contributing $500 to the privately sponsored Board of Education for Colored Schools.[9] In February, 1866, it decided to engage directly in educating blacks and authorized that "one or two schools be established as soon as suitable rooms can be obtained for that purpose." The board justified its decision by asserting that the new law demanded serious attention to colored education, that "common justice to the colored people as taxpayers" required it, that the "best good of the community" would be served, and that "public sentiment approves it."[10] However valid the appeal to law, justice, and the public good, the board was plainly wrong in its assessment of the public's mood. As soon as the decision was announced, the outcry began.

There are few records extant of the role of the freedman in the ensuing controversy. The documentation that remains largely concerns a conflict that divided the white community. This division was in microcosm a reflection of a national conflict that was carried on by Radical Republicans and Democrats. On a local level, the discord was exacerbated by the ethnic animosities that aggravated relations between the German Republicans and the Irish Democrats. The question of colored education was only one of a number of issues outstanding between the political parties, and the success of black schooling was dependent on Republican victories.

The *Missouri Republican*, the leading organ of the Democratic or Union party, embarked on an anti-colored school campaign by denouncing the school directors as being frivolous with public monies for planning to build "extravagant school houses" for blacks. Moreover, they were condemned for caring too much for Negroes: "If they [Radical Republican directors] like to associate with the niggerdom, as would seem to be the case, let them go to them, but not at the expense of the white men." The expulsion of the

9. Felix Coste, "President's Report," *Annual Report, 1865*, pp. 11–12.

10. "Public School Matters," *Missouri Republican*, February 17, 1866.

directors from public office was fitting punishment for such behavior.[11]

Superintendent Ira Divoll responded by reminding the critics that eight schoolhouses were being planned for white students and that no comparable outlay was contemplated for blacks. He added that Negroes had been paying $15,000 per year into school revenues through property taxes from which they had not benefited. Chiding his critics with an appeal to justice mixed with subtle racism, Divoll suggested that whites would no longer wish to benefit from such money and that the best way to dispose of it was to expend it on Negroes. Blacks, not whites, Divoll concluded, "had the right to complain."[12] Divoll's response did not persuade the critics, and the issue became further enmeshed in the city's politics.

Between the board's February policy statement and the municipal elections of April, 1866, the Democratic press mounted a bitter and vicious campaign against the School Board, radicalism, and blacks. The language of the attacks is indicative of the social and political context out of which the first public, colored schools struggled to be born. The *Missouri Republican*, for example, exhorted the city's voters to stand against "the bigoted spirit of Radicalism and Radical Negro equality, not only on the street cars but everywhere else, to come out to the polls on next Tuesday and vote for such men as would reflect the wishes of the people." It accused Radicals of "supporting lazy Negroes and building fine school-houses for colored abecedarians." The paper also applauded anti-Negro action on the national level. For example, it supported President Johnson's veto of the Civil Rights bill of 1866 with the headline: "The President Puts His Foot Down on Nigger Equality, Amalgamation and a Centralized Despotism." A legend that preceded a plea for the anti-Radicals connected national and local politics: "In Favor of President Johnson's Policy

11. "Union Meetings on Thursday Evening," *Missouri Republican*, March 20, 1866.

12. "Office of the Superintendent of Public Schools, St. Louis, March 20, 1866, to the Editor, *Missouri Republican*," *Missouri Republican*, March 23, 1866.

. . . Against Negro Equality . . . Opposed to $450,000 Additional School Tax. . . ." Castigating the Radicals as the "Negro Equality Party," the Union party claimed that the "thinking man must choose between two tickets—one supporting the President, the Constitution and the restoration of the Union; the other, in Radical opposition, and in favor of making this a Negro government, and saddling the city with an enormous increase in taxation."[13]

The "thinking man" chose every anti-Radical candidate for school director and most other city offices, striking radicalism with its worst defeat of the decade. The *Missouri Republican's* victory statement claimed that the results were "a direct, emphatic and unmistakable condemnation of the proposition to largely increase the assessment of property for the erection of additional buildings to accommodate and do especial honor to colored juveniles."[14] Had the victory been complete, it could have pitted the board against the new state law and its own superintendent, and could have prolonged the exclusion of the Negro. Radicals, however, retained a slight majority, as only one-third of the directors were elected each spring, and they continued to control the board during the next decade even as they did most municipal offices. The Radical program, although obstructed and under constant attack, was not ended.

During the course of the next school year, the divided but still Republican board acted to establish three schools for 437 black students. The board wished to do more, as this number represented only a small proportion of the potential black student population, but community prejudices extended beyond the ballot box and prevented the opening of a larger number of schools. Not until December, three months after classes began for whites, could the board locate someone who was willing to rent a few rooms for black pupils. The problem of finding space was so acute

13. "City Election—The Issues," *Missouri Republican*, March 29, 1866; "Another Veto," March 28, 1866; "Union Nomination," March 29, 1866; Ibid.; April 3, 1866.
14. "The School Board," *Missouri Republican*, April 5, 1866.

that a special committee was created to conduct a city-wide search. In January, it reported that on every occasion it contracted for the rental or purchase of a suitable house the other parties "ascertained the use to which we intended to put it, and backed out." After receiving the report, the board resolved to advertise in the English and German newspapers for two weeks in order to rent two houses and empowered the committee to purchase suitable accommodations if this failed. Through these means they finally acquired a home and rented basement rooms in different sections of the city. So dilapidated were these facilities, however, that additional funds had to be appropriated to make them suitable for classes. Even after repairs, the house was described as "a small one, rather ancient in appearance, and not very attractive inside or out."[15]

The prospects for finding proper schoolrooms changed very little in the next few years. The general condition of black schools was so bad that they were continually abolished and moved to new locations. In 1869, for example, when teaching in "Colored School No. 3" became impossible because of dampness and general unhealthfulness the school was discontinued, and students were moved to some unoccupied rooms in another building. This kind of instability made it difficult to assign district boundaries to colored schools and to maintain the standard graded curriculum, two reforms recently introduced into the system. In addition, since the schools' locations were determined by the availability of rooms, some black pupils had to walk more than two miles for classes. At best, blacks would inherit an old "white" schoolhouse that had been abandoned for more modern facilities. More often, however, Negroes were educated in inadequate, inferior, and occasionally distant buildings, sometimes pursuing instruction at a different location each year.[16]

15. *Annual Report, 1867*, p. 31. "PBPS, December 11, 1866," *Missouri Republican*, December 12, 1866; "PBPS, January 15, 1867," January 16, 1867; "PBPS, February 26, 1867," February 27, 1867; June 11, 1867.

16. For discussion on the conditions of Negro schools, see,

Faced with these conditions, blacks frequently complained to the board about capriciousness in the handling of colored schools and the lack of concern for their children that this indicated. On one occasion, they were so anxious for a good school at a convenient location that they built one at their own expense and then transferred it to the board on condition that it undertake the obligation of sustaining and maintaining the building. They sought more than just improved physical conditions; blacks wanted for their children what was available to whites. They requested evening schools, kindergartens, training for their teachers, and a high school. Apparently the only element of public education they did not seek was German, which even among whites had limited appeal beyond the German community.[17]

The founding of Sumner High School suggests the kind of resistance Negroes encountered in their struggle for parity. For the first nine years of segregation there was no high school for Negro students. In September, 1875, one was temporarily introduced in some vacant rooms in a colored school, but it was discontinued within a month. This resulted in the demand of blacks, under an appeal to separate and equal facilities, either for the reinstitution of the classes or for the admittance of blacks to white high schools. The board responded immediately that the mixture of races was forbidden by the Missouri constitution. However, Robert Rombauer, the board's attorney, then advised that under the same constitution the board was "to provide for and maintain a high school for colored children in this city, and that a total discontinuance of such school is not within the legal power of the Board." Faced with Negro pressure and Rombauer's opinion, the board agreed to establish Sumner High School.[18]

Sumner High, however, was not all that its title suggests.

"PBPS, December 22, 1868," *Missouri Republican*, December 23, 1868. *Annual Report, 1869*, p. 72; *Annual Report, 1870*, p. 104; *Annual Report, 1872*, p. 99.

17. "PBPS, July 14, 1868," *Missouri Republican*, July 16, 1868.

18. *Official Proceedings*, 2, September 14, 1875, 59.

While white high schools were provided with the highest paid teachers in the system, the black "high school" was staffed with "third assistant" teachers, or the lowest paid. This was perhaps appropriate, as Sumner High was largely an elementary school with most of its student body in the first four grades. In 1880, for example, of the school's 411 students, only 76 were doing high school work. Moreover, on the average, three times as much money was spent on white high school students as on their black counterparts. All the board had really done was change the classification of the school, not genuinely respond to black demands or the requirements of the law.[19]

In addition to attempts to achieve equality in facilities, there was also pressure for symbolic equality and for respect. With the exception of Sumner, colored schools were assigned numbers, not names as were white schools. No remembrance of presidents, statesmen, or local heroes graced the entry to colored schools. In 1878, the Colored Educational Association requested that they be named for deceased Negroes, suggesting Alexandre Dumas, Crispus Attucks, and Toussaint L'Ouveture, among others. The board, however, was unwilling to grant so racist a request and countered with the offer of calling them after "men who have distinguished themselves in the cause of the colored race." In 1890, the issue again came before the board, which offered the names of Wendell Phillips, William Lloyd Garrison, John C. Frémont, Ulysses S. Grant, and others, generally Republicans, who might be considered friendly to blacks. After rejection of this proposal, approval was finally given to labelling black schools with the names of distinguished Negroes.[20]

The difficulty of realizing such a modest goal reflects not only the paternalism with which even relatively sympathetic boards viewed black education but the limited pressure that blacks could bring to bear in gaining their objectives. In this

19. *Annual Report, 1880*, pp. cxvi-cxxv.
20. Leidecker, *Yankee Teacher*, p. 647. *Official Proceedings*, 3, August 13, 1878, 112. Gersman, "The Development of Public Education for Blacks in Nineteenth Century St. Louis, Missouri," pp. 42–43.

period, during which the system was undergoing tremendous expansion and redefinition in response to population growth, the apportionment of public resources was not made by a more or less objective assessment of what constituted a group's educational requirements. The application of funds and the concern for special needs were largely influenced by the distribution of power among groups that contended for control over the system. The success of the German community in obtaining their demands provides the most striking illustration of the importance of group pressure in the politics of education, and even in this case, they were successful only for a limited time. They were able to frustrate their opponents because of basic demographic and political facts: The Germans constituted the largest single minority in the city, outnumbering the Irish, who were their most active opponents, by as much as three to one. They were also cohesive enough to be able to muster mass meetings and present petitions that contained as many as 40,000 signatures. If the Irish, who were represented on the board and were a major force in municipal politics, failed in their protests over board policy, the chances for successful black protest were even slimmer. In the postwar generation, the Negro was considered an appendage and a captive of the Republican machine, and his threats to play an independent and more effective role were not taken seriously.

Given this reality, the city's most recent, impoverished, and powerless immigrants were forced to seek an accommodation in a community that, at one extreme, viewed them with candid hostility and, at the other, with limited benevolence. In effect, this meant accepting segregation. Members of the Negro community recognized this boundary and endorsed it. In 1870 the Colored Convention, an organization composed largely of blacks, met in Jefferson City to discuss the condition of the Negro in Missouri and especially his educational problems.[21] The convention recommended that

21. "Lincoln Institute—A Protest," *Missouri Democrat*, February 5, 1870. Among the leadership were men like James Milton Turner, an ex-slave who became Minister to Liberia and Monrovia in the 1870s and was active in Negro political and educational affairs in Missouri, and James Yeatman, the white president of the Western

"separate schools" be established with "the same advantages" as schools for white chldren. Only when there were not enough colored children in a district to warrant the creation of a separate school did the convention recommend that blacks and whites attend the same classes. The proposal received wide support from leaders of both races and was enacted into law in 1876.[22]

Integration was not at issue during the postwar period. The maximum to which even sympathetic whites would assent was equal, though segregated, facilities. A petition sent to Congress protesting a proposed civil rights bill was one of the rare occasions the board felt compelled to express itself on the subject. The bill required that white and colored children be admitted to the same classes where schools were supported by taxation. The board claimed that it was maintaining separate and equal schools and that should the bill be passed, "irreparable injury if not total destruction would result to the school system." It argued that the white children would be withdrawn from the schools and the opponents of public education would then be able to muster support for repeal of the school tax.[23] This was probably an accurate assessment. The *Globe-Democrat*, a Radical Republican organ that was sympathetic to Negro education, likewise claimed that "integration would work a great deal of mischief, and could do no good except in the satisfaction of a little false pride on the part of colored children and their parents."[24]

Blacks sought to satisfy their "pride" in other ways that, ironically, served to strengthen the patterns of segregation. In the fall of 1874 a group of Negroes petitioned the Board of Public Schools to change recruitment policies, asking

Sanitary Commission, who was active in many philanthropic affairs in St. Louis. Irving Dillard, "James Milton Turner: A Little Known Benefactor of His People," *Journal of Negro History*, 19 (October 1934), 373–411.

22. "Colored Schools," *Missouri Democrat*, January 27, 1870. W. Sherman Savage, "Legal Provisions for Negro Schools in Missouri," *Journal of Negro History*, 16 (July 1931), 309–21.

23. *Official Proceedings*, 2, June 9, 1874, 430–41.

24. *Globe-Democrat*, March 16, 1877.

"if the time hasn't arrived when teachers for colored schools may not be selected from among ourselves."[25] The board agreed in principle, but it was not until the fall of 1877 when another group, the Colored Educational Council, again petitioned that substantive action resulted. While the council's petition stated that they were *"greatly aggrieved"* by a system that segregated "all classes of American citizens" from those "known to have *African blood coursing through their veins,"* it did not advocate integration. Instead, the council pressed for the replacement of white teachers with qualified blacks on the basis that this would improve the quality of instruction. The petition pointed out that many of the better-trained whites would not consider teaching colored children because of "the social stigma attached to such a position." Furthermore, it maintained that "white teachers are not the best teachers for colored schools," since they have been inculcated with "certain false and wicked ideas" that impair their effectiveness when standing before black children. Black teachers, on the other hand, were better equipped and more desirable: Through contacts with colored children and parents, they "know better the wants of their pupils and how to supply them"; "they are free from unfavorable social surroundings" that breed prejudice, so that they have a great "zeal and power for good"; and, since they were themselves black, "by example and intercourse," they could elevate the aspirations of the black child.[26]

At one meeting of the council James Henry, a white minister, voiced opposition to the petition. He feared that if only Negroes taught in segregated schools the "color line" would be reinforced and a fundamentally inequitable and pernicious situation would be perpetuated. Even though some benefits, such as employment for blacks, might be attained, Henry advised not to extend the "color line" but to destroy it. He insisted that the council press for complete

25. *Official Proceedings,* 1, October 13, 1874, 367.
26. "Colored Teachers in Colored Schools; Rooms of the St. Louis Educational Council, St. Louis, February 26, 1877—To the Honourable President and Officers of the St. Louis School Board," *Globe-Democrat,* March 14, 1877.

equality. Just as qualified whites should instruct in black schools, qualified Negroes should teach in white schools. Furthermore, he insisted that the Negro community should demand to have their children admitted to every department of the system and, if necessary, use the courts to enforce the demand for integration. Henry's statement was received with applause, but the Negro leadership successfully pressed forward with their own petition.[27]

An important factor in the council's rejection of Henry's proposals was the recognition that segregation would benefit educated black adults. In this respect, the St. Louis debate was an extension of a controversy that was taking place in secondary schools and colleges in the South. As James McPherson has shown, Negro educators sought to secure positions in and to obtain control over northern-sponsored educational institutions that were vital to their interests during the postwar decades in what amounted to a nineteenth-century version of "black power."[28] Since for St. Louis blacks there were few opportunities for advancement beyond unskilled or service jobs, the approximately seventy teaching positions available in the public schools during much of this period were of special importance. This view is supported by statistics on the sex of teachers that show that 95 per cent of the teachers in white schools were female, while about half of the positions in colored schools were filled by males.[29]

The council's assessment of the impact of Negro teachers proved remarkably accurate. In the first year of their introduction, 1877–1878, the number of black pupils rose by 35 per cent. When he evaluated this increase in the *Annual Report*, Superintendent Harris credited it to the changeover to black teachers. After the second year he attributed

27. "The School Question: Father Henry is Opposed to the Color Line in Schools," *Globe-Democrat*, June 10, 1877. The same point is made in a speech at the St. Paul M.E. Church, "Educating the Africans," *Globe-Democrat*, June 28, 1877.

28. James M. McPherson, "White Liberals and Black Power in Negro Education, 1865–1915," *American Historical Review*, 74 (June, 1970), 1380–86.

29. The appendixes of the *Annual Reports* contain the names of the system's teachers from which sex distribution can be established.

another increase of 20 per cent to the same cause. In the third year, 1880, the black public schools increased their enrollment by another 27 per cent. From 1876, the year before black teachers were hired, through 1880, enrollment had more than doubled, from about 1,500 to more than 3,600 pupils, even though the city's black population had remained constant. Clearly, the demand for black teachers arose not only from the leadership of the community or from aspiring teachers but enjoyed popular support. As Harris testified, large numbers of blacks preferred to keep their children out of public schools so long as there were unqualified or hostile instructors. What had occurred, in effect, was a boycott of public schools, although it was unaccompanied by the mass public demonstrations and legal protests that characterized such actions in later decades in other cities.[30]

This boycott parallels the action taken by other St. Louisans when confronting a hostile educational environment. Thousands of Lutherans and Catholics chose to establish their own schools rather than have their children subjected to the nonsectarianism of the public system. The German community, too, developed its own institutions in large measure as a consequence of the refusal of the public system to offer instruction in German. The boycott is remarkable, however, in that blacks lacked the alternatives available to others.

Although it is not possible to differentiate between blacks who sent their children to school even before black teachers were hired and those who did not, it is possible to ascertain how important public schools became to the city's blacks once the critical issue of teachers had been satisfactorily resolved. To this end a collective biography of St. Louis children, containing information on school attendance, child employment, and the nature of the family, was created by an analysis of the 1880 manuscript census. The biography comprehends 12,274 white and 1,078 black children from ages one through twenty. These materials are especially

30. *Official Proceedings*, 3, June 11, 1878, 72; March 11, 1879, 197; January 13, 1880, 366; April 13, 1880.

useful in analysing school attendance among blacks, as the only institution available other than the public system was a Catholic parochial school that had perhaps 100 black students. Since the census indicates school attendance but does not discriminate between public, private, and parochial institutions, the precise relationship between whites and the public schools cannot be defined solely through this body of information. The collective biography can, however, be applied with confidence to the black public school student.[31]

The following information is part of a larger discussion of the social structure of education and of the public schools that follows in Chapter 7. For purposes of analysis, the population is divided into groups based on race, age, and class. Because analysis of the white community shows that class was an important determinant in both educational and vocational advancement, and since very few black fathers were engaged in middle-class occupations, valid comparisons of white and black children must be drawn from parallel cohorts of working-class children.

In comparing white and black working-class children during the peak ages for school attendance, six through twelve, 81 per cent of whites attended school as compared with 68 per cent of the blacks. Among ten-year-olds, 91 per cent of the whites and 88 per cent of the blacks attended. The higher percentages of whites for the entire age group reflect the fact that whites may have attended school for a year longer on average, dropping out after the third grade, while blacks dropped out after the second; but it is apparent that children of both groups went to school (Tables 6 and 19).

In the thirteen- through sixteen-year age group blacks attended more than whites, 63 per cent as compared with 38 per cent (Table 19). Indeed, the percentage of blacks who were children of unskilled or blue-collar workers ap-

31. *The Priests and People of St. Elizabeth's Mark the Seventy-Fifth Anniversary of the Founding of Their Parish* (St. Louis: 1933?), pp. 7–8. See appendixes A and B for the tables relating to the following section.

proaches that of white children whose fathers were white-collar workers, who averaged 70 per cent attendance (Table 21). The higher proportion of thirteen- through sixteen-year-old blacks in 1880 did not mean that they remained in school longer than whites but may have been a consequence of their refusal to enroll until black teachers were hired. Support for this hypothesis comes from the public school records, which report that few older blacks were found in the third grade or above and fewer still in the high school, the logical place for students at these ages. One additional observation is in order here. When the percentages are broken down by sex, black girls, like their white counterparts, attended school a year or so longer than boys (Table 20). Thus, as soon as the atmosphere of the public schools was made receptive by the hiring of black teachers, blacks were as eager as whites for schooling and closely conformed to the parameters that characterized attendance among white children of the same class.

The enthusiasm with which blacks ultimately flocked to schools is striking when two other factors are considered: the nature of the black household and the birthplaces of parents. Contemporary writers have commented on the debilitating effects of nonnormative family life on the aspirations and achievements of children of blacks and of the poor, in general. Analysis of the data confirms the applicability of such a perception to patterns of school attendance. When children lived at home with fathers, and with mothers who were occupied as housewives, they were more likely to have a better education. Thus, only 74 per cent of the white children aged six through twelve who were not in such families went to school as compared with 82 per cent of the children with families. Between thirteen and sixteen the gap widened to 48 per cent for family children and only 28 per cent for children not in the family. One might, therefore, have expected that blacks would have made even less use of schools, since many families were fatherless and were headed by a working mother. For example, between the ages six and twelve only 55 per cent of black children as compared with 84 per cent of whites had both parents. Of the remaining 45 per cent, 24 per cent lived in a household headed by the mother, 13 per cent lived with other relatives, 6 per cent were boarders or otherwise living outside the family, and 1 per cent lived only with their fathers. Moreover, whereas 87 per cent of white mothers of young children were full-time housekeepers, only 54 per cent of black mothers were similarly at home. Conditions for thirteen- to sixteen-year-olds were even less favorable. Thus, blacks maintained a high level of enrollment even though they came from a higher proportion of one-parent and even parentless families (Table 22).

As one last indicator that measures the enthusiasm of blacks for an education that conformed to their standards, consider the birthplaces of the parents and children. Sixty-four per cent of the fathers and 54 per cent of the mothers were born outside of Missouri, largely in the South, and except for 2 per cent of the fathers whose origins are unknown, the remainder were born in Missouri. Nearly all of the parents, therefore, grew up in places where education was either forbidden or limited. Indeed, even 30 per cent of the children were born outside of Missouri, again largely in the South and very likely in locations where education was not as accessible as in St. Louis. Without a tradition of education and in the absence of compulsion from municipal authorities who had not yet discovered the truant officer, these children came to school out of an internal dynamic present in the black community. Moreover, their movement into the schools was unsolicited and therefore unique. During the postwar period, the School Board actively sought to serve the poor by kindergartens; the middle class through the high school; immigrants through evening classes; and Germans through German language instruction. There is no record, however, that suggests that the board ever campaigned to bring in blacks. In this first generation of contact with public education, blacks expressed their desire for and faith in education not merely by individual and group agitation but through massive participation. By sending their children to school, they demonstrated that they considered education one of the necessities for urban living and a requirement for free men.

Historians such as Willie Lee Rose, Joel Williamson, and Henry Bullock have written that, during Reconstruction, freedmen in the South were possessed by an almost mystical enthusiasm and faith in the value and power of schooling. The data collected from the census confirm this assessment for postwar St. Louis. As the incident of the boycott demonstrates, however, they would not act blindly on this faith. Blacks had well-developed ideas about the kind of instruction they wanted, and only when basic conditions were met did they commit their children to the schools.[32]

There is an additional insight derived from the data that is appropriate here, and this concerns the significance of schooling as a preparation for life. The collective biography points out that it was after schooling that the most profound differences between whites and blacks occurred. Beginning at age twelve, both whites and blacks moved into the labor force, but there developed in the teen years an increasingly sharp differentiation in the kinds of work they performed. White teenagers initially found employment as unskilled laborers and semiskilled workers, and by age sixteen appreciable numbers had risen to skilled workers and clerks. By age eighteen, for example, 24 per cent are skilled workers and 27 per cent were in white-collar positions. While children of white-collar workers had a greater opportunity for skilled positions or better through the teen years, such opportunities also existed for white children of the working classes. On the other hand, blacks entered the labor market at the lowest positions, as unskilled and semiskilled laborers, and stayed there. Significantly, in the population study of 259 black males between the ages of twelve

32. Henry A. Bullock, *A History of Negro Education in the South: From 1619 to the Present* (Cambridge: Harvard University Press, 1967). Willie Lee Rose, *Rehearsal for Reconstruction: The Port Royal Experiment* (Indianapolis: Bobbs-Merrill, 1964). Joel Williamson, *After Slavery: The Negro in South Carolina during Reconstruction 1861–1877* (Chapel Hill: University of North Carolina Press, 1965).

and twenty that was derived from the census, there were but three clerks, two musicians, and one skilled worker. The pattern established for teenagers also held for their parents. Whites, of course, were distributed throughout the occupational hierarchy, while blacks were overwhelmingly concentrated in the lowest rungs. The 1891 *Annual Report*, for example, specified the occupations of the parents of about 4,000 black students, 97 per cent of whom were unskilled and semiskilled workers (Table 18). Clearly, whatever the success of the black community's agitation for better education, the larger aspiration for improvement outside the school was to be denied. Since schooling did not serve as a prerequisite for social mobility, the seeds of frustration over the value of education that was subsequently voiced were sown during these years. The tragedy for blacks during the postwar period was that their enthusiasm for schooling was neither cultivated nor rewarded.

Nevertheless, black children attended school as much and, in some cases, even more than comparable whites. More sensitivity to the needs and aspirations of blacks would undoubtedly have been well-received. However, as the twelve-year delay in acceding to the request to name colored schools after leaders of the black race indicated, the board was unable to advance from paternalism to understanding and compassion. Instead, blacks usually confronted reluctant, evasive, and even hostile boards. Moreover, the failure to deal more justly with blacks stands in striking contrast to the treatment accorded other groups, particularly the Germans. The *Missouri Republican* expressed the reason for the difference: "We have never tried to assimilate with the Indians; we should never try to amalgamate with the Africans. It is altogether different with European nations, especially those of German origin."[33] For those who were not as well favored as the Germans, there were alternatives. Dissatisfied Irish, Catholics, and Lutherans were able to create separate school systems. This was not a possibility for the black immigrant. More than most groups,

---

33. "Destiny of the German Nationality in the United States," *Missouri Republican*, November 11, 1878.

the black was dependent on the public system. The St. Louis schools, which were generally eager to overcome divisions of class and nationality, were singularly hesitant and compromising in confronting the problem of race.

Finally, in creating a subsystem of colored schools, these post-Civil War boards set the course of public instruction for almost a century. Not until 1954 did segregation and its attendant inequality officially end. In the face of such deeply rooted prejudices, the first post-Civil War generation of Negro immigrants, anxious for the education of their children, attained as much as possible from a largely antagonistic community. They were unable to achieve more because the schools, although promising openness and equality, in fact closely mirrored the prejudices and limitations of the society they represented and served.[34]

34. After 1954, *de jure* segregation became *de facto*. For analysis of the place of the Negro in contemporary St. Louis see, Herbert Semmel, "Race and Education in St. Louis, Missouri," unpublished report submitted to the United States Commission on Civil Rights, 1967; Monroe Billington, "Public School Integration in Missouri, 1954–1964," *Journal of Negro Education*, 35 (Summer 1966), 252–62.

5

The Beginning of the Public School
Kindergarten Movement

The establishment of the first public school kindergarten
in St. Louis in 1873 represented the nation's first large-scale
involvement with "pre-school" instruction. It was also an
indication of the growing awareness of the role of public
education in equipping children, particularly those who
came from the slums, for the demands of urban life. Kindergartens did not, of course, originate within the public
schools. Prior to the 1870s they had won considerable popularity through the operation of numerous private and
charity institutions. Developing in the 1830s out of the
ideas of the Swiss educator Friedrich Froebel, who believed
that through play a child's personality was enhanced and
his intelligence trained, kindergartens spread to western
European countries, primarily the German states, France,
Italy, and Holland. In the 1850s, Froebel's teachings crossed
the Atlantic with German immigrants who established
German-language play-schools in St. Louis and other midwestern cities. The first, private, non-Germanic kindergarten opened in Boston in 1860, and it was widely imitated.
In this context of the growing influence of the kindergarten
movement, Superintendent Harris and Susan Blow, a young
woman from a prominent local family, studied and recognized the possibilities of kindergartens for the city's public
schools.[1]

1. For the early history of the kindergarten movement, the writ-
ings of early kindergarteners are especially helpful. See Susan E.
Blow, "Kindergarten Education," in Nicholas Murray Butler, ed.,
Education in the United States, 1 (Albany, N.Y.: J. B. Lyon, 1900),
33–76. Also, Nina C. Vandewalker, *The Kindergarten in American
Education* (New York: Macmillan, 1913). For Harris's understanding
of the flow of the movement and its relation to St. Louis see William
Hyde and Howard Conrad, eds., *Encyclopedia of the History of St.
Louis* (St. Louis: Southern History Company, 1899), pp. 2013–19.

Harris's appreciation for the kindergarten stemmed from his experiences as the chief officer of one of the nation's larger school systems. Soon after becoming superintendent in 1868, he ordered a series of studies, "block reports," to investigate the distribution of children in the city so that he might better assess the educational requirements of different parts of the community.[2] These reports revealed that in some areas, especially the levee and factory districts where children were "surrounded by the haunts of vice and iniquity, and they have everything to struggle against if they set out on the path of virtue and culture," many attended school for three years or less. In 1870, Harris proposed dealing with this problem by taking slum children into the schools at a younger age than usual so that they might spend more time under the benign influence of a well-disciplined and moral atmosphere. He therefore proposed suspending the legal requirements that fixed six as the minimum age of attendance.[3]

Unable to accept Harris's proposal, the school board was forced to raise the age of admission to seven in several crowded manufacturing districts because schools could not accommodate all of those who wished to attend.[4] In 1871, therefore, Harris made another plea for the downward definition of the admission age and, for the first time, explicitly referred to the implementation of the kindergarten idea. He suggested that Froebel's system provided "valuable hints" for dealing with slum children. Since the prob-

Kindergartens were supported in St. Louis by German immigrants in the 1860s and perhaps earlier. See, "The Schools Collection," Missouri Historical Society, St. Louis, for a brochure dated April 9, 1863, advertising "Kleinkinderschulen (auch Kindergarten, oder Vor– und Spielschulen genannt)." This was a school for children between the ages of two and seven with German as the language of the classroom. Also see, *Annual Report*, *1868*, p. 80.

2. The minutes of board meetings carry reference to block reports that inquired into the number, ages, and backgrounds of the children in all of the city's blocks. Unfortunately, they are no longer extant.

3. "PBPS, October 11, 1870," *Missouri Republican*, October 13, 1870. *Annual Report*, *1870*, p. 26.

4. Felix Coste, "Report of the President," *Annual Report*, *1870*, p. 9.

lem of reclaiming the children was so pressing, he recommended that, at the minimum, an experimental class be established immediately from which lessons might be learned about how to make instruction in the district school more effective. He was careful to point out that such an experiment would not be conducted "with a view of extending our system to the kindergartens themselves." By the following year, 1872, he had become more specific in his call for remedial education and asked for decisive action. No longer suggesting only a class from which techniques could be gleaned for application to the normal curriculum of the primary school, he advocated kindergartens for children three years old and up as a fixed feature of the school system. In two years Harris had moved from isolating the problem to a program for its solution.[5]

As he refined his thought during his term as superintendent, his *Annual Reports* to the board included large sections devoted to propagating, analysing, and justifying the kindergarten. He defined the obligation of the educator as "reach[ing] all of the population of the community, and of subjecting it to the beneficent influences of the schools." It was clear to him that the children who grew up "in poverty and crime" were those who required the most immediate attention:

> Living in narrow, filthy alleys, poorly clad and without habits of cleanliness, "the divine sense of shame," which Plato makes to be the foundation of civilization, is very little developed. Self respect is the basis of character and virtue; cleanliness of person and clothing is a sine qua non for its growth in the child. The child who passes his years in the misery of the crowded tenement house or alley, becomes early familiar with all manner of corruption and immorality. The children thus unhappily situated are fortunate if they are placed at work even in their tender years, and taught habits of industry, though deprived of school education. The unfortunate ones grow up in crime. But if they can receive an education at school besides the education in

5. *Annual Report, 1871*, pp. 9–10; *Annual Report, 1872*, p. 18.

useful industry they are more than fortunate, their destiny is in their own hands.[6]

The lack of discipline and the propensity for crime that slum children exhibited was, Harris believed, but a reflection of the maladjustment of large numbers of poor people in the city. Beginning in 1870, he wrote that this problem grew out of the breakdown of the traditional processes of socialization. Sensitive to the novelty of the urban environment, he believed that people in cities were "living on the frontiers of national life, and are continually acting the part of pioneers." However, this participation in the creation of a new community and of novel forms of social organization exacted a heavy price from those who were unable to cope with the consequences of change.[7]

The basic problem was that the traditional socializing agents—the family, church, vocation, state, and school—were moving into a new balance that was dictated by modern conditions of life. Of prime concern to Harris was the diminishing role played by the family. He saw that especially slum families lost control of their children as early as the third year and the child was therefore in danger until age six or seven, when he entered school. These formative years, the "plastic" period of the child,[8] were "not well provided for either by family life or by social life in the United States."[9] During this critical time of transition from the "nurture" of the family to the influence of the classroom, the child was threatened with malformation or perversion by life in the city's streets. The great object of the kindergarten was to step into this breach in the child's development and redeem him for society.[10]

6. *Annual Report, 1876,* p. 79.

7. *Annual Report, 1872,* p. 77.

8. *Annual Report, 1872,* p. 26. Harris elaborated on the decay of the family in urban-industrial society in a pamphlet commissioned for international distribution by the Bureau of Education. Duane Doty and William T. Harris, *A Statement on the Theory of Education in the United States of America, as Adopted by Many Leading Educators* (Washington, D. C.: Government Printing Office, 1874), pp. 11–14.

9. *Annual Report, 1879,* p. 136.

10. *Annual Report, 1879,* p. 217; *Annual Report, 1872,* p. 18.

Harris's partner in the kindergarten movement, Susan Elizabeth Blow, came to much the same position from a different point of departure. Miss Blow, the daughter of one of the city's leading business and political families, was motivated to commit herself to aiding slum children by a sense of personal responsibility and obligation. Born in 1843 to Henry T. Blow, who made a fortune in the lead industry, she was given the finest private education that the city could provide. When this proved inadequate, her father imported a teacher from Philadelphia and established a private school for her and a few friends. At sixteen she went to New York for more training and in the next few years she traveled and studied in Brazil and Europe. Aside from the education derived from schools, tutors, and the Grand Tour, her family experiences molded her personality and concept of responsibility in a way that led her to choose kindergarten work.[11]

In a letter to Harris, she described her early life as typical of "every girl brought up in a Christian family"; she taught Sunday School, did church work, instructed her brother and sister, and tended a very large family. Looking back on these years spent within the bosom of a religious, active, and affluent family, Miss Blow wrote that this upbringing had made her aware of "an irresistible impulse to action, and a hunger for something which might seem worthwhile doing. I suppose I had the feeling the Catholic call Vocation." Returning to St. Louis at the age of twenty-eight, she served for a brief period in 1871–1872 as a substitute teacher in the public schools. In that role she discovered precisely the form of that vocation.[12]

While substituting, she experimented with some of Froebel's techniques of play, which she had observed when traveling in Germany. "This," she wrote, "may be said to be the outside occasion of the beginning of the work." After this experience, she went with the approval and en-

---

11. Susan E. Blow, Cazenovia, N.Y., to William T. Harris, Saratoga, N.Y., July 9, 1892, *William Torrey Harris MSS*, folder marked "Blow Letters, Susan E., 1890–1896," Missouri Historical Society.
12. Ibid.

couragement of Harris to New York to study kindergarten methods with Maria Kraus–Boelte, a leader of the movement, who had recently arrived from Holland to open a kindergarten in that city. In May, 1873, Harris urged her to return to St. Louis where, he advised, in September finally she could commence the work in the public schools on an experimental basis. In September, 1873, the professional educator and the bachelor woman of mission joined hands to establish the first public school kindergarten.[13]

Working together, they devised and publicized the new institution for the redemption of the slum child. They designed a curriculum that bridged the "nurture" of the family and the established program of the district school. Much of their effort was devoted to teaching the young child a complex of virtues and values that were necessary for his integration into the manners and discipline of community life. Thus, great emphasis was placed on "moral discipline," and the child was taught to be neat and clean and to practice the amenities and etiquette of polite living. He was trained also in those virtues that formed such an important part of the district school curriculum—habits of regularity, punctuality, silence, obedience, and self-control. In short, the child was taken from the culture of the streets, poor neighborhoods, and undisciplined families, and was conditioned in the skills of community living or, as Harris put it, the techniques "which enable him to combine with his fellow man in civil society and the state."[14]

Borrowing directly from Froebel's kindergarten concept, Blow and Harris used "games" as a primary pedagogical tool. In a typical game the children were assembled in a

13. Susan E. Blow, Cazenovia, N.Y., to William T. Harris, Washington, D. C., June 5, 1892, *William Torrey Harris, MSS*, folder marked "Blow Letters, Susan E., 1890–1896"; Susan E. Blow, New York, to William T. Harris, St. Louis, November 14, 1872; William T. Harris, St. Louis, to Susan E. Blow, New York, March 23, 1873, *William Torrey Harris MSS*, folder marked "Blow Letters, 1872–1889," Missouri Historical Society.

14. *Annual Report, 1873*, pp. 18–19; *Annual Report, 1879*, pp. 194, 212–14.

circle for a group recitation that was accompanied by appropriate gestures which were carefully contrived to impart the desired ethic. As with the following game, the child was expected to act out and enunciate the value of social combination or association:

> Whatever singly thou has played
> May in one charming whole be made.
> The child alone delights to play,
> But better still with comrades gay.
> The single flower we love to view,
> Still more the wreath of varied hue.
> In this and all the child may find,
> The least within the whole combined.[15]

There were many other verse-games that spoke of the good grandmother, happy and wholesome family life, going to church, and the like. For the child, the games gave enjoyment and relief from life on the streets. From the educator's point of view they formed a course in personal and civic morality.

Harris was careful to distinguish between games of the sidewalk and of the kindergarten. He explained that the schools were not operating a child's garden in the sense of a juvenile paradise, where all was mere frolic and play, with the operating assumption that the child would naturally develop his innate goodness to his and society's advantage. Indeed, he opposed such kindergartens "where too much sentimentalism prevails on the paradisaical nature of childhood." Rather than draw inspiration from Rousseau's Emile, he heeded Hegel's warning that "education through play is liable to result in the evil that the child learns to treat everything in a contemptuous style." In Harris's own phrase: "The Apotheosis of childhood and infancy is a very dangerous idea to put into practice."[16] Such elevation of the child did not take place. Instead, treated as an object to be manipulated, he was made to

15. *Annual Report, 1879,* p. 210.
16. *Annual Report, 1876,* p. 95; *Annual Report, 1879,* p. 218; *Annual Report, 1876,* pp. 90–91; *Annual Report, 1876,* p. 95; *Annual Report, 1879,* p. 214.

conform to a pre-determined pattern of social behavior and was taught a set of practical skills.

The games were intended to enable the child to acquire those skills that would be of value to the child and the city's industry. In a "manner half playful, half serious," the kindergarten imparted twenty "gifts" that prepared the student for a life of work. The first six of these gifts shared the common object of familiarizing the child with some elementary notions of geometry. While building with such solid forms as the cube, sphere, and cylinder, he learned elementary addition, subtraction, fractions, and division. Through manipulation of these objects he acquired the skills necessary for elementary arithmetical operations.[17]

The second group led him from the manipulation of thin blocks or tablets to drawing with a pencil on paper ruled in squares. Through drawing, the child's eye and hand muscles developed coordination. At this point, the gifts were explicitly related to industrial uses, for the "art of drawing" was considered a basic industrial skill. It was claimed that such ability was best developed while the pupil was still a child, because "as age advances, it becomes more difficult to acquire new phases of manual dexterity." Harris further advanced the claim that even one year of such training would remain with the individual throughout his life.[18]

The third and subsequent groups of gifts were even more clearly and directly related to the arts and trades. Manual dexterity, measurement skills, and intellectual activities required in geometry were developed through instruction in embroidery. These skills were further encouraged in the fourth group, weaving and plaiting. Finally, the production of solid forms was taught through modelling. Harris envisaged that the gifts would endow the child with the capacity to engage successfully in a wide variety of employment, from the needle trades and the foundry to the preparation of foods in the home. He also believed that the same skills necessary for the factory or the home would be

17. *Annual Report, 1879*, pp. 129–30.
18. Ibid.

useful in better utilizing leisure time. He thought, for example, that female graduates might "practice elegant employments" like embroidery and the males might become more accurate and dexterous marksmen, hunters, fishermen, bowlers, and baseball players. In short, the kindergarten was to become the molder of the *uomo universale* of the industrial city.[19]

It should be pointed out that, despite these claims and rhetoric, the kindergarten was not a vocational school. Proponents were interested in developing habits of mind and mechanical skills that would be beneficial in the growth of children.[20] They expected that the kindergarten's immediate impact would be to serve as an "antidote" to the evil of the city's streets, and the long-term influence would be to contribute to a better-disciplined and mechanically skilled work force. On this basis, the kindergarten received the support of the board and reached into most sections of the city. From the fall of 1873 to 1880 it had grown from an experiment of 68 pupils, conducted by Susan Blow and 3 unpaid assistants, to a network with 166 paid teachers and 60 unpaid assistants serving 7,828 children.[21]

The kindergartens also enjoyed great popularity among the public. When it was suggested in 1875 that the board should close them because of the expense, 1,500 people signed a petition opposing such action.[22] Letters flowed into the city's press urging the kindergartens' continuation and expansion. One writer suggested that "if it be true (as usually alleged) that the chief object of the public school system is to reach the children of the poor," then the board must not abandon the experiment. Another wrote that the

19. *Annual Report, 1879*, pp. 131–34.
20. This was made clear by the board's steadfast refusal to permit any form of vocational training in its schools. The issue directly occurred first in a controversy between William Harris and Calvin Woodward in 1880 and continued till the turn of the century. *Official Proceedings*, 3, July 13, 1880, 478. This struggle over vocationalism forms the major theme in Chapter 8.
21. *Official Proceedings*, 1, April 14, 1874, 323–24. *Annual Report, 1880*, pp. 152–53.
22. *Official Proceedings*, 2, July 13, 1875, 41; June 15, 1875, 35.

results of its work merited support: "So thorough and efficient had been the work so far, that the children who, six months ago, were timid, untutored and probably in some instances 'unwashed,' now present a tidy, brightened, cultured appearance, far beyond their years."[23] Concurring with these opinions, the board denied that the kindergarten was too great a burden and rejected the petition for termination.[24]

In the following year, however, finding itself financially unable to support the kindergarten's expansion but valuing its social usefulness and "industrial features," the board moved to a compromise that would allow for continued growth on a self-supporting basis. It introduced a fee system of $1 per quarter but allowed free entry for those who could not pay.[25] During the first year of the plan, 1876–1877, 40 per cent were admitted free. At the beginning of the 1878 school year, the board was so impressed with the kindergarten that, ending the charge, it declared that the period of experimentation was over and that the kindergarten was an integral part of the public school system.[26] The final step in the kindergarten's acceptance was its extension in 1881 to the city's Negro children, who were segregated into a separate network of schools.[27]

Of great importance to the survival and growth of the kindergartens in the early years was the extensive use of female volunteers. Chief among them was Susan Blow, who gave not only of her time but of her money for the purchase

23. "Kindergarten," *Globe-Democrat*, June 17, 1875; July 6, 1875.
24. *Official Proceeings*, 2, July 13, 1875, 46–47.
25. *Official Proceedings*, 2, November 14, 1876, 180–81. In addition to fees they were placed on a "modified Lancasterian system" or ninety were placed in each class. *Official Proceedings*, 2, December 18, 1877, 405.
26. *Official Proceedings*, 2, November 14, 1876, 182; *Official Proceedings*, 3, September 10, 1878, 186.
27. There was generally a lag in extending innovations to black children. The appropriateness of kindergartens for them was well expressed in the 1882 *Annual Report*: "This [the opening of the first 'colored kindergarten'] was just and proper. No reason or justification for any discrimination existed; but if there was any, the most helpless and dependent class in the community is the one especially entitled to kindergarten facilities." *Annual Report*, 1882, p. 50.

of equipment.[28] In 1876–1877, 150 women volunteered, and 139 and 65 served in the following two years. Paradoxically, this decline reflected the success of their efforts, as the kindergarten had won such recognition that the board attempted to professionalize the large number of assistants. After 1876, if a volunteer received certification on completion of a special examination, the board was willing to pay her a salary.[29]

The possibility for remuneration was only one motive for kindergarten work. Some were attracted to the "novelty of the thing"; others found it a kind of insurance in the event that, after marriage, "untoward fortune" would necessitate self-support; and still others were "filled with a sublime enthusiasm, and devoted themselves, like missionaries, to a work which they believed to be potent for the regeneration of society, morally and intellectually."[30] In addition, at a time when there were limited opportunities for young ladies, the work offered a bridge for the years between school and marriage. Harris considered the kindergarten "a most excellent preparatory training for a young lady for the duties of life." This, he believed, was especially appropriate for the daughters of comfortable households that did not demand early marriage or participation in obtaining the family's income. The kindergarten not only was an instrument for the redemption of the poor, but also a kind of "finishing school" and a way-station for the young ladies of St. Louis's better-established families.[31]

28. *Annual Report, 1876*, p. 88; *Annual Report, 1879*, p. 195. Miss Blow was acting in the family tradition. Her father donated land to the public schools in 1870. "PBPS, July 12, 1870," *Missouri Republican*, July 15, 1870.

29. *Annual Report, 1879*, p. 195. *Official Proceedings*, 2, November 14, 1876, 182.

30. *Annual Report, 1876*, pp. 85–90.

31. *Official Proceedings*, 2, December 18, 1877, 404–5. The economic and social background as well as the moral concerns of Susan Blow and the kindergarteners bear great resemblance to those of the young ladies who would engage in social redemption in the social settlement house movement in the 1890s and beyond. See, Allen F. Davis, *Spearheads for Reform: The Social Settlements and the Progressive Movement, 1890–1914* (New York: Oxford, 1967), pp. 26–39, and Christopher Lasch, *The New Radicalism in America [1889–*

Although the kindergarten enjoyed much popular and official support and the enthusiasm of the city's young ladies, it was occasionally subject to bitter opposition. As was discussed earlier, the attack on German in 1878 included criticism of the kindergartens. Typically, one critic claimed that "it is not an American institution" and damned it for its association with Germans. There were other grounds for objection. Some argued that since the board's charter provided only for the education of children from the ages of six to twenty, and not three-, four-, or five-year-olds, the kindergarten was "unlawful." Others found fault with it because of the cost, insisting "it is a luxury which the public cannot afford." There were yet others who remained unconvinced of its necessity or effectiveness.[32] During March and April, 1878, such complaints were gathered into a petition, which was signed by 3,000 citizens, calling for the abolition of the kindergartens. These criticisms and the petition were rejected by the board on this occasion as they were on others.[33]

A more serious and damaging attack was made through the courts. In a series of legal battles running from 1878 through 1883, the board was forced to defend not only the kindergarten but also the departure from traditional education that it represented. In November, 1878, suit was brought against the board, challenging its operations on two grounds:

First: "That the Schools in the charge and control of the defendant [the Board of President and Directors of the Public Schools], are *common* schools, where only the rudiments of an English education can lawfully be taught; and that it is not competent for the defendent, to expend its revenues in the teaching of the branches

---

1963]: *The Intellectual as a Social Type* (New York: Vintage, 1965), pp. 3–68.

32. The letters appeared in a special section dealing with the German question in the *Globe-Democrat* in March and April, 1878. See, "Against the Kindergarten," March 18, 1878; "L.S.J., Common School Education," March 15, 1878; "M.A.J., Thoughts of a Former Kindergarten Teacher," March 19, 1878.

33. *Official Proceedings*, 3, March 12, 1878, 42; April 23, 1878, 54.

of learning mentioned in the petition. Second: That children under six years of age, cannot rightfully be admitted or instructed in said schools."[34]

The definition of common education as developed in the suit excluded Greek, Latin, German, science, and the higher English branches. The nature of the criticism was such that the suit brought into question the existence of the high and normal schools and the Public School Library as well, and could have thrown the system back to the age of the "ragged school."

The board, on the other hand, contended that the charter required it to provide instruction in such "knowledge and intelligence" as was necessary for rendering its pupils "good and useful citizens." A broad definition of this imperative justified the entire range of the schools' activities both in terms of curriculum and the ages of students. This interpretation was upheld by the courts in three rulings. However, it was only partially vindicated by the Supreme Court of Missouri in 1883. The courts had decided that "common" and "public" were interchangeable and that neither term connoted a particular type of education. Furthermore, they affirmed that the board had within its discretion the determination of the subject matter appropriate to its schools. Basing itself on the provisions of the board's charter, the Supreme Court, however, reversed the previous decisions on the question of age by prohibiting the use of public money for children under six years. It was this eventuality that had been most feared, and it was for this reason that the suit was almost always mentioned in the board's *Official Proceedings* together with the discussions on kindergarten education. The board understood from the beginning that the suit's major target was the kindergarten and that the danger to it was genuine.[35]

34. *Official Proceedings*, 4, July 10, 1878, 556–57.
35. Ibid. Also see, *Official Proceedings*, 3, March 12, 1878; November 12, 1878; December 10, 1878; April 8, 1879; April 29, 1879; March 11, 1880. Roache's action was similar to that undertaken in other parts of the country as traditionalists challenged broadening definitions of public education. The most famous case was the one concerning the Kalamazoo, Michigan, high school in 1872. See Ell-

The Supreme Court's decision impelled the board to implement compromise measures in order to salvage the kindergartens. The age of admission was raised to five, and a $1 per quarter charge was instituted for these children. The plan provided, however, for free instruction for those six and seven.[36] This prevented the board from carrying out its mission of reclaiming younger children from the pernicious influences of the city's streets and slums. In effect, these pioneering efforts to meet the problems of the post-Civil War industrial city were checked by a legal document drawn for a smaller and less complicated society, the St. Louis of 1833. This turn of events dramatically showed how far the city's educators and school managers had progressed in redefining their responsibilities to the community; it also demonstrated the persistence of a more conservative view of public education.

Even as the limits of age contracted, the definition of kindergarten work expanded in new directions. Initially it had been justified as necessary for saving the children of impoverished families from an unwholesome environment. By the end of the 1870s, it was considered worthwhile for children from rich homes and good neighborhoods. In 1879, Harris wrote that "a child of poverty . . . is saved by the good associations and the industrial and intellectual training he gets. It he is a child of wealth, he is saved by the kindergarten from ruin through the self-indulgence and corruption ensuing on weak management in the family." As if to emphasize the affluence of the new clientele, Harris criticized wealthy parents for too fully entrusting their children to the care of servants. This new rationale was reflected in the spread of the kindergartens beyond the levee and manufacturing districts. By 1880 the kindergartens were located along with the schools in every section of the city.[37]

---

wood P. Cubberly, *Public Education in the United States: A Study and Interpretation of American Educational History* (Cambridge: Riverside Press, 1947), 262–64.

36. *Official Proceedings*, 4, July 10, 1883, 556–58.

37. *Annual Report*, 1879, p. 190.

Harris elaborated on why the children of the wealthy must be included during the following years. In a call for the formation of the St. Louis Kindergarten Association in 1889, which he drafted in the capacity of United States Commissioner of Education, he argued that the educational system must incorporate children from age four, because their innate abilities might otherwise go underdeveloped or become misdirected. These children suffered, not from the danger of evil streets, but from the success of parents who perforce neglected them because of "public and social duties." The consequence was that they became "incorrigible by the time they are sent to ordinary school and go to ruin in early manhood." Harris thought the only solution was the kindergarten, which was "especially adapted to occupy their restless minds and to unfold in a normal way their directive power for good."[38]

The kindergarten had come to offer something to all the city's children. It would help the tenement child grow up a moral person, properly disciplined and capable of taking his place in the home or the city's factories; and it would aid the rich child to develop his character and his creative powers so that he might take his place in the direction of the community's affairs. This view presupposed that children of different classes would have different futures for which the schools must equip them. For all classes, the kindergarten idea represented the belief that urban living required a new public agency to assist in the "transition between life of the Family and the severe discipline of the School."[39] So important did Harris consider the kindergarten for "the children of poverty and the children of wealth" that in 1895, fifteen years after he left St. Louis, he was using the prestige of his national office to urge an amendment to the Missouri constitution to lower the school age to four.[40] While the attempt to bring the kindergarten

38. "Rough Draft by W. T. Harris for formation of the St. Louis Kindergarten Association, 1889," *William Torrey Harris MSS*, Missouri Historical Society.

39. Ibid.

40. Susan E. Blow, William T. Harris, *et al.*, *The School Age in*

to younger children failed, the widespread appreciation of the value of play among educators resulted in the incorporation of the pedagogical techniques of the kindergarten into the lower grades of the district school during the first two decades of the twentieth century.[41]

Bringing children "under healthful school influence, as soon as they are able to walk and talk" was a new development in public education. It emanated from the desire of St. Louis educators to fill the needs of city children. For their benefit, an agency that was at once prophylactic, remedial, and redemptive was created. The innovation spread to other cities, and St. Louis played a major role by providing the model and many of the key personnel. Through the *Annual Reports*, which were distributed nationally, Harris and Blow explained the need for kindergartens and detailed techniques for their economical management, thereby paving the way for their adoption by the nation's city school systems. In many cities, including Boston, Baltimore, and Chicago, people trained in St. Louis either introduced or supervised the work. Twenty-five years after Susan Blow began her experiments, there were almost 190,000 children in kindergartens.[42] This movement, born of the conviction that "the kindergarten is the best institution ever devised for the reform of the children of the slums," and extended to include the children of the wealthy, was an important precedent for the commitment of public resources in dealing with the special problems of growing up in the modern city. The almost 8,000 students who attended the St. Louis kindergartens in 1880 were in the vanguard of those legions of children whom the schools would try to save in the years ahead.[43]

Missouri: Some Arguments in Favor of the Proposed Constitutional Amendment, located in "St. Louis Board of Education: Public Schools Various (uncatalogued)," State Historical Society of Missouri.

41. A similar development is described in Marvin Lazerson, *Origins of the Urban School: Public Education in Massachusetts, 1870–1915* (Cambridge: Harvard University Press, 1971), pp. 62–73.

42. Blow, p. 2.

43. Statistics on kindergartens can be found in Blow, "Kindergarten Education," p. 42. Among those involved in the spread of the movement were Caroline Hart, who supervised the kindergartens

of Canada and Baltimore, and Laura Fisher, who headed the Kindergarten Normal School in Boston. See, "Rough Draft by W. T. Harris." In addition, social settlements featured kindergartens in their activities and, indeed, many settlements were outgrowths of private kindergarten societies. Davis, pp. 43–59. Robert A. Woods and Albert Kennedy, *The Settlement Horizon: A National Estimate* (New York: Russell Sage Foundation, 1922), pp. 131–37. Robert A. Woods and Albert Kennedy, *Handbook of Settlements* (New York: Russell Sage Foundation, 1911) contains specifics on the relationship in the individual sketches of settlement houses.

6

The Significance of Schooling for Nineteenth-Century Children

> It is both encouraging and gratifying to the members of this Board to witness the unexampled success of our school system, and the great popularity of the schools. This is still the more gratifying, when we feel a consciousness that this popularity is deserved; and that the more our schools are tried and the closer their operations are examined, the greater will be their popularity, and the confidence reposed in them.[1]

So Isaiah Forbes concluded his annual report as president of the St. Louis Board of Public Schools in 1855. Mid-nineteenth-century school directors, superintendents, and heads of departments universally echoed this confidence in the success of the schools and their continued growth. Moreover, the educators attempted to substantiate their claims with an impressive array of statistics that both summarized yearly operations and placed them in historical perspective. The break with parochial schools in the generation after 1860 and the successful introduction of kindergartens in the 1870s served to strengthen further the pervasive celebrationist manner in which educators analysed the results of their efforts. Beginning with Forbes's report, successive boards published through the end of the century, in English and German, an average of 5,000 to 7,000 copies of the *Annual Report* for local and national distribution to broadcast the triumphs of the public schools.

These *Annual Reports* dramatically delineate the expanding popularity of the public schools both in absolute and relative terms. Between 1840, or shortly after the first schools were established, and 1880, when they had evolved into a complex and diversified system ranging from kinder-

1. Isaiah Forbes, "President's Report," *Annual Report, 1855,* p. 6.

gartens to evening, high, and normal schools, the student body had grown from 266 pupils to 55,870. When correlated with the city's total population, these numbers show that between 1840 and 1850, its first full decade of operation, the system reached about one in fifty of the city's population. By 1880, one out of every six or seven persons came into contact with the schools, with the greatest proportion of this rise occurring in the post-Civil War period.[2] By this date, the schools had become one of the city's most important social institutions, touching the lives of more people on a daily and continuing basis than perhaps any other.

Nevertheless, while public education expanded, some of the system's basic features remained constant. Despite its increased complexity and size, it performed much the same kind of work in 1880 that it had in previous decades. In the 1850s, the period when good records become available, as well as during the next two decades, the average student was between nine and ten years of age.[3] Furthermore, little change took place in the length of schooling, since the burden of the system's work was devoted to instructing seven- through twelve-year-olds who were in the first three grades. Thus, the board continued to be involved primarily in teaching fundamentals of reading, writing, arithmetic, some geography, and group singing.[4] These subjects comprised the natural limits of public education, for the majority of parents permitted their children to drop out despite the availability of free higher schooling.

From the perspective of the present, these seem like minimal accomplishments that hardly justify pronouncements of satisfaction. In order to understand this frame of reference, it is necessary to appreciate what parents perceived the role of schooling to be in the lives of their chil-

2. *Annual Report, 1880*, pp. cxxviii–cxxix. *Tenth Census of the United States, 19*, Pt. 2, 567.

3. In 1860 the proportion under ten was 66 per cent; in 1865, 54 per cent; in 1870, 49 per cent; in 1875, 53 per cent; and in 1880, 56 per cent. *Annual Report, 1860*, p. 55; *Annual Report, 1880*, p. 31.

4. The curriculum is broadly outlined in *Annual Report, 1879*, p. cvi.

dren. It is important, therefore, to distinguish first between those who remained from those who left, and to determine what factors influenced their decisions. Secondly, it must be established how educators interpreted these facts. To that end, this chapter is divided into two parts: a statistical analysis of the nature of school attendance; and a discussion of the introduction of evening schools and the public school library, which throw into relief the fundamental assumptions of midcentury schoolmen.

I

Of prime importance in exploring school attendance are the cumulative tables in the *Annual Reports* that deal with such matters as enrollment, age and sex of pupils, occupations of parents, and the number in each grade. Since it was uncertain how representative school records were of the patterns operating in society at large, however, and since the variables present in the tables are limited, a collective biography of more than 15,000 children, drawn from the manuscript census of 1880, was established. The biography yields a cross section of the community's economic, social, and racial groups and is based on an analysis of about 45,000 persons, or one-eighth of the nation's fourth-largest city, in twenty-six selected election precincts.[5]

In addition to emphasizing the importance of elementary education, the *Annual Reports*, by themselves, suggest that the major difference between those who left school and those who remained was the level of the fathers' occupations. Although St. Louis educators prided themselves on an open and democratic system, clearly children in higher economic groups used the schools to better advantage. Table 5 shows that about 50 per cent of the system's students were children of unskilled or skilled workers with an approximately equal division of the two categories between 1860 and 1880. Despite their large representation in the

5. For an analysis of the methodology of the *Annual Reports*, see Appendix A, and for that of the manuscript census, see Appendix B.

system as a whole, Table 5 illustrates their disproportionately low distribution in the higher reaches of the system. For example, they comprised about 21 per cent of the high school and only 18 per cent of normal school students.

The relationship between class and education becomes even more striking when the children of unskilled laborers are isolated and examined. In 1880, for example, they comprised 27 per cent of day students; that is, pupils in the district, high, and normal schools; but supplied only 3 per cent to the high and 7 per cent to the normal school. Breaking this category down into its constituent parts, it becomes clearer how few advanced beyond elementary instruction. There were 8,262 children of "laborers," the major component in the unskilled classification, in the district schools, but there were only 23 in the high and 2 in the normal school. Similarly, only one child of a "laundress" was found in the high school and none were preparing for teaching, but 1,711 were in the district schools. Yet another component, "draymen and teamsters," made the same kind of showing, sending 1,984 to district schools, 4 to the high and 2 the normal school. On the other hand, "professionals," with a number approximate to that of "laundresses" and to "draymen and teamsters," sent 113 to the high school, 9 to the normal school, and 1,866 to the district schools. This pattern of unequal distribution by class, established with the first high school class in 1857, remained one of the constants in the social structure of the schools.[6]

Sex is another area of maldistribution. While there is no way in which differentiation can be made by grades, it is possible to delineate differences between levels. In the day schools as a whole, there was approximately equal distribution of males and females, with males predominating by 1 per cent in 1860 but with 1 to 2 per cent more females during the 1870s. In the high school there were somewhat more males than females in the early years, but after 1865 an increasing proportion of girls enrolled. Between 1855

6. *Annual Report, 1855*, pp. 116–21. For a discussion of a parallel structure in Massachusetts, see Michael B. Katz, *The Irony of Early School Reform*, pp. 39–40, and Appendix C.

Table 5. Occupations of Parents of Students in Day Schools, 1860, 1870, 1880, by Percentage

Occupations	Unskilled labor	Skilled labor	Clerk & minor white collar	Businessmen & managers	Professionals	Unclassified	Total number
1860							
TS*	22	31	8	20	4	14	10,908
DS	24	32	8	19	4	13	10,413
HS	13	9	12	36	6	24	387
NS	1	19	4	23	13	39	108
1870							
TS	27	24	9	26	4	11	24,347
DS	27	24	8	26	3	11	23,817
HS	5	18	17	30	13	16	391
NS	4	21	9	20	8	38	139
1880							
TS	27	26	11	24	4	8	51,261
DS	27	26	11	25	3	8	50,146
HS	3	18	18	28	13	20	953
NS	7	11	15	24	5	38	162

* TS indicates total number of students; DS, those in the district schools; HS, those in the high school; and NS, those in the normal school. See Appendix A for source of data.

and 1860 enrollment was 46 per cent female, but between 1875 and 1880 it was 59 per cent. The normal school, however, was from its beginnings in 1857 almost completely a female institution.[7] These data suggest that, commencing in the postwar period, girls were receiving more schooling in the teen years. Such a conclusion may be unwarranted, since it does not take into account the opportunities available for males at nonpublic institutions found in the city and elsewhere. Indeed, for a refinement and elaboration of all the information described above—ages of attendance, the significance of class and sex for educational advance-

7. *Annual Report, 1881*, p. 100.

ment—as well as additional factors influencing attendance, it is necessary to turn to the manuscript census.

An important advantage of the collective biography is that it relates school to other experiences, allowing for a profile of the stages in the development of children. Table 6 shows that schooling began at age six for 56 per cent; the peak years of education were from ages eight through eleven when about 90 per cent enrolled. Then, beginning at twelve, ever-larger numbers of youngsters left school. The exodus became so massive that less than half of the fourteen-year-olds and less than a fifth of those aged sixteen continued to take advantage of St. Louis's diverse schools. Based on the patterns of education and employment in Table 6, children can be divided into four age groups: one through five; six through twelve; thirteen through sixteen; and seventeen through twenty. Only the second group was involved with schooling *en masse*, confirming the data drawn from the *Annual Reports*. Thereafter, most children either became "unknowns," probably returning home, or graduated into the world of work.[8]

The kind of job a child was able to obtain when he dropped out was related to the age at which he left school. Since girls tended to go to school longer than boys and found different kinds of employment, Table 7 separates the sexes in order to define more precisely what children did between the ages of ten and twenty. Throughout this period there was an expansion of the work force in all the

8. Unknowns represent those for whom the census enumerators marked "at home" or left a blank. It is assumed that these omissions represent those who were neither employed nor at school and they are, therefore, calculated with those whom we know to be "at home." The assumption is based on three considerations. First, since the enumerator is accounting for nearly all children between nine and twelve, with an average unknown of about 8 per cent, it appears unlikely that the enumerator was less accurate or less avid in determining occupations or school attendance at other ages. Second, the curve reflected by unknowns is so well-ordered as to suggest important meanings rather than chance. Third, the pattern of employment and school attendance conforms to expectations. We know from school reports that children began dropping out in large numbers at about age twelve when they gradually began to be absorbed into the work force.

Table 6. Education and Employment from Ages 5 to 20, by Percentage*

Age	Attending school	Employed	Unknown	Total number
5	19.5	0.0	80.5	625
6	56.2	0.0	43.8	657
7	80.6	0.2	19.2	573
8	89.0	0.4	10.6	546
9	90.1	0.6	9.3	494
10	90.9	2.1	7.0	573
11	89.3	3.6	7.1	524
12	82.0	9.4	8.6	545
13	70.7	17.5	11.8	532
14	48.9	33.0	18.1	585
15	35.1	43.1	21.8	536
16	19.3	60.0	20.7	576
17	11.6	64.2	24.2	541
18	5.4	68.7	25.9	710
19	3.7	71.1	25.2	678
20	1.7	76.1	22.2	769

* Source: See Appendix B.

categories and movement into jobs of greater status and complexity with the advance of years. For example, whereas 20 per cent of the twelve-year-old boys had left school, only 58 per cent of these had jobs, and most of them, 88 per cent, were employed in semiskilled or unskilled occupations. At age sixteen, 15 per cent remained in school. Of their peers who left, 86 per cent were employed: 47 per cent were semiskilled and unskilled workers; 15 per cent had moved to skilled positions; 21 per cent held white-collar jobs as various kinds of clerks; and 3 per cent were in the higher occupations. At eighteen and twenty, at least 50 per cent of all males were skilled workers or better.

While a few girls also began to work at age twelve, a greater proportion of twelve- to sixteen-year-olds stayed in school. At ages twelve, fourteen, and sixteen there were

Table 7. Occupations of White Males and Females, Ages 10–20, by Percentage*

	Attending school	Higher occupations	White collar	Skilled workers	Semiskilled workers	Unskilled workers	Unknown	Total number
Age 10								
M	90.4	0.0	0.0	0.4	0.7	2.9	5.7	280
F	91.5	0.0	0.0	0.0	0.0	0.3	8.2	293
Age 12								
M	79.6	0.4	0.0	1.1	4.6	6.0	8.5	284
F	84.7	0.0	0.4	0.0	0.4	5.7	8.8	261
Age 14								
M	46.0	0.7	2.1	7.0	11.6	21.8	10.9	285
F	51.7	0.3	0.3	2.0	0.0	20.7	25.0	300
Age 16								
M	14.8	2.8	18.0	12.7	14.1	26.1	11.6	284
F	23.6	2.1	1.7	3.4	0.3	39.4	29.4	292
Age 18								
M	4.6	5.3	21.4	23.5	13.3	21.1	10.9	285
F	5.9	2.4	2.8	3.8	1.6	47.5	36.0	425
Age 20								
M	2.4	5.8	22.7	23.3	13.9	24.5	7.3	330
F	1.1	3.0	1.4	3.9	1.4	55.8	33.5	439

* Source: See Appendix B.

5, 6, and 9 per cent more girls in school than boys. By eighteen and twenty, there was a return to parity as education became increasingly less significant for both sexes. When females left school, however, it was for experiences fundamentally different from those of males. Fewer girls worked. At age twelve, 6 per cent less were employed; at fourteen, 20 per cent; at sixteen, 27 per cent; at eighteen and twenty, 25 per cent. Moreover, those employed generally worked as maids, seamstresses, laundresses, or kept house for their own families. By the late teens, only about one out of ten girls had left the household, whether her own or someone else's, for the factory, shop, and office.[9] After several years in school, large numbers simply returned home. At sixteen, 30 per cent were unemployed and in the family. Between seventeen and twenty, the average rose to 36 per cent. By contrast, only about 9 per cent of the boys were similarly disengaged from both work and school.

One wonders why more girls, faced with the prospect of staying home without contributing to the family income, did not take greater advantage of the city's schools. The fact that they did not, even though they received on average more schooling than males, probably means that education was not considered of particular value for girls and reflects indulgence and minimal parental economic expectations as they awaited their real vocation. While for boys school was a prelude to a lifetime of work, for most girls it served as a hiatus between the freedoms of early childhood and the responsibilities of marriage. Thus, despite this distinction, the most significant trend for children of both sexes was their abandonment of education in their early teens.

The relationship of a child to his household is another factor that affected the length and quality of his school experience. Children who lived with both or even one of their parents were at a decided advantage. Those living in institutions, in households headed by a relative other than a parent, or as boarders, went to work earlier. In their case, too, the beginning of adolescence marks a convenient demarcation point. While children in families in the six-to-twelve group had a somewhat greater opportunity for going to school, Table 8 shows that their chances of leaving school increased to almost two to one through the teen years.

9. Of 734 girls aged seventeen through twenty-one who were listed as unskilled laborers, 66 per cent (488) were servants and maids, 20 per cent (144) were keeping house, 9 per cent (63) were seamstresses, and 5 per cent (39) were in various other occupations, including 15 prostitutes.

Table 8. School Attendance and Family Status of White Children, Ages 6–12, 13–16, 17–20*

Ages	In family	Percentage in school	Not in family	Percentage in school
6–12	3,765	82.4	107	73.8
13–16	1,795	47.5	379	28.2
17–20	1,491	7.3	1,125	3.4

* Source: See Appendix B.

Not only did the educational gap between children within and without the family grow wider through the teen years, but those children who resided outside the family attended school under less favorable circumstances. For example, in the thirteen-to-sixteen group, less than 1 per cent of family children who went to school also held jobs, as compared with 28 per cent of those who were not in the family. In the seventeen-through-twenty group, the proportions become 4 per cent as opposed to 29 per cent. Clearly the family provided a protective umbrella for the child in its midst, giving him an opportunity for prolonged schooling and for an education without the distractions of work.

In addition, children who lived at home were not required to work as soon or in the same numbers as those who were on their own. In the seventeen-to-twenty group, 11 per cent of the males and 55 per cent of the females living with their families were unemployed, as opposed to only 3 per cent of those who were outside the family. The family, then, also provided some young men and especially the young ladies with a base of support where they might await the creation of their own households. It therefore may have made it possible for some women to choose such avocations as reform and charity work.[10]

For children living at home, the school and job experience was further influenced by their fathers' occupation. Its in-

10. For a portrait of comfortable females who made reform their vocation, see Christopher Lasch, *The New Radicalism in America [1889–1963]*, chapters 1, 2, and 4.

fluence was minimal for youngsters between six and twelve. At this stage, with an average of 82 per cent in school, there was a large measure of equality of experience. For example, children of unskilled and skilled workers had attendance rates of 83 and 80 per cent, while children of professionals and petty officials and businessmen had rates of 88 and 87 per cent. Moreover, if a child were not in school he was at home. Age, not economics, was important.

The earnings and status of the father were of greater importance in the thirteen- through sixteen-year-old group, for as participation in education diminished, significant variations based on class occurred. Table 9 indicates how distinctions between subgroups widened as the average attendance dropped from 81 per cent for six- to twelve-year-olds to 43 per cent for thirteen- to sixteen-year-olds. We find, at one extreme, children of professionals with 80 per cent in attendance, and at the other the children of unskilled workers with 32 per cent. While from ages six through twelve there was a difference of 5 per cent between children in these categories, for the four-year span after twelve the gap had widened about tenfold to 48 per cent. It made little difference whether the father of a child aged eight or twelve was a physician or a boatman; for most children it made all the difference a few years later.

Based on a hierachy of parental occupations, Table 9 also delineates a critical factor for the nineteenth-century dropout. The community of dropouts was initially and largely drawn from the male children of skilled, semiskilled, and unskilled workers. These sons had attendance rates ranging from 32 per cent to 36 per cent with a median of 33 per cent. Sons of fathers with higher occupational levels had a median of 65 per cent with a range of 56 per cent for petty officials and businessmen to 80 per cent for professionals. The clear point of division was whether one's father wore a white or a blue collar.

While unemployment rates were nearly identical with sons of blue- and white-collar workers at about 11 per cent, significantly more working-class children were employed. Although sons of blue-collar workers had more than dou-

Table 9. Crosstabulation of Fathers' Occupations by Sons' Occupations, Ages 13–16, by Percentage*

Sons	At school	Higher employment	White collar	Skilled	Semiskilled	Unskilled	Unknown	Percentage of total sons	Total number
Fathers									
Professional	80.0	2.9	11.4	0.0	0.0	2.9	2.9	3.8	35
High official or businessman	70.0	0.0	12.5	1.3	5.0	2.5	8.8	8.6	80
White collar	64.1	2.6	9.0	5.1	6.4	7.7	5.1	8.4	78
Petty official or businessman	55.9	2.2	7.5	5.4	3.2	6.5	19.4	10.0	93
Skilled	32.0	0.0	10.0	12.1	12.1	25.1	8.7	24.9	231
Semiskilled	35.9	0.0	6.4	3.8	16.7	21.8	15.7	8.4	78
Unskilled	31.7	0.8	4.0	8.7	6.3	37.3	11.1	13.6	126
Unknown	36.2	2.4	7.7	6.8	15.0	22.2	9.7	22.3	207
Average of total	43.4	1.2	8.3	7.1	9.9	19.7	10.3	——	——
	(403)	(11)	(77)	(66)	(92)	(183)	(96)	——	(928)

* Source: See Appendix B.

bled the employment rate, 57 per cent to 25 per cent, and entered the labor force at an earlier age, they held inferior jobs, with the majority in unskilled positions. Some sons of white-collar workers also took unskilled jobs when they left school, but many more of them worked as clerks or filled other white-collar positions. For example, sons of unskilled workers had eight times as much chance to be themselves unskilled as to hold a white-collar job, while children of high officials and businessmen had a five-to-one chance to avoid unskilled labor and find white-collar jobs. In sum, sons of households with higher occupational levels could not only stay in school longer, but could also begin at a better job than children from working-class homes.

The disparity between children of different classes was most marked among the seventeen-through-twenty group. The higher the father's position, the greater the son's chance for schooling, the better his job, and the smaller the chance of unemployment. As an illustration of the critical importance of fathers' occupations, sons of blue-collar workers had one-third the chance to become clerks and twice the likelihood of holding unskilled jobs as those who came from white-collar families. The same inequalities affected the experiences of the daughters. Girls from blue-collar families were more likely to leave school and enter domestic service, while daughters of white-collar workers remained in school longer or stayed at home. Class distinctions impinged on the experiences of children of both sexes.

As was anticipated, the social structure of education as revealed in the census complements the information in the *Annual Reports*. It is now clear that schooling was nearly universal during midcentury, with about 90 per cent of all children between eight and eleven in school and the great majority in public schools. The efforts expended by public and nonpublic institutions to reach the mass of the city's children and to create generations of literate individuals were successful.

As both the census and school records also indicate, several factors were responsible for a significant divergence in experience and opportunity for children beyond age twelve. Sex played a minor role, as girls retained a narrow majority in the public schools, although this may not have been the case in the nonpublic academies. Also, presence in a family headed by a parent was significant, probably because it provided the kind of security necessary to delay entry into the labor market. The importance of economic security is underscored by the critical impact of the fathers' occupations. While some working-class children went beyond the district school, prolonged education was more likely to occur in white-collar families. Thus, while the system was open and free, children of different classes did not make equal use of it. Equipped with a basic education, working-class children in particular embarked in large numbers during the early teens into an increasingly industrialized and complex society. The stratification of the public system necessarily mirrored society at large. Class became the most important parameter and, in effect, controlled the length of childhood and the nature of the options available to the young.

That many children from the lower classes failed to attain more schooling is not surprising. Large numbers had to work to assist their families. No data are available on children's earnings or on family income, but numerous writers have commented on the phenomenon of nineteenth-century urban families that required the income of their offspring. Before the widespread adoption of cash registers, telephones, and child labor laws, there was ample opportunity for unskilled work as cash boys, messengers, and light manual laborers.[11]

While drawing attention to the importance of economics, the census data suggest that other factors also contributed to extended schooling. Working-class children may have entered the work force earlier through press of circumstances, but many children of businessmen and especially white-collar workers also left. They departed in smaller numbers and perhaps a year or two later, but most ended their education in the early teens instead of taking advantage of the public high school and similar institutions. Of all the groups, it is the sons of professionals, who had themselves experienced extensive training, that have the highest and most persistent attendance records. Not only income but attitude kept the lawyer's son in school and sent the businessman's or clerk's son out to work. The extraordinary percentages of professionals' children in school reflects the value that their households placed on learning.[12]

11. A classic progressive account of poverty is Robert Hunter, *Poverty: Social Conscience in the Progressive Era*, ed. by Peter d'A. Jones (New York: Harper and Row, 1965). An example of contemporary scholarship is Stephan Thernstrom, *Poverty and Progress: Social Mobility in a Nineteenth-Century City* (Cambridge: Harvard University, 1964).

12. Although the census does not include information on income, it is possible to establish occupational hierarchies that reflect both status and wealth. The occupational matrix for the group biography is an adaptation of the one developed by Stephan Thernstrom and Peter Knights in their studies of occupational mobility in Boston and has been modified to include children's and women's vocations. See Peter R. Knights, *The Plain People of Boston 1830–1860* (New York: Oxford University Press, 1971), Appendix E.

On the other hand, if children outside the working class were not required to augment the family income, their employment suggests that the experience of working in factories, offices, and stores was deemed by their parents as being more worthwhile than the classical or modern curriculum of the high school. Employment for these sons was viewed as a quasi-apprenticeship system. Professionalization, or the concept of attaining the skills required for modern industrial society through formal education, was just forming in late nineteenth-century America.[13] Thus, while elementary instruction was widely appreciated by both parents and schoolmen alike, clearly the value of more education was far less understood. It is because of this perception that the *Annual Report*s express no dismay over the fact that there were ten times as many children enrolled in the first three grades of the district school as in the three years of high school.[14]

Indeed, the patterns of school attendance and employment that emerge from the St. Louis census and school records in 1880, when placed together with data from early twentieth-century studies conducted by the system and outside sources, suggest a broad continuum of practice and attitudes. Only during the 1910s was significant progress made in retaining teenagers, due to the popularization of the high school, the introduction of vocational and commercial courses, and effective compulsory attendance laws. From the middle of the nineteenth century, when St. Louis developed extensive public and parochial systems, through the first decade of the twentieth century, the patterns of

13. On professionalization see Robert H. Wiebe, *The Search for Order, 1877–1920* (New York: Hill and Wang, 1967), pp. 11–132. Also, the teen years were not yet defined as a distinct period in the life-cycle, and special attention in the form of institutional care had not yet developed. Hence, the shift from the fourth or fifth year of school into the factory or office was considered natural. On attitudes towards teens, see John Demos and Virginia Demos, "Adolescence in Historical Perspective," *Journal of Marriage and the Family*, (November 1969), 632–38.

14. *Annual Report, 1880*, pp. cxviii–cxix. There were 22,954 in grades one through three but only 2,233 in grades seven through nine.

school attendance remained the same—a few years of schooling in the preteen period. Thus, 1880 is a midpoint for a condition that spanned several generations. Certainly educational practices in the first ten years of this century were more similar to those current in mid-nineteenth century than to our own.[15]

The continuity of educational practices may be further inferred from Joseph Kett's recent analysis of children in rural New England from 1800 to 1840. Among his conclusions, he determined that children attended school between the ages of eight and twelve, after which sons passed into apprenticeship or employment. Sons of ministers and of wealthy parents, who correspond to professionals' children in this study, tended to stay in school longer than children of mill owners and manufacturers, demonstrating the importance of parental values. The continuum of behavior in these aspects of growing up between rural New England in the first part of the nineteenth century and St. Louis in the latter part suggests that for the history of childhood and education there are limits to the significance of a rural–urban dichotomy and to a chronology that would divide the nineteenth century. Rather, traditions firmly rooted in American culture persisted throughout the period.[16]

Certainly St. Louis educators accepted as natural and even desirable the practice of initiating children into the work force after a few years of formal learning. They expected that a major portion of the child's education and especially that part which related directly to the acquisition of vocational skills would be achieved independently of classroom experiences. These beliefs found institutional expression in two midcentury innovations, the public school library and evening classes. While the evening schools illustrate how anxious educators were to ensure a basic schooling—and, indeed, how minimal this schooling could

15. The process of transition to modern patterns of attendance as well as the causes of change are the themes of chapters 8 and 9.
16. Joseph F. Kett, "Growing Up in Rural New England, 1800–1840," in *Anonymous Americans: Explorations in Nineteenth Century Social History*, ed. by Tamara Hareven (Englewood Cliffs: Prentice–Hall, 1971), pp. 1–16.

be—the justification of the public school library demonstrates how heavily they relied on personal initiative to advance beyond these fundamentals. These reforms were consistent with popular expectations of the kind and amount of schooling necessary, and help explain why the comparatively low levels of attendance were not a source of concern.

II

In partnership with Washington University, the board held the first evening classes in 1854. In 1859, consciously following the example of eastern systems, the directors decided to assume complete control. By the 1870s, St. Louis supported a network of evening schools that was the largest, proportionate to population, of any city in the country. From less than 1,000 students in 1860, enrollment reached a peak of 6,417 in 1877–1878 and then dropped to less than 2,000 in the following decade.[17] Not until the first decade of the twentieth century was the high of the 1870s reached and surpassed. During the nineteenth century, the evening school functioned as a center for remedial education, offering an opportunity for literacy to immigrants or to those who had not completed their elementary schooling. At the beginning of the twentieth century, these schools achieved a new efflorescence as they added vocational courses and served a new wave of immigrants from eastern and southern Europe.[18]

Evening schools were introduced in the 1850s to supplement the work of the day schools especially among the city's laborers, "the bone, sinew, and muscle of the body politic," who missed schooling because they went to work at too early an age. Fearing that uneducated native Americans or foreigners would be dysfunctional socially and politically,

17. *Annual Report, 1859*, pp. 19–40; Felix Coste, "Report of the President," *Annual Report, 1874*, p. 16.

18. A convenient summary of many of the essential statistics can be found in Mildred and Robert Fletcher, "Trends in Evening School Education in St. Louis, 1859–1928," *Journal of Educational Research*, 24 (November 1931), 293–98.

Superintendent Tice advocated such training as would make them literate, capable of self-improvement, and qualified members of a democratic society.[19] That these were essentially the same goals of the district schools was reflected in the curriculum. With the exception of the foreign born, who spent all their time in mastering basic reading, writing, and speaking skills, students enrolled in four half-hour meetings per week, totaling fifty-six in a fourteen-week session, which were devoted to advanced reading and writing, arithmetic, and geography. In effect, this constituted an abbbreviated version of the day school curriculum. Even the same textbooks were used, with the most elevated reading matter, a fifth-grade primer.[20]

Since day and evening programs were so similar, there was concern that parents would allow their children to skip the district school and withdraw them early so that they might augment the family's income and get a head start on their careers. In order to forestall competition with elementary schools, the minimum age was set at twelve, the age of adulthood for many St. Louisans. The result was a student body of working youths. Nearly all the students were employed and averaged between sixteen and seventeen years. From 10 to 20 per cent were females and nearly all of these were employed as house girls, laundresses, seamstresses, dressmakers, nurses, sales clerks, and milliners. Almost all the boys were employed in about sixty occupations including bakers, bricklayers, errand boys, glass workers, office and store boys, machinists, and laborers.[21]

This working population offered an excellent opportunity for instituting vocational courses. However, rather than follow the European model of transforming evening schools into training centers for textile manufacturing, watchmaking, or other specialized activities, the School Board adhered to Tice's insistence that "there be no difference between the mental discipline and training of the evening

19. *Annual Report, 1856*, pp. 46–47.

20. For a typical distribution of students in the various courses see *Official Proceedings*, 2, December 12, 1876, 188–89.

21. *Annual Report, 1875*, pp. 106–7; Fletcher, "Evening School Education," p. 297.

and day schools."[22] Harris echoed this, arguing that the board must not succumb to the temptation to produce specialized laborers.[23] Even though the schools lost a chance to train workers with special skills, he felt that the community's interest would be better served by encouraging them along the path of self-improvement. This appeared to be a plausible position, since nearly all evening school students were gainfully employed and apparently had no difficulty in satisfying the city's appetite for relatively unskilled labor.

Only the O'Fallon Polytechnic Institute, the evening high school, offered explicitly vocational education. Established in 1855 as part of Washington University, it joined the public schools in 1868 when the university, unable to maintain it, tendered it to the board along with 7,000 books and a $100,000 endowment.[24] The board accepted and a partnership developed wherein the institute was a free public school with its students nevertheless considered part of the preparatory department of the university and listed in its catalogue. The institute was designed to teach "something of practical value."[25] Its curriculum comprised "a higher course" in algebra, natural philosophy, chemistry, and "such other branches of technological instruction" for superior students who had completed the lower evening schools. With enrollment generally ranging between 200 and 300, or 5 per cent of the evening school population, the institute was a peripheral and even accidental area in the system's work.[26]

In only a very limited way was the curriculum designated to benefit directly the city's businesses. Divoll thought that the evening schools should emphasize writing so that the students should have "a good business hand."[27] Similarly, Robert Rombauer, a director and attorney for the board,

22. *Annual Report, 1856,* p. 46.

23. *Annual Report, 1870,* pp. 111–13.

24. Scharf, *History of St. Louis,* p. 856. *Annual Report, 1869,* pp. 73–83.

25. Calvin Woodward, "Polytechnic Evening School," *Missouri Republican,* February 25, 1868. *Annual Report, 1873,* p. 131; *Annual Report, 1869,* pp. 76–77.

26. *Annual Report, 1871,* p. 91.

27. *Annual Report, 1860,* pp. 40–41.

commented that schools should "lay special weight on the writing of letters and copying bills and receipts."[28] With the exception of drawing in the district schools, this was as close as the system came to connecting specific courses with particular vocations. The concern of educators was with offering a general, not an industrial, education.

The rationale for a public school library, which separated from the system in 1894 and became the St. Louis Public Library, similarly reflected an appreciation for the importance of self-education as the key to advancement. Superintendent Divoll, who was most responsible for its introduction, argued that it was a legitimate and logical extension of the system's efforts, since the board had an obligation not only to make people literate but to furnish them with reading materials on the assumption that the student must continue learning after school. Thus Divoll began his library campaign in 1860, claiming that "the engrafting of these libraries upon the common school system constitutes the most substantial improvement that has been made in education reform during the last quarter century."[29]

At the end of the Civil War, which had interrupted his plan, a charter was secured from the legislature in 1865 for the Public School Library Society of St. Louis. The society was made legally independent of the board, but since several directors, including the president, the superintendent of schools, and the principals of the high and normal schools were trustees, there was an intimate relationship between the two. Furthermore, all officers, teachers, and pupils of the public schools were eligible for membership in the society. The legal fiction was soon dropped, and in 1869 the library was formally integrated into the system.[30]

In the meantime a membership and fund drive was initiated. Beginning in 1866, John Bailey, the librarian, made visits to the district schools to publicize the advantages of the library and to convince the students to pay the $1 annual fee. Recognizing that rhetoric alone would not suffice,

28. *Official Proceedings*, 2, September 11, 1877, 337.
29. *Annual Report, 1860*, p. xviii.
30. *Annual Report, 1865*, pp. 36–39.

Bailey's "remarks (to hold the attention of the children)" were "interspersed with humor and closed with a fairy story." At the same time, he conducted a campaign outside the schools to attract subscribers and donations of books. He organized lectures, put on tableaux of music and readings that featured pupils, teachers, and "distinguished amateurs" and staged a "fairy spectacle, entitled 'The Way of Life.' "[31]

While appealing to all citizens, the library was primarily interested in students, technicians, and professional people. Although in 1874 the board opened the reading room to the general public, it continued to restrict home circulation to paying members. The only exception, and a highly significant one, was made for evening school students who, having attended punctually for sixty out of sixty-four sessions, gained privileges without charge. The same was true of O'Fallon Institute students, who were granted free life membership if they attended faithfully for two years. Presumably, they were industrious laborers eager to advance their skills, and therefore merited the dispensation. This program was not only important for the development of the library but for the evening schools as well. Presidents of the board and Harris repeatedly claimed that the lure of free admission was the greatest factor in the rapid rise of evening enrollment. About 2,000 earned library membership in this fashion between 1873 and 1875.[32]

The library also tried to become the city's central agency for the advancement and diffusion of useful knowledge by drawing professional and technical societies into association with it. In the usual arrangement, a group not only paid a reading and borrowing fee but also determined how the money was spent. Under this system the St. Louis Medical Society, Institute of Architects, Engineer's Club, Local Steam Engineer's Association, and the Academy of Science affiliated, and collections in a variety of scientific and technical

31. *Annual Report, 1865*, p. 37.
32. For testimony on the attractions of the library see *Annual Report, 1869*, p. 73. The statistics are found in *Annual Report, 1874*, p. 16; *Annual Report, 1875*, p. 103.

areas were quickly built up. In 1875, the library was receiving 162 journals, primarily in English and German, 85 of which were of a practical nature.[33]

The library also built up a substantial literary collection, and its presence in the reading room and that of novels on the shelves became a source of conflict. Although who the protagonists were is not clear, the issues reveal much about the purposes of the library and of public education in general. Insisting that the business of the library was the diffusion of the useful and the moral, some trustees urged that offensive matter be removed so as "to coerce readers into reading what is called solid books." An "experiment" to this effect took place in 1874, but in the following year the life members, who voted on library policy, overwhelmingly overturned it. Bailey claimed this was a reflection not only of reading tastes but of a fear that they might lose members to the Mercantile Library, a well-established private association, which was gaining at their expense. Noting that since "majorities rule, and since the majority of users of a public library want novels," he stated it was appropriate that their wishes be considered. He also felt that it was better to read than find other amusements.[34]

Nevertheless, moralistic and utilitarian prejudices remained. This was evident in the student's ideal reading list compiled by Bailey's successor, Frederick Crunden. Aside from a nod to novels like *Arabian Nights*, "to charm and cultivate the imagination," Crunden emphasized readings like *Boy Engineers*, *The Young Mechanic*, *Amongst Machines*, and *Growth of the Steam Engine* to "procure aid in his special calling," and Hughes's *Tom Brown* "to instil sentiments of manliness and morality." In a similar vein, he apologized for the presence of so much fiction, advising that "the library is accumulating the 'literature of instruction' rather than of 'entertainment,' [and] that it is growing in an educational direction."[35]

33. *Annual Report, 1875*, pp. 147–49, 171.
34. John Bailey, "Historical Sketch," *Annual Report, 1875*, p. 141.
35. Frederick Crunden, "Report of the Librarian," *Annual Report, 1879*, pp. 161, 171–72.

Harris, too, conceived of the library not so much as a place for people to enjoy good books, but rather as an arm of the schools with which they might continue to guide and shape a productive populace. The emphasis on this aspect of library work was derived from the limited instructional time available. Because of the short duration of the average student's education, especially in the evening classes, much energy was spent on developing reading skills. Fortunately, Harris could boast that "if St. Louis schools have any strong feature, it is this one of teaching the pupil to master the art of reading in the shortest possible time." It was on the basis of this accomplishment that the expectation for the library could be justified.[36]

Implicit in the rationale for the library was the ethic of the self-made man. As Irvin Wyllie has shown and as the Horatio Alger novels testify, belief in the self-made man and in the reward of virtue and industry was deeply ingrained in the values of Harris's generation.[37] Harris stressed that the uniqueness of the educational system was rooted in "the American idea of self-help."[38] In the American experience he found "a national history whose biographical side is the story of the 'self-made' man" and that "aspiration is the leading characteristic of the people."[39] If the system succeeded, it would produce skilled readers with habits of diligence and discipline, and the process of education would never cease. This would be in keeping with the fundamental purposes of the curriculum, which Harris characterized as "the providing of the pupil with the mental discipline, and an equipment of tools of intelligence, so that he may help himself. This cannot be repeated too often."[40]

36. *Annual Report, 1877*, p. 189.
37. Irvin Wyllie, *The Self-Made Man in America: The Myth of Rags to Riches* (New York: Free Press, 1966).
38. *Annual Report, 1867*, p. 71.
39. *Annual Report, 1873*, p. 56.
40. *Annual Report, 1872*, p. 150. Harris, in fact, never tired of repeating himself. In 1900, as United States Commissioner of Education, he wrote: "In the United States the citizen must learn to help himself in this matter of gaining information, and for this reason he must use his school time to acquire the art of digging knowledge out of books." William T. Harris, "Elementary Educa-

Such attitudes help explain why St. Louis educators were content with the structure of school attendance as revealed by their data and the findings of the collective biography. They were convinced of the possibility of individual and social betterment with only a relatively short period of formal schooling. Inequalities of attendance in the higher reaches of the system aroused little concern in a society that did not especially demand formal and specialized instruction. Since the schools were representative during the important few years of nearly universal education, the fact that the higher grades were undemocratic in character and rather poorly attended troubled neither professional educators nor the public. Significantly, St. Louisans in the 1860s and 1870s complained that the system offered too much rather than too little education and charged that the high school's curriculum was aristocratic, not that its student body was unrepresentative. In a society where schooling consumed such a small portion of childhood, and where its relation to work was still imprecise, inequities did not command serious attention.

The lack of concern for educational equality is related to a fundamental difference in attitudes over the role of schooling between the nineteenth century and the present. Pointing to the relationship of educational attainment and job level, the sociologists Lipset and Bendix have written concerning mid-twentieth century that "education was the principal avenue for upward mobility in most industrialized countries." Furthermore, they suggest that an open society is supported by the openness of the educational system through which even the poor can advance.[41] In this society, the deprivation or obstruction of individual or group access to schooling of quality has important and measurable economic and social consequences. Similarly, failure to exploit opportunities can be disastrous. With the widespread recognition that so much is at stake, the assessment of the edu-

tion," in *Education in the United States*, ed. by Nicholas M. Butler, 1 (Albany, N. Y.: J. B. Lyon, 1900), 11.

41. Seymour Martin Lipset and Reinhard Bendix, *Social Mobility in Industrial Society* (Berkeley: University of California, 1964), pp. 91–101.

cational system and of its relationship to society becomes an issue of paramount importance. In addition, as society came to expect so much from schools, they also came to demand a great deal from the child, exacting a seemingly ever-increasing commitment of time and energy.

While much was also expected of education in the nineteenth century, the popular investment in schooling was far less. The mass of society, from unskilled workers to businessmen, shared this belief. They gave it expression by insisting that their children go to school and then by withdrawing them by the early teens in the expectation that they were now adequately equipped to begin their careers. Except for males headed for the professions, for females destined to be teachers, and for those few whose families valued higher learning, the encounter with education was relatively brief. Its brevity testifies to how little direct impact school made on one's career. Among the most telling evidence for the lack of a measurable connection between school and vocation is the fact that girls stayed in school, on the average, longer than boys. Parents were generally reluctant to delay the entry of sons into the world of work.

Thus, in mid-nineteenth century, young children attended as popular and democratic an educational system as the nation ever possessed. Divorced from the stigma of a charity venture, the public schools were not yet marked by hierarchies of quality and specialization, as their importance was not recognized. The result was a remarkable homogenization of experience that was enhanced as the graded curriculum was standardized. The ideal of a common school where children from all segments of society would have a common experience was approximated. It was this achievement that led St. Louis schoolmen to broadcast with such confidence the progress of their schools.

7

Bureaucracy and Discipline: Common Schooling Institutionalized

"The history of city systems of schools makes it evident that in the matter of administration the tendency is towards a greater centralization and permanency of authority and that this tendency is in the direction of progress and improvement." So concluded John Philbrick, the former superintendent of the Boston schools, in his famous 1885 survey of American urban school systems.[1] Fearing chaos and disorder as they confronted the difficulties of coping with the multitudes who came to their schools, educators approved of centralization and strict control. The magnitude of their problem can be appreciated by realizing that systems grew proportionately more rapidly than cities, adding thousands in a year and tens of thousands in a decade. In addition, they came to employ hundreds of teachers annually and to manage revenues and property valued in the millions. Aside from such organizations as modern armies and large-scale manufacturing enterprises, there was no precedent for institutions of such size. Moreover, like Horace Mann and William Harris, "professional" educators were often men of letters with good intentions but with little or no administrative experience.

The ethic of uniformity and control carried over into the classroom for, to use Philbrick's phrase, there was not only the "one best way" of hiring teachers and building schools, but also of arranging desks and teaching reading or penmanship. Uniformity of methods meant conformity in behavior. This was acceptable to nineteenth-century schoolmen, who interpreted conformity as proof of their success in establishing discipline and a commonness of experience

1. John D. Philbrick, *City School Systems in the United States*, Bureau of Education, Circular of Information No. 1 (Washington, D. C.: Government Printing Office, 1885), p. 19.

for the city's young. In this way, institutional needs reinforced moral and social objectives. Philbrick was not alone in judging that the St. Louis schools had found the "one best way," for particularly during Harris's administration St. Louis became a model for educators throughout the country.[2] Harris, however, was not responsible for creating the efficient system. Rather, he rationalized and advertised what had already been accomplished during the 1850s, when an earlier generation of superintendents and directors developed the means for effectively controlling the system and its students.

The shifting of responsibility from directors to a superintendent was the first step toward strong central controls. The advance of public education as measured in the amount of revenues and numbers of children and schools had placed great responsibility on the shoulders of the directors. According to the St. Louis school system's Act of Incorporation, the directors, who numbered two to each ward, controlled the lands belonging to the schools, the appointment of teachers, the character of the curriculum, and the management of the pupils. In brief, they were responsible for all operations connected with the public schools. However, the conditions under which directors were chosen and the complexity of their tasks worked against the intent of the charter.[3]

All free white males above the age of twenty-one who had paid the city tax had the right to vote for directors. The voters, through lack of interest in elections, encouraged a situation in which inept and improper administration usually prevailed. Director William Garwood wrote that directors rarely received more than a third or a half of the votes given other candidates. The behavior of the directors reflected the indifference of the public. Their record of June, 1840, is perhaps indicative. Four meetings were held in June, all without a quorum; salaries were not paid on time; and only two or three directors attended the examination of students, which was one of the most important functions of the year.

2. Philbrick, pp. 8, 14–19.
3. *Annual Report, 1860*, p. 63.

At the examination in December, only one of the eight was present. The apathy of the public received its just rewards.[4]

After 1848, candidates for the directorships were nominated by parties. These endorsements failed to arouse interest in the position, however, because it was discovered that nominations meant very little to the voters or parties. There was almost no concern with qualifications or dedication. As the *Missouri Republican* commented: "As a general thing it is considered a sufficient recommend at the election to say of the nominee that he is a *sturdy Democrat*, or an *unwavering Republican* or a *heroic Know Nothing*."[5] Superintendent Tice complained that good candidates were elected by "more the result of accident than design; the prevalent feeling being that any one will do for a school director."[6]

Even if the public had exhibited greater interest in choosing directors, it is doubtful that their performance would have been significantly better. The conditions of the office hampered the directors in fulfilling their numerous responsibilities. Most were successful businessmen too busy to carry out their duties and freely admitted their laxity. In 1855, the president of the board politely recommended that the members read the *Annual Report* carefully so they might become more familiar with the system. William Garwood claimed that the public had little right to demand more assiduous and dedicated service. While expecting directors to give attention to and develop an expertise in educational finance, teacher selection, and classroom evaluation, he complained citizens were also expecting them to serve without compensation.[7]

The logic of the situation and the willingness of directors to delegate or abdicate authority resulted in the naming of paid officers, including a superintendent, secretary, attorney, land or business agent, and clerks. In addition, the

4. *Missouri Republican*, July 3, 1857. *Daily Evening Gazette*, June 23, 1840; December 26, 1840.

5. *Missouri Republican*, July 3, 1857.

6. John Tice, "Education in Missouri," *Teachers and Western Educational Magazine*, 1 (May 1853), 46.

7. *Annual Report*, 1855, p. 6. *Missouri Republican*, July 3, 1857.

board subdivided into permanent standing committees that operated with considerable freedom. With the fragmentation of responsibility, it became desirable to place the diverse affairs of the system into the hands of the superintendent. A telling indicator of the growing importance of this office was the rise of compensation. In 1839, the first superintendent received a salary of "thanks." The next officer served from 1841 to 1842 for $300, which was $300 less than teachers were receiving. The office was not filled again until 1848, when it became permanent. The superintendency and secretaryship were joined between 1848 and 1852 as the salary for both rose from $900 to $1,500. After 1852, with the exception of one year, the superintendent held only one office and was thereafter the highest-paid employee of the board.[8]

The size of the salary indicated that the superintendency was considered a full-time job. Superintendent Divoll left a record of the time and energy required. He spent an average of six hours a day visiting schools. The rest of the time he spent in meetings with committees, examining applicants for teaching positions, arranging cases of discipline, and making reports. In the course of one school year he made over 700 visits to schools and twice that number to individual classrooms. Though some talked of abolishing the office, the superintendent gained increasing respect and influence and emerged as the "executive officer of the system."[9]

The word "superintendent" reveals a great deal about the nature of antebellum administrative reforms. Finding no precedent in educational institutions for such a vast undertaking, the directors looked to the experience of a comparable organization for guidance and found it in the large business corporation and factory. The term "superintendent" itself is borrowed from the terminology of the business world. Superintendent Tice perhaps understood this best when he wrote:

8. *Annual Report, 1854*, pp. 98–99.
9. *Annual Report, 1858*, p. 9. "PBPS, February 17, 1855," *Missouri Republican*, February 21, 1855. *Annual Report, 1855*, p. 82.

Every kind of business requiring the employment of persons to conduct it is under the supervision of someone, either the employer or some special agent to watch over it, and see not only that the work is well done, but how much of it by each person. Everybody knows that without this personal supervision, if either by the employer or his agent, no business would be carried on well or profitably.

The directors' abdication of their mandate, through neglect, indifference, or incompetence, elevated the importance of the superintendent in the "business" of education.[10]

The superintendent, as the agent of the directors and the chief executive of the school system, devoted most of his energies "to the more economical and effective administration of the public school system."[11] Every *Annual Report* and the minutes of innumerable board meetings preached the doctrine of efficiency and economy. It was in this spirit that major reforms were instituted in the operation of the public schools. Confronted with the problem of educating legions of children at a minimum cost and at maximum efficiency, the board made a major effort to institute uniform instruction.[12] Uniformity was achieved by introducing the graded curriculum, the district plan, standardized architecture, and a specially trained, professional teaching staff.

Prior to the educational reforms of the 1850s a modified Lancasterian system was employed in the schools. Under this system a principal teacher was responsible for 150 or 200 students. He might also be aided by one or two assistants. Although this arrangement was practical in a small-scale operation, it proved unworkable when applied to a large city system. A description of the Franklin School illustrates the problem of managing numerous monitorial

10. Tice, pp. 136–37.
11. *Annual Report, 1855,* p. 7.
12. Michael Katz has written that this was the basic question of midcentury reform: "How amidst an expanding population and increasing social complexity could the operation of the schools be both economized and improved?" See, "The New Departure in Quincy, 1873–1881: The Nature of Nineteenth Century Educational Reform," *New England Quarterly,* 40 (March 1967), 6.

groupings: "It is not one school, but five, having five independent organizations, five principals, five different methods of discipline and government, etc. It is not to be expected that a school so organized will work so smoothly in all details."[13]

In order to increase the efficiency of instruction, the board instituted graded schools in 1857. By 1860, four-fifths of the schools had been converted to the new system, which separated the students into six classes, three primary and three grammar.[14] Each grade followed a prescribed course of study, and advancement depended upon achieving a specified percentage of a standard examination. This procedure facilitated the transfer of students from one level to another and from one school to another. Through this course of action the board expected "to establish uniformity and to locate way-marks which shall tell precisely where each school is standing." In effect, their reforms were aimed at establishing and gaining control over educational assembly lines that would turn out, according to schedule, a standardized product in every part of the "factory." This vision was clearly perceived in the original plan:

> The program of one school shall be the program of all, the same grade shall recite in the same study at the same hour all over the city.[15]

The change in the system was prompted by economic considerations as well; it was cheaper. For a board that was hard pressed to find money for new schools and teachers, this factor was very important. The monitorial system required about twice as many principals. Under the new system the principal was a kind of "local superintendent," who devoted most of his time to supervising other teachers and managing the school building.[16] Although more teaching

13. *Annual Report, 1860*, p. 31.
14. *Annual Report, 1860*, p. 8.
15. "PBPS, November 10, 1857," *Missouri Republican*, November 13, 1857.
16. James D. Logsdon, "The Development of Public School Administration in St. Louis, Missouri," (unpublished Ph.D. dissertation, University of Chicago, 1946), p. 75. *Annual Report, 1859*, p. 51. "PBPS, August 24, 1858," *Missouri Republican*, August 28, 1858.

assistants were thereby required, this was altogether desirable from the standpoint of economy, since an assistant was paid only from one-half to one-third as much as a principal. It was estimated that the change would save two or three dollars per pupil. For a system of 10,000 pupils the yearly saving was $25,000.[17]

Uniformity of instruction was also desirable for several other reasons. If the high school was to function properly, different scholars from the separate grammar schools had to enter with the same level of knowledge and preparation.[18] Also, since a child who remained in the system for six years was likely to have six different teachers, it was essential that the teachers instruct in the same way and according to the same plan. Tice pointed out that "if each of the teachers is permitted to employ his or her own method, or no method at all, it is evident that the ideas of the pupils must be obscure, confused and chaotic, just in proportion as these methods conflict with one another."[19]

Another reform aimed at making the system more efficient and manageable was the district plan. In June, 1857, a few months after the board placed the schools on the graded system, the city was divided into school districts. This was done to encourage greater stability in the schools' population; to minimize confusion over records; to discourage pupils from changing schools merely out of disaffection with a particular teacher; and to prevent the exclusion of children from schools in their own neighborhood by children from distant parts of the city. Since St. Louis was "a city where families are constantly changing their residences and consequently their schools," the job of keeping track of students was difficult enough without allowing for free movement among the schools.[20]

As the mechanism for ordering the transmission of knowledge and the movement of students was being worked out, the board found it necessary to standardize schoolhouses.

17. *Annual Report, 1858*, pp. 14–16.
18. Tice, p. 150.
19. *Annual Report, 1856*, p. 13.
20. "PBPS, June 30, 1857," *Missouri Republican*, July 3, 1857. *Annual Report, 1858*, p. 12; *Annual Report, 1854*, p. 16.

In 1858, the board owned an assortment of buildings ranging from a converted dwelling with room for a teacher and sixty students to a three-story building with twenty-four rooms for more than a thousand pupils. This assortment included specifically designed school buildings, converted churches, private dwellings, and even bars. Their general condition can be surmised from Divoll's comment that converted bars were often better than buildings expressly constructed as schools. One had deteriorated to such an extent that the students had to be moved to temporary classrooms in the basement of a neighboring school. Since even poor housing was in short supply, the board was forced to rent rooms in various parts of the city.[21]

The board's solution was, characteristically, an attempt to impose a rational plan throughout the system. In 1859, nine schoolhouses were built according to uniform specifications designed to meet the requirements of the graded system. The older schools, built for the monitorial system, generally consisted of a large room in which the principal sat elevated before the pupils, and several smaller rooms, set off to the side, where assistants heard recitations. The new arrangement, which altered the role of the principal and upgraded that of the assistants, consisted of a set of equal rooms, each with a capacity of about sixty seats. The basic plan provided for a school of 224 pupils and larger schools were built as multiples of this unit. Thus, in 1859, the board erected six structures for 224 pupils, two for 448, and one for 672. The new architecture was a case of form following function, the standardization of the buildings following the standardization of the curriculum.[22]

One more reform was needed to ensure the efficiency and effectiveness of the system. The *First Annual Report* included the names of the men and women who taught in the public school between 1838 and 1854. Of the 230 listed, 122 were employed for one year or less; 49 taught for two years

21. *Annual Report, 1858*, p. 13. "PBPS, June 29, 1858," *Missouri Republican*, July 1, 1858; "PBPS, March 9, 1858," March 12, 1858.

22. *Missouri Republican*, January 30, 1860. *Annual Report, 1858*, pp. 13–16.

and 20 for three years. Only 59 taught for a longer period, and 1 remained for ten years. Since the average period of employment was less than two years, and given a high rate of transfer, a teacher's stay in any one school was little more than a year. The lack of a qualified, permanent staff was described by Tice "as a canker gnawing at the vitals of our system, from which it must be freed, or else it must be destroyed by it." On one occasion the board was forced to send to the East for fifteen teachers. This was unsatisfactory as a permanent solution. The only way to remove the "canker" was to provide a local teacher-training facility.[23]

The Normal School, which was established in 1857, proved an excellent instrument with which to train prospective teachers in the methodology and curriculum of the graded system. Specifically created for this purpose, it allowed a student to matriculate for the two-year course at no cost, with even books and stationery supplied, if he would take an oath that he would work for two years in the St. Louis public schools. Those who had come from outside St. Louis or who had begun teaching before the establishment of the Normal School were trained in Saturday classes, which in 1857 were made a part of the Normal School and became compulsory. The Normal School was so productive that by the 1870s St. Louis had a surplus of teachers.[24]

The importance attached to the Normal School and Saturday classes is summed up in a particularly apt metaphor that Tice drew from the experience of the assembly line. He compared the entire graded system to "some of the large manufacturing establishments where each workman has his alloted work to perform upon the article manufactured, and then hands it over to another and so on until it is finished." Tice saw that the success of the operation depended on well-trained workmen who discharged their duties with precision and devotion.[25]

---

23. *Annual Report, 1854*, pp. 99–109, 62, 73; *Annual Report, 1855*, p. 93.
24. *Annual Report, 1859*, p. xliii. "PBPS, February 24, 1857," *Missouri Republican*, February 27, 1857. *Annual Report, 1880*, pp. 55–56.
25. *Annual Report, 1854*, pp. 17–18.

In 1859, as Superintendent Divoll looked back at the reforms of the previous few years—the graded curriculum, the district plan, school architecture, and teacher training—he was pleased. He pronounced the system "to be complete in its outline and capable of expansion to any extent."[26] Divoll's assessment proved correct. As the institution grew to more than 50,000 students in 1880, these reforms became further entrenched and elaborated. By the time Harris assumed the superintendency in 1868, he had only to make some refinements in the manner of classifying students and in the supervision of the schools. Future managers of public education administered according to the principles established in the 1850s.

Harris did, however, contribute an explanation for the reforms of his predecessors, justifying the transformation of the one-room schoolhouse into the urban, factorylike school. Drawing upon his own experiences, which began in "the 'red school house' in the woods and [extended] through several private schools called 'academies,'" Harris concluded that traditional "laissez-faire" education resulted in "a wholesale slaughter of the time and opportunity of well-disposed youth." He explained that even as the "germinal school organization" of the one-room, one-teacher school grew into the village school with several teachers and several rooms, its operation remained inefficient and its education defective. The improper classification of children, the lack of uniformity in textbooks, and the ill-prepared teacher made for confusion and a loss of opportunity.[27]

In Harris's view, the reformation of the schools was accomplished by copying the system of the factory, thereby taking advantage of the size of the city's population. The principle of the "division of labor," which brought order and efficiency to the manufacturing process, was employed to redeem education. Harris critically compared traditional schooling to the "antiquated process by which the gun was made throughout—lock, stock and barrel—by one gunsmith." He asked his readers to consider the advantages of

26. *Annual Report, 1859*, pp. 13–14.
27. *Annual Report, 1874*, pp. 136–37.

"the division-of-labor systems in the Springfield armory, or the watch manufactories at Waltham or Elgin, where each manipulation has a different workman to perform it." The adaption of these factory techniques created an efficient and uniform educational system that successfully mitigated the chaos of traditional education.[28]

The threat of chaos and the availability of the factory model determined the course of school administration and the character of the educational experience from these formative years. Contemporary observers have also written of the parallels between the school and the factory. For example, Raymond Callahan's *Education and the Cult of Efficiency* has shown how Taylorism, industrial engineering, and the model of the business experience have shaped the administration and character of education in the twentieth century.[29] However, the transformation of the schools into factories and of educators into executives and managers did not, and indeed could not, await the development of the science of professional business management in this century. It was born of necessity as educators first confronted the problems of managing a rapidly expanding and increasingly complex institution.

Ironically, these reforms created a system that future generations, in their turn, would seek to change. Even as the educators of mid-nineteenth-century St. Louis attempted to destroy the little red schoolhouse, contemporary reformers want to remake the factory–school, which they believe encourages conformity and stultifies individual expression.

28. Ibid. There are many other examples of the influences of the factory-model. The following excerpt from Felix Coste's "President's Report," *Annual Report, 1869*, p. 10, serves as an example of how the language of the business manager has been adapted to the purposes of public education: "A system of management that answers well for a business for one stage of its growth, has to be radically changed when that business has expanded well beyond its original limits. It is this fact that I bear in mind when I say that our own school system has arrived at that phase which requires a thorough remodeling of the machinery by which its internal management is carried on."

29. Raymond E. Callahan, *Education and the Cult of Efficiency; A Study of the Social Forces That Have Shaped the Administration of the Public Schools* (Chicago: University of Chicago Press, 1962).

It is interesting that even the first generation of reformers were aware of the potential dangers of their system and recognized that the application of the factory ethic to the school might inhibit individual freedom and spontaneity. Nevertheless, they continued to affirm that individualism could be provided for in a disciplined and standardized framework.[30]

What little evidence remains of conduct in the classroom suggests that this belief was not justified. Given the emphasis on uniformity, standardization, and order, it would have been surprising if freedom and individuality were not suppressed. In a series of articles published in the *Forum* in 1892, the muckraking pediatrician, Joseph Mayer Rice, exposed the dangers inherent in the excessive supervision and discipline of the St. Louis system. Rice pointed out that teachers worked under the constant pressure of regular city-wide examinations. Anxious to obtain praiseworthy results, the teacher directed instruction to ensure a good rating. The consequence was that children were treated in a manner that "cannot be considered otherwise than barbarous":

> During several daily recitation periods, each of which is from twenty to twenty-five minutes in duration, the children are obliged to stand on the line, perfectly motionless, their bodies erect, their knees and feet together, the tips of their shoes touching the edge of a board on the floor. The slightest movement on the part of the child attracts the attention of the teacher. The recitation is repeatedly interrupted with cries of "Stand straight," "Don't lean against the wall," and so on. I

30. Most of the arguments for and against the reformation of the schools can be found in *Annual Report, 1874*, pp. 121–48, in a special section, "Grading and Classification." In the first portion of this report Harris presented the opinions of educators from all over the country who reacted to his justification for the organization of pupils and the curriculum in St. Louis. The following portions of the report contain a historical explanation for the evolution of these reforms and of how they operated in the St. Louis schools. For an example of another urban system which underwent similar reorganization see David Tyack, "Bureaucracy and the Common School: The Example of Portland, Oregon, 1851–1913," *American Quarterly*, 19 (Fall 1967), 475–98.

heard one teacher ask a little boy: "How can you learn anything with your knees and toes out of order?" The toes appear to play a more important part than the reasoning faculties. The teacher never forgets the toes; every few moments she casts her eyes "toe-ward."[31]

Regimentation helped to promote a method of instruction that Rice characterized as "mechanical and calculated to crowd the memory with cut-and-dried facts." While admitting that these techniques made it possible to teach "a large number of facts" and to develop reading skills in a shorter period than in most systems, Rice also noted that "the price they pay for them is a terrible one." He found that during recitation "all spontaneity is suppressed. Whenever a pupil volunteered to express an idea suggested to him by the recitation, he was cut short by some such remark as "Speak when spoken to,' 'Don't talk, but listen,' 'You mustn't raise your hand.' "[32] If the organizational reforms of the late 1850s did not directly bring about such oppressive, if efficient, conformity, they certainly paved the way for it.

The discipline found in St. Louis schools was not universal. Rice discovered in Indianapolis a more sympathetic method of supervision that produced a learning environment which accommodated noise and motion. Spontaneity was encouraged by personal discussions between supervisors and teachers through periodic group meetings. The most important forum was the "principals' club" where on each Tuesday evening during the school year teachers analysed pedagogical writings and would consider topics like "The Rights of the Child in School," "How to Treat Children," and "How to Manage a School so that its Administration Shall of Itself Enforce Ethical Laws." The objective of these sessions was to aid teachers in giving "such training as shall make self-active, powerful, helpful, beautiful, happy human beings—what we call in our school law 'good citizens' in the best and true sense." Such experimentation and

31. Joseph Mayer Rice, *The Public School System of the United States* (New York: Century Co., 1893), p. 98.
32. Ibid., pp. 99–100.

methodology were rare, however, both because they demanded a unique assembly of people and because they were all too susceptible to institutionalization and standardization. Indeed, as normal schools took over the responsibility of training new legions of teachers, amateurism and spontaneity ended. St. Louis, not Indianapolis, pointed the way to the future.[33]

If the management of large numbers, the quest for standardization, and the professionalization of teachers led to strict discipline, Harris found this a satisfying result. Ever-present in his evaluation of educational reforms was a comparison with rural schooling. He recognized "that more than anything else it [the urban school] gives the appearance of a machine, and the American city schools are often condemned for their mechanism." He believed, however, that there was a great advantage when "the whole school seems to move like a machine." Despite the loss of the "delightful individuality" of the rural school and the criticism that urban school behavior appeared "at first to be so much waste of energy," he preferred the latter because "the moment the question of moral training comes to be investigated, the superiority of the education given in the large school is manifest." An important advantage was that it encouraged children to develop habits conducive to proper social behavior. It taught self-restraint, curbed unruliness, cultivated a sense for the student's "own time and that of others," prepared him "for concerted action," and, by "moving to and fro by a sort of military concert and precision," stimulated "the impulse to behave in an orderly manner, to stay in his own place and not get in the way of others."[34]

Harris also credited the schools' discipline with mitigating urban violence: "That the public schools have worked great and favorable changes to the advantage of civil order cannot be doubted. They have generally broken up the feuds that used to prevail between the people of different precincts. Learning to live without quarreling with school-fellows is an efficient preparation for orderly and peaceful

33. Ibid., pp. 102–13.
34. Harris, "Elementary Education," pp. 15–16.

life with one's neighbors." In sum, he found that the "city school is a stronger force than the rural school because of its superior training in the social habits named—regularity, punctuality, orderly concerted action and self-restraint." The internal organization of the urban school reinforced its ability to inculcate moral attitudes.[35]

In addition, with the triumph of standardization, nine-teenth-century educators had found the means of dealing with the social divisions of their society, if only temporarily. During those few years between ages eight and twelve when attendance was universal and most of the children were in public schools, there was an approximation of a common experience, since in each grade of every school of the city children received the same kind of instruction both in terms of content and presentation. As far as they possibly could, educators had constructed a series of city-wide classrooms, which were socially diverse but homogeneous in content and environment.

Looking backward in 1900, Harris wrote that the reformation of American education originated in the common school movement of the Jacksonian period and singled out the appointment of Horace Mann to the Massachusetts state board of education in 1837 as the critical event. Traditional interpretation by twentieth-century scholarship similarly focuses on the crucial importance of this period and also points to Mann's leadership. Unlike the contemporary view, which emphasizes the ideological antagonisms and democratic crusades as catalytic agents for educational reform, Harris interpreted Mann's activities as being largely concerned with adjusting traditional education, conceived and organized in a rural society, to fit the conditions of an urban environment. Mann assumed his position, Harris pointed out, "just at the beginning of the epoch of railroads and the growth of cities," and his contributions included attacking "with unsparing severity the evils of the schools as they had been."[36] The result was that successive generations of

35. Ibid., pp. 17–18.
36. Ibid., pp. 123–24; Cremin, *The Wonderful World of Ellwood Patterson Cubberley*, pp. 25–26, 45.

educational reformers had developed techniques that served not only as a means but as an end. For at the same time and by the same means that they solved the problems of school management, they attempted to shape the lives of the young and thereby the future of the city.

8

New Directions:
From William Harris
through Calvin Woodward

This is a sad state of things, yet it should be known to every citizen of St. Louis, that every year a vast army of public school boys and girls, who are thirteen and fourteen and fifteen years old, in the middle of the district school course, for one reason or another, stop going to school. These facts have much the nature of a public calamity, and it is the solemn duty of those in responsible charge of the schools to point out as clearly as possible the probable causes and the most practicable remedies.[1]

Reviewing in 1900 the same statistics on school attendance that had been available for about half a century, Calvin Woodward, the president of the board and one of the leaders of the manual training movement, judged that they evidenced a "public calamity" rather than provided a source of satisfaction as they had for the generation of Harris. Underlying Woodward's assessment was a new concept of the role of schooling in the life of the child and in the community. Woodward believed that children were not in school long enough to be trained adequately for modern society and that therefore they and the community suffered. Identifying himself as a reformer, he promised to explore the "probable causes" for the deficiencies in attendance and to offer the "most practicable remedies." By 1900, Woodward had already invested about twenty years in the search, and his conclusions contributed to the most important changes in educational thinking and practice since the inception of the system.

His reforms stemmed from a concern with the education

1. *Annual Report, 1900*, p. 21.

of what would become the schools' new constituency—the city's youth, especially those who ordinarily dropped out after age twelve. This was a radical departure from the emphasis that previously was placed on elementary instruction. In the 1870s, Harris had tried to increase the duration of schooling by expanding the lower limits of attendance through the kindergarten rather than attempt to retain pupils through the teen years. Not until after the turn of the century did the high school dramatically grow in St. Louis, as elsewhere, and not until the 1920s did it become an integral part of the experience of a large proportion of American youth. As this transformation in attendance began, educators came to focus increasing attention on the teenage population that was located both within and without the schools. During the first two decades of the twentieth century, Woodward and similarly motivated St. Louisans succeeded in introducing an interrelated package of reforms that, in attempting to deal with these groups, substantially changed the nature and character of the system. Their work resulted in compulsory education and child labor laws, an expanded and diversified high school curriculum, the junior high school, manual training and vocational education courses, vocational guidance, special classes for juvenile delinquents and for defective children, and the collaboration of the schools with agencies of social reform and with the city's major businesses.[2]

Concern with teenagers was a widespread phenomenon of the period. As recent scholarship has shown, "adolescence" was discovered just before the turn of the century, primarily through the work of the psychologist G. Stanley

2. The studies that have been most helpful in dealing with this period of transition are Marvin Lazerson, *Origins of the Urban School; Public Education in Massachusetts, 1870–1915* (Cambridge: Harvard University Press, 1971); Lawrence A. Cremin, *The Transformation of the School; Progressivism in American Education, 1876–1957* (New York: Vintage, 1964); Arthur G. Wirth, *Education in the Technological Society; The Vocational–Liberal Studies Controversy in the Early Twentieth Century* (San Francisco: Intext Educational Publishers, 1972); and Edward Krug, *The Shaping of the American High School* (New York: Harper, Row, 1964).

Hall.[3] Yet the attention lavished by educators on youth was not so much a consequence of new psychological insights as of a more precise understanding of the need for preparing workers for a technological society. It was the development of the urban economy into a more advanced industrial phase that provided the impetus for change. It is not at all incidental that Woodward was a professional scientist active in the training of engineers while Harris, who was perhaps his most formidable opponent both in St. Louis and in a larger national debate, thought of himself as a philosopher. Harris also understood that education was necessary for productivity and progress, possessed a deep and abiding interest in science and technology, and appreciated the change taking place in economic organization. Nevertheless, he steadfastly resisted the growing demand to transform the schools into an apprenticeship agency for American industry. The system's new directions and emphases can perhaps be most profitably viewed through the shift of perceptions and prejudices from a man of letters to those of a practicing engineer.

William Torrey Harris was born on a Connecticut farm in 1835 to a well-to-do family that had roots in the early Puritan migration. After spending some terms at Phillips Academy in Andover and at Yale College, he went West as did his father and brother who were lured by the opportunities for profits in land speculation in Missouri and Kansas. He arrived in St. Louis in 1857 at the age of twenty-two, eager for business opportunities. As a young man without capital but with a good education, he turned to teaching and offered classes in phonography, the nineteenth-century version of shorthand. Failing at this, he accepted a teaching post in the public schools. This was not an unusual course, for many young men of this period temporarily became teachers while training for a profession or before moving on to a career in business. For Harris, however, this was the beginning of a twenty-three year association with the

3. Dorothy Ross, *G. Stanley Hall; The Psychologist as Prophet* (Chicago: University of Chicago Press, 1972).

St. Louis schools and the start of a career that would take him to the summit of the American educational establishment, serving as United States Commissioner of Education from 1889 to 1907.[4]

His reputation grew primarily out of the *Annual Reports* of the thirteen years of his superintendency, 1868–1880. These volumes contained a comprehensive guide on how to build and manage a large urban system and offered a rationale for its work. Widely distributed in English and German, they earned him a preeminent place among educators in the period between the generation of Horace Mann and Henry Barnard and that of John Dewey. In recognition of his talents, he was offered such posts as the superintendency of Boston and the presidencies of Johns Hopkins University and the University of California at Berkeley. In addition, between 1867 and 1880 Harris founded and edited *The Journal of Speculative Philosophy,* which provided a vehicle for the writings of America's leading intellects including Charles Peirce, John Dewey, and William James, as well as Harris's own work on Hegelian and Greek philosophy, thereby establishing himself as a philosopher of the front rank. Finally, his talents in administration were so well appreciated that he was offered the presidency of the largest lead-mining company in the country. Not foregoing the opportunities of the marketplace entirely, he became a successful educational entrepreneur editing several series of widely used textbooks. A man of many abilities and interests, and with a range of opportunities before him, he preferred to devote the major portion of his enormous energies

4. The best sources of information on Harris's thought are Leidecker, *Yankee Teacher*; and William H. Goetzmann, ed., *The American Hegelians: An Intellectual Episode in the History of Western America* (New York: Knopf, 1973). A brief but insightful essay is contained in Merle Curti, *The Social Ideas of American Educators: With New Chapter on the Last Twenty-five Years* (Paterson, N.J.: Littlefield, Adams, 1959), Chapter 9. The most complete bibliography of his writings is Charles M. Perry, *The St. Louis Movement in Philosophy: Some Source Material* (Norman, Okla.: University of Oklahoma Press, 1930), pp. 96–148. Valuable materials are also located in the *William Torrey Harris MSS,* Missouri Historical Society, St. Louis.

to improving public education and adapting it to the requirements of an urbanizing and industrializing society.

Throughout Harris's writings, there is a spirit of boosterism and enthusiasm for the growth of cities, technological innovation, and material progress. Unlike those who dwelled on a nostalgic vision of a less complicated and more rural life, he welcomed change and was a prophet of the future. It is perhaps for this reason that he found the philosophy of Hegel so congenial. Standing with the right wing of Hegelian interpretation, Harris saw human history as a process of synthesis and evolution that he judged to be inevitable and desirable. For the individual, this meant accepting and subordinating himself to existing institutions in which the divine plan worked itself out. These included the city, the corporation, the state, established religions, and the industrial system. Through a process called "self-realization," a person elevated himself to embrace the social order by overcoming his "natural self." Harmony with one's social environment was the mark of a civilized man. Since the schools were "the means of the preservation of civilization," it was their task to reflect and support society. As instruments of the existing order, they were to train the individual to adapt to and to function in his environment.[5] Therefore, the first responsibility of the educator was "that of orienting himself from time to time by the movement of society at large." What Harris perceived was the development of a new stage of civilization:

> In our own time we behold the spectacle of the rapid growth of urban life. Cities that had apparently attained their full growth have taken again a vigorous start and others have increased their rate almost incredibly. In our newly-settled border land, gigantic cities have sprung into existence within a score of years, and we are now in full tide of progress. This tendency to urban life is not a capricious phase of our civilization, but the effect of the application of machinery to productive industry. Through this application, the productive power of man has been so greatly mutiplied, that

5. Curti, pp. 312–21.

immense populations can now be supported in cities where a comparatively small percent of society could be spared from the field two centuries ago.[6]

One implication of such a vision was the necessity of molding a rural population into an urban one. As we have seen in his defense of the public schools from the attack of religious sectarians, Harris placed great importance on the inculcation of morality and the fashioning of an urban discipline. Hence, the schools taught obedience to authority and stressed the acquisition of desirable "habits" such as punctuality and regularity. Moreover, as was evidenced in the discussion over assimilation of the Germans and the nature of kindergarten games, Harris was anxious that children learn to cooperate with one another by acquiring the skills of "social combination." The schools' extraordinary emphasis on proper behavior, while attributable to other motivations, was also usually justified in terms of the creation of a new kind of citizen for a new form of social organization.

A second imperative was that the schools assume a role in providing a labor force and managerial class for the new industrial economy. Harris observed that as a result of the division of labor system that was characteristic of modern economic organization there was a tendency toward specialization and the creation of new vocations. No longer could a man become a jack-of-all-trades or be content to rely on an inherited fund of knowledge. By way of example he suggested "the literary profession," which had become progressively fragmented into numerous specialties "including journalists, printers, publishers, authors, bookmakers, booksellers, telegraph employees, artists, including musicians, painters, sculptors, photographers, actors, etc." Moreover, several of the specialties must always work in harmony with each other for efficient production. Using a favorite analogy, Harris asked if one would "think for a moment of the business of the management of a railroad, requiring as it does, a system of subordination of all parts

6. *Annual Report, 1873*, p. 119.

and members to one hand directing it, so complete, that all shall be a perfect unit." In a wonderfully symmetrical vision, Harris perceived that the system would equip children for their varied roles, and toward this end every department had a special assignment. The high school would encourage a select few to develop "directive power," while the district and evening school would drill an army of skilled workmen accustomed to the rhythm of machinery. Such a plan might not be necessary in a "more agricultural country not penetrated by railroads and other transit facilities," Harris continued, but "the closely organized society that grows into existence with the instrumentalities of commerce and inter-communication finds popular education simply an indispensable provision."[7]

From this understanding, it naturally followed that there would be a direct connection between education and success. The examination for principals, for example, required that the candidates explain "why should an educated factory operative and day laborer be more successful in his vocation than an uneducated one." The answer was supplied by the *Annual Reports*, which repeatedly correlated the acquisition of even a minimal education with the attainment of wealth. Relying on statistics compiled by the United States Commissioner of Education in 1870, Harris found that "all the various trades and occupations of men in this country are directly and beneficially affected by education. The replies from the superintendents of the various departments of commerce and transit testify with great uniformity to the fact that the mere ability to read and write . . . increased the productive power of the laborer from ten to sixty percent and his wages accordingly." Furthermore, advancement to the higher grades of the district school or the high school "increases his value fifty percent more, and his wages in the same degree." Harris noted that the need for education was accentuated by industrialization and that "the common laborer, who depends merely on his hands, has a poorer chance to earn his livelihood [today] than three hundred years ago." This fact, he believed, "is a

7. *Annual Report, 1874*, pp. 78–80.

startling one to the educator of youth. Unless the child be trained by education into the rational use of his intelligence, unless he be made a directive power, he will scarcely escape the pauper's doom when he grows up." In a similar vein, he warned that all must learn new skills and get at least a minimum of schooling or suffer the consequences: "The men not able to understand and successfully direct a machine cannot earn a respectable livelihood."[8]

What was necessary for the individual was also required of cities and nations. Massachusetts, one of Harris's favorite examples, was cited as an educationally advanced society that achieved prosperity despite a lack of natural resources. Looking to Europe, he noted that since the 1850s "there has been inaugurated an immense movement towards special education of the laboring classes of the people in order to increase the results of productive industry." He pointed out that "property itself has sought investment through the municipal organization of the community in founding numerous schools," which would give instruction in a host of skills ranging from horticulture to manufacturing. This movement was born out of the belief that schooling "increases in a direct and potent manner the productivity of the community." As further evidence, he claimed that the educational exhibits of the international expositions of Vienna, Paris, and London, and "the colossal victories of Prussian arms at Sadowa and Sedan have aroused statesmen and political economists to the study of public education as essential to the national strength in industry and in the field of battle as well."[9]

Political economy also taught "that the community flourishes best with diversity of employment at its doors." He warned that unless St. Louis possessed a large reservoir of people skilled in a multitude of tasks it would become economically stagnant and dependent on distant communities

8. *Annual Report, 1873*, pp. 30, 130; *Annual Report, 1872*, pp. 102–3; *Annual Report, 1879*, p. 118.
9. *Annual Report, 1870*, pp. 71–72; *Annual Report, 1872*, pp. 102–5; *Annual Report, 1873*, p. 55.

for the manufacturing and consumption of its raw materials. The iron ore of Missouri must not be sent off to Pittsburgh or Birmingham; it must be processed and then fabricated at home. "If the expenditure of capital will develop skilled industry," he promised, St. Louis would never descend into the status of a colony: "It is the verdict of the civilized world . . . that the community must see to it that general and special education be fostered if it would thrive in the accumulation of wealth."[10]

The school system could do more than equip men with the new skills demanded by an industrial society. It could also spawn the kind of creativity essential for progress. "How many cities," Harris asked, "like Manchester and Lowell, have been made almost entirely by the invention of the power loom? Where would be the wealth of this Mississippi Valley, had no adventurous Fulton invented the steamboat?" Harris was pointing out that the *"directive intelligence"* of the creators and managers of the community's wealth were indispensable to a vigorous economy. For example, when such genius is channeled into the generation of new industry, "laboring people flock near," causing "real estate to double and treble in value," and merchants and others soon follow. "The whole wealth of the community," Harris continued, "arises from the application of directive intelligence, and the corollary deduced is this: No other investment pays so well as a good system of schools, kept up to foster the growth of directive intelligence." Indeed, the "investment" in education could be so productive that "one educated directive man of the community creates wealth enough to pay all the tuition in all the schools of his town or city."[11]

In a eulogy for his predecessor, Superintendent Harris summed up Divoll's concept of the political economy of the schools as well as his own: "His [Divoll's] ideas are shared by the people of this great land. Education in the public schools is essential to the prosperity of the country.

10. *Annual Report, 1872*, p. 104.
11. *Annual Report, 1869*, p. 20.

Wherever the great mills and shops shall rise, there also shall arise the school house, equally a symbol of an industrial civilization."[12]

Most educators, including Woodward, had no quarrel with Harris's ideas. There had been general agreement since Horace Mann that schools must be purveyors of desirable habits and valuable skills so that they might benefit the economic development of the community and guarantee the successful integration of the young into vocations. The debate that emerged between Harris and Woodward was over what kinds of skills were essential for future workers. Woodward came to believe that the curriculum should emphasize instruction in industrially oriented skills and specifically in manual training, a novel concept in whose development he played the major role during the 1870s. His commitment to manual training naturally led him in the 1880s and 1890s to make perhaps the earliest analyses of the education of American youth, and his findings convinced him to advocate far-ranging proposals to further modify the curriculum and institute still more novel courses. Moreover, since many of his recommendations were intended for children between the ages of twelve and sixteen, Woodward could no longer tolerate, as did Harris, their exodus from the schools. Using both the force of law and a curriculum that was calculated to appeal to this age group, he launched a movement that retained thousands of children in the classroom who previously would have returned to the streets or entered the work force.

Like Harris, Woodward was a transplanted Yankee, born in western Massachusetts in 1837 into a family that also traced its origins back to early Puritan immigrants. His success in local schools won him a scholarship to attend Harvard. He graduated in 1860, winning an award as the outstanding student in mathematics. After a brief career as a Union officer and as principal of a high school in Newburyport, Massachusetts, he accepted an invitation to come to Washington University in St. Louis. He quickly distinguished himself there as a leading instructor in its sci-

12. *Annual Report, 1871,* p. 166.

entific departments, teaching mathematics, geometry, topographical drawing, and applied mechanics. By 1871, at age thirty-four, Woodward was dean of the polytechnic school and held an endowed professorship. Actively concerned with the education of scientists, chemists, physicists, engineers, and others who expected to hold positions of leadership and responsibility in industry, he devoted much of the next forty years seeking to improve the quality of preparation of youth for an industrializing society. Not content with improving the curriculum only at Washington University, from the mid-1870s through 1909 he was continually involved in trying to influence the policy of the St. Louis schools and served intermittently as a school director and as president of the board. In an effort to expose his theories to an even larger audience, from the 1880s and through the rest of his life he was a frequent speaker at assemblies of educators and engineers and a prolific contributor to professional and popular journals. Ironically, his ideas were better received outside St. Louis than at home. While he was able to change the curriculum of Washington University and found many admirers and imitators in other cities both in the United States and England, Harris and successive superintendents, as well as the majority of school directors, opposed his reforms. Not until the turn of the century did Woodward and a coterie of like-minded reformers, some of whom had been his students at Washington University, capture control of the St. Louis board.[13]

Washington University was a fitting locus for his work. At its founding, engineer William Chauvenet, the first chancellor, expressed his desire for "a department for the benefit of industrious mechanics and no others." Indeed, such a department preceded the establishment of the more traditional scientific and literary curricula. Beginning in 1856, Washington University offered day and evening classes for the city's young workers in mechanical and industrial drawing, algebra, and mensuration, in addition to the traditional "common branches." These courses were

13. *Dictionary of American Biography*, 20, p. 507. *National Cyclopaedia of American Biography*, 9, p. 469.

organized in 1857 into the O'Fallon Polytechnic Institute, the establishment of which was intended to "prove useful and advantageous to the manufacturers of St. Louis." The institute was, in effect, part of a widespread movement to create schools that would benefit young men who wished to advance into industrial vocations and serve the needs of local industries. In his inaugural speech as principal of the institute, John Howe formally recognized this, affirming that his school was modeled on "the mechanics' institutes of our country, and those of Berlin, Vienna, and other cities of Europe."[14] Such schools spread in New England and New York during the 1840s generally in the form of mechanics' institutes and trade schools and tried to reach youths in the late teens or above. In a few cases small colleges offered manual training but their courses were designed to benefit the institution, as the sale of student products became a kind of tuition. Usually, courses were geared to fitting students for positions in local industry and therefore served as a kind of surrogate apprenticeship system. Teaching specific skills rather than theory, these small college courses were a form of vocational training.[15]

Until the 1870s, the approach of Washington University's manual training program was consistent with those of other institutions. Change came under Calvin Woodward, although it was gradual and initially without clear direction. Dissatisfied with the preparation that the future engineers in his courses were receiving, Woodward began to experiment with a graded curriculum that he came to believe would be of value not only to students in his courses but to any child, even if he were not preparing for a career in industry. He also argued for lowering the age at which most had thought manual training would become beneficial, thus broadening its potential constituency to include all children. These ideas crystallized under the im-

14. Charles Penney Coates, *History of the Manual Training School of Washington University*, Bureau of Education, Bulletin, 1923, No. 3 (Washington, D. C.: Government Printing Office, 1923), pp. 7–9.

15. Berenice M. Fisher, *Industrial Education; American Ideals and Institutions* (Madison: University of Wisconsin Press, 1967), pp. 14–49.

pact of the educational theories of Victor Della-Vos, a Russian educator who had modified the Swedish version of manual training called *sloyd*. President John Runkle of the Massachusetts Institute of Technology was one of the few who noticed Della-Vos's display at the Centennial Exposition at Philadelphia in 1876—hidden as it was under a stairwell in a corner of the Exposition Hall—and grasped its significance. Runkle began propagandizing Russian *sloyd* immediately, pointing out that it had universal application for all students. Woodward was already coming to the same conclusions in his St. Louis experiments. Both Runkle and Woodward, sensitive to the value of the new curriculum and desiring to increase the readiness of college-bound engineers, established preparatory schools based on manual training as adjuncts to their universities.[16]

The motto of the St. Louis Manual Training School, which opened its doors in 1880, expressed Woodward's aim: "The Cultured Mind—The Skillful Hand." The curriculum was rich not only in manual training, which consisted of shop activities, especially carpentry, and of mathematics and the sciences, but also in courses designed to provide a good general education with a generous and rigorous English program. In addition to technical studies, he placed much importance on traditional subjects, although he advocated "a judicious abbreviation of the time devoted to literary work." Woodward believed that the training given his students was sufficiently broad to have educated the "whole boy." While he expected that most of his boys would pursue scientific or industrial careers, he was convinced that the preparation he had given his students would enable them to succeed in any academic discipline and in any area of endeavor. In fact, the graduates of his school pursued a variety of vocations, becoming bookkeepers, accountants, merchants, manufacturers, salesmen, teachers, lawyers, and physicians, as well as engineers and scientists.[17]

16. Coates, pp. 49–76.

17. Calvin M. Woodward, *Manual Training in Education* (New York: Scribner and Welford, 1890), p. 45. Coates, pp. 45–46.

Underlying Woodward's pedagogical theory was the belief that the schools must change with society. "With every new phase of civilisation," he wrote, "has come a new phase in education." Like Harris, he saw that "educational progress has been first the effect of progress, and then the cause of more progress." Claiming that "never was there a century or half-century so progressive," and that the most marked advances came in industry, science, and commerce, he argued that the schools must depart from the standard curriculum to ensure further growth. Although he acknowledged the need to produce men with "intellectual vigor" and with "practical power," he was appalled that the schools "persisted in ignoring or decrying the value and necessity for scientific and industrial training as compared with an almost exclusively literary culture." With the exception of the kindergarten "games," he deplored the absence of the "useful branches" in the elementary school curriculum and was most critical of instruction in ancient languages in the high school, which he saw as a wasteful and unnecessary conformity to tradition. The specific target of his criticism was Harris, who defended a curriculum based on arithmetic, geography, history, grammar, and literature—his famous "five windows of the soul." This curriculum was deficient, Woodward maintained, for it was based on the assumption that "all the activities of life may be learned from books." Instead, he argued: "We need to know more of the concrete, less of the abstract; more of primary knowledge, less of secondary; more personal experience, less of memory. We need more of life, more action, more interest, more of the executive, and less of the passive; more of growth, less of absorption." Such changes could be accomplished through manual training, which Woodward saw "as a sort of general culture which acts beneficially upon every branch." While the manipulation of tools, making of diagrams, and building of objects had a practical and immediate value for only a few, their ultimate worth was that they sharpened the intelligence and gave satisfaction to all. The coordination of the hand with the eye and the execution of a carefully designed plan that concretized the abstract were both necessary correctives and natural extensions of the traditional curriculum. In place of Harris's "five windows," Woodward offered his own—mathematics, literature, science, drawing, and manual training.[18]

Harris did not accept Woodward's claims for the benefits of manual training. He blocked its incorporation in the schools during his superintendency and challenged it at national educational meetings during the 1880s and 1890s. Maintaining that Woodward's assessment of the intellectual value of manual training was based on faulty psychology and pedagogy, Harris argued for adherence to the traditional courses, including the classical languages, which afforded an excellent means for disciplined intellectual growth. His objections were also based on a traditional bias that manual training was beneficial only for those who could not meet the standards imposed by the established curriculum. Since the 1830s and 1840s, with the spread of houses of refuge and industrial schools, practical courses were offered to delinquents, orphans, and the intellectually substandard— a biased practice that would continue well into the twentieth century. Harris insisted on a common curriculum that excluded practical courses, for he still believed that the mass of children could learn what is necessary for modern society after having acquired discipline and the capacity to progress through self-study. He would brook no departure from the "culture" of the public schools.[19]

Harris was fighting a rear-guard action, however, for throughout the post-Civil War period pressure was building for practical courses. The interest aroused by Woodward's techniques bears testimony to this. Soon after the opening of the St. Louis Manual Training School in 1880, numerous imitations appeared in American cities. There was an impressive succession of visitors from cities throughout the country, including Chicago, Toledo, and Boston,

18. Woodward, pp. 3–6, 41–46.
19. Woodward's frustration with Harris's opposition is a constant theme in Woodward's early writings. See *Manual Training in Education*, pp. 2, 41–51, 148, 218–19, 264. For discussions of the controversy between the two see, Wirth, *Education in the Technological Society*, pp. 9–15, and Fisher, pp. 72–84.

who came to observe and learn. There was also a steady stream of students and instructors who went out from St. Louis to teach in new institutions. In 1885, Woodward's reputation attracted the attention of Englishmen who invited him to visit Manchester and other English cities, which soon founded their own schools. Moreover, exhibits of the St. Louis methods were shown at major world fairs, including Vienna in 1889, Chicago in 1893, and St. Louis in 1904. The president of Mexico, Russian princes, members of Parliament, educators, businessmen, and "philanthropists" from most of the industrializing countries of the world came to inspect the school and leave their names in the visitors' register. Woodward's school had become an important and influential showcase for a pedagogy that promised to produce the skilled workers required by industrial society.[20] By 1891, the National Educational Association, the most important professional association of educators in the country, has established a "Department of Industrial Education and Manual Training."

Yet Woodward's victory was more apparent than real and not without irony. Manual training achieved a brief efflorescence around the turn of the century, but even then more narrowly defined, skill-oriented, vocational courses began to overtake Woodward's innovation. The popularity that manual training enjoyed can be attributed, at least in part, to the ambiguity of the concept. Although Woodward considered both parts of his school's slogan, "The Cultured Mind—The Skillful Hand," of equal importance and mutually reinforcing, many educators and noneducators, particularly the businessmen who funded private manual training schools in St. Louis and elsewhere, were more interested in skillful hands. "Manual training," "industrial," "polytechnic," and "vocational" education were loose terms that Woodward himself and later educators and historians have found it difficult to define with precision. Under the rubric of manual training, students made neckties, bookcases, and powder puffs; they hammered, colored pictures,

20. Coates, pp. 76–82.

and blew bubbles; and they learned to become domestics, auto mechanics, and engineers.[21] On occasion, even Woodward despaired of what was carried out under his name and spent much time reaffirming that his intention was to produce a well-rounded, intelligent, and able person. His pedagogy had symbolic, not explicit, aims. As Woodward put it: "In a manual training school the aim is not the narrow one of learning a trade. Neither is dexterity sought in special operations which may be only small parts of a trade. The object of every feature is education in a broad, high sense. Its influence is subjective." In an unsuccessful effort at clarification, he suggested that manual training be called "manual culture."[22]

Woodward also encouraged the movement to vocational courses with his studies on school attendance that attracted national attention during the 1890s. A summary of these analyses formed the burden of his "President's Report" for the St. Louis schools in 1900. In a survey of major American cities, Woodward confirmed that the massive exit of children between twelve and sixteen years of age that had characterized midcentury enrollment records continued. He judged that a small portion of this exit could be considered "a reasonable loss" and attributed it to "a certain death rate, a certain amount of pinching poverty, and a certain amount of incapacity which practically shuts out pupils." What did concern him was identifying and correcting the causes for "abnormal withdrawals." Refusing to grant that among most healthy and able children there was a genuine need to supplement family income as soon as possible, he labelled the claim of poverty an "excuse." The real reasons for dropping out were that parents lacked an appreciation for the value of more schooling and that children were bored with their classes. Sympathizing with these attitudes, he placed the ultimate blame on the schools.

21. *Annual Report*, *1912*, pp. 118–21.
22. Woodward, pp. 60–72. Paul H. Douglas, *American Apprenticeship and Industrial Education*, Columbia University Studies in Economics, History and Law, 95, No. 2 (New York: Longmans, Green and Co., 1921), 178–84.

More specifically, he faulted neither teachers nor facilities, which he found to be good, but the curriculum.[23]

Woodward was not surprised that boys and girls became discontented after age twelve. Biological and psychological changes impelled them to engage in a more active life and made it difficult for them to submit to the sedentary and passive behavior demanded in the usual classroom. This, Woodward thought, was particularly true of boys, who "long to grasp things with their own hands; they burn to test the strength of materials and the magnitude of forces; to match their cunning with the cunning of nature and of practical men." Inevitably, the energies of these youths found expression in the streets or in the factory, office, and home. Manual training for boys and domestic science for girls was the answer, for these courses were "suited to their tastes."[24]

Woodward also suggested ways for assuaging the discontent of parents. The first challenge was to persuade them that the schools were teaching their children something that could meet their needs as future wage earners. This, too, could be met by a new curriculum that was of a "more practical character" than the traditional literary one. Second, he urged the distribution of free books in all grades of the system. In St. Louis, this meant extending the free-book program beyond the fourth grade, a practice that was introduced in 1891. This was important, not because the cost of books inhibited enrollment, for Woodward discounted poverty as a significant deterrent to attendance; rather, he suspected that in limiting free books to the lower grades the system confirmed the belief of many parents that an elementary education was sufficient. The distribution of books through the high school would encourage an appreciation for a more complete education.[25]

Between 1900 and 1920, the problem of "elimination," as the phenomenon of early withdrawal from school was called, became the subject of numerous reports sponsored

23. *Annual Report, 1900*, pp. 15–16.
24. Ibid., p. 27.
25. Ibid., pp. 27–29.

by city and state boards of education, the Russell Sage Foundation's Department of Child Hygiene, the National Committee on Vocational Education, and the United States Bureau of Education.[26] The studies generally focused on cities, although there was a widespread feeling that conditions were even worse in rural areas. Not only did rural areas provide many pressures as well as opportunities for work, but their resources for a more advanced education were limited. These studies were remarkably similar to Woodward's description of the problem and his findings for its causes. Based on a study of 318 cities, George Strayer, a professor at Columbia University's Teachers College writing under the auspices of the Bureau of Education, produced in 1911 the most comprehensive report, which showed that the public schools lost one-half of their students between the ages of thirteen and fifteen. Strayer suggested that the way to deal with the problem was to create a differentiated curriculum that segregated the college-bound from those who would want to or need to find work. He argued that "it is manifestly unfair to provide a rigid curriculum which leads straight to the college or university." To be truly democratic, the schools must offer each student "that training which will best fit him for his life's work." The point of Strayer's study was to make a case for vocational training. Unlike Woodward, who had envisioned manual training as a part of a general curriculum

26. Paul Douglas has an excellent survey of the literature in *American Apprenticeship*, pp. 85–108. Among the more noteworthy studies are *Report of the Commission on National Aid to Vocational Education*, House Document 1004, 63rd Cong., 2nd sess. Luther Gulick and Leonard Ayres, *Why 250,000 Children Leave School; A Study of Retardation and Elimination in City School Systems* (New York: Charities Publications Committee [Russell Sage Foundation] 1909). George D. Strayer, *Age and Grade Census of Schools and Colleges; A Study of Retardation and Elimination*, United States Bureau of Education, Bulletin, No. 5, 1911 (Washington, D. C.: Government Printing Office, 1911). George Counts made major contributions to this study in the 1920s and 1930s. See, George S. Counts, *The Selective Character of American Secondary Education* (Chicago: University of Chicago Press, 1932). The outpouring of analysis in the early twentieth century is further testimony that the dropout was not a nineteenth- but a twentieth-century problem.

from which all students might benefit, Strayer was typical of a current of opinion that advocated the abandonment of a common curriculum and favored the separation of youths into different tracks, which predicted that large numbers of students would enter into specialized, vocational courses. Like others, Strayer had modified Woodward's earlier studies in another significant way. Strayer wanted the schools to include all children, even those whom Woodward put into the category of "reasonable loss." He therefore called for "special schools" that would accommodate the "unusually deficient either mentally or physically," and applauded the movement to enforced compulsory education. Like most early twentieth-century educators, Strayer joined reforms that would engender new, positive attitudes toward advanced schooling with reforms that would coerce the unpersuaded.[27]

As with Woodward's studies, Strayer's was based on the assumption that more children would attend school if the curriculum emphasized more practical courses. A large body of statistics confirmed Woodward's belief that the majority of children used poverty as an "excuse" for withdrawing from the schools. In 1910, for example, the Federal Investigation into the Condition of Women and Child Wage-Earners offered the following analysis for "elimination": "Child help desired though not necessary"—27.9 per cent; "Child's dissatisfaction with school"—26.6 per cent; and "Child's preference for work"—9.8 per cent. Thus, about 65 per cent of the children were potential students if parents and children could be persuaded that more schooling was worthwhile. Only 30 per cent were in the category "Earnings necessary to family support," and 5.7 per cent were accounted for by "other causes," which included mental and physical problems. This commission's figure of 30 per cent for children whose earnings were necessary for family support was about average but higher than the 20 per cent reported by the Public Education Association's study of New York in 1912, and the Douglas Commission's 24 per cent for Massachusetts in 1906. Furthermore, investigators

27. Strayer, pp. 11, 139–40.

felt that these genuinely poor children were not necessarily lost to the schools, for they believed that poor families might be willing to make the sacrifices necessary to prolong their children's education if the value of education were sufficiently demonstrated to them. The net effect of these studies by educators was to convince them that with the appropriate reforms they could reach a very substantial number of youths.[28]

The necessity for doing so was buttressed by studies conducted during the 1910s on what children did upon leaving school. The most comprehensive survey, undertaken in Philadelphia, inquired into the vocations of 14,000 children. Of these only 3 per cent were in skilled positions. The same was true in surveys taken in Chicago and in Worcester, Massachusetts. St. Louis came out somewhat better but recorded that 88 per cent of the children were in unskilled positions such as bellboys, cash, or messenger boys, or in wagon and delivery service. The same studies showed that the average daily wage of a child was but $3.00 to $3.50, or one-third that earned by men. In addition, employment was of a temporary nature. In another series of studies conducted at the same time, it was shown that children tended to work at one job for only a few months. At Swift and Company of Chicago, children worked an average of only three and a half months; in Hartford, Connecticut, children averaged two and a quarter jobs per year; and in Maryland, which compiled the best statistics, more than 50 per cent of children under sixteen worked for two months or less, and 15 per cent for only two weeks. While there are no comparable figures for St. Louis, it was apparent that children who left school, particularly for unskilled work, held a very insecure place in the job market. This meant that there was little likelihood for a steady, dependable income and, what was of great importance to educators, little opportunity to learn new skills. The career of the early

28. *Report on Conditions of Women and Child Wage-Earners in the United States*, Senate Document 645, 61st Cong., 2nd sess., 1 (Washington, D. C.: Government Printing Office, 1910), 46. Douglas, pp. 89–90.

dropout was marked by shiftlessness, unemployment, low skills, and low wages.[29]

Paul Douglas, a reformer and academic who later became senator from Illinois, best summed up in 1920 the work of the previous two decades. He described the experience of many children as drifting "from job to job, from industry to industry, still unskilled, and exposed to all the social and industrial evils which threaten adolescence." Typically, when the child matures into manhood, he finds that his position is vulnerable because of the incessant influx of younger unskilled workers into the labor force. The result is that he "finds himself one of the class of the permanently unskilled with the attendant low wages and unemployment of his class." As a final judgment, Douglas noted: "He had nothing to sell but his youth; he sold it, and received nothing in return." Surely, the press of family circumstances and the dissatisfaction with schooling had to be very great to sustain the willingness of the tens of thousands of youths to confront these possibilities.[30]

The heightened concern for teenagers that was expressed in these studies stemmed from an appreciation that the urban economy had developed into a more industrial phase and that, therefore, unschooled teenagers had become a liability to society and to themselves. So long as teenagers were able to find gainful employment, and even unskilled work could be considered a necessary or valuable prelude for future advancement, it was possible to be complacent with both a relatively abbreviated duration of schooling and a lack of vocational instruction in the curriculum. Prior to the twentieth century, there were many more openings in service occupations that required minimum skills and in laboring positions that demanded less than adult strength. Thus large numbers of children were employed in factories, stores, and offices as cigar makers, messengers, cash boys or cash girls, delivery boys, wrappers, markers, and the like. But around the turn of the century the introduction of cash registers, pneumatic tubes, paper-folding machines,

29. Douglas, pp. 96–105.
30. Ibid., p. 85.

and telephones, to suggest only the more obvious, necessarily made many of their jobs obsolete or reduced the need for their services. An advancing technology had not only brought about job insecurity or unemployment for legions of adolescents but had contributed to the demand that schools be used to improve youth's preparation for a modern industrial system.[31]

These studies ultimately served to elaborate and make more precise a problem that concerned many educators around the turn of the century—the decline of apprenticeship. Woodward connected it with industrialization: "The invention of machinery and the use of costly machine tools so far modified and limited apprenticeship as to almost ruin it."[32] Manual training was his response to the problem. Increasingly, the answer came in the form of vocational and trade schools that were usually privately sponsored by businessmen and philanthropists. For example, in addition to Woodward's St. Louis Manual Training School, which was founded with the financial support of the city's leading industrialists and merchants, there were four other private trade schools operating in 1910.[33] Aside from the relatively few instances of vocational courses in several systems, apprenticeship training took place outside of the public schools, so that the great mass of urban youths was not affected. During the first decade of the twentieth century, a national movement of educators, businessmen, and organized labor collaborated in such organizations as the National Society for the Promotion of Industrial Education and pressed for

31. The impact of technological innovation on the displacement of youth from the work force is detailed in Selwyn K. Troen, "The Discovery of the Adolescent by American Educational Reformers 1900–1920; An Economic Perspective," a paper presented at the American Historical Association meetings, Chicago, December 1974.

32. Calvin Woodward, "Manual, Industrial, and Technical Education in the United States," *Report of the Commissioner of Education for the Year 1903*, 1 (Washington, D. C.: Government Printing Office, 1905), 1021.

33. Lewis Gustafson, "The Recognition of Industrial Education for Apprentices by Organized Labor," *National Society for the Promotion of Industrial Education*, Bulletin No. 20 (New York: NSPIE, 1915), pp. 134–35.

the inclusion of vocational courses in the public school curriculum. On a national level, their work resulted in the passage of the Smith-Hughes Act of 1917, which allocated federal funds for the first time on behalf of vocational training.[34]

The movement toward vocationalism was most clearly evidenced in the shift of emphasis in two influential studies commissioned by the National Education Association—the Report of the Committee of Ten of 1892 and the Cardinal Principles of Secondary Education of 1918. The 1892 statement, which was formulated by some of the most distinguished educators in the United States, was concerned with defining the curriculum of the high school so that there would be a better correspondence between its work and the uniform entrance requirements to which many of the nation's colleges had recently agreed. Commissioner of Education Harris, who wrote the section on the ideal high school curriculum, not surprisingly emphasized the traditional subjects of English, mathematics, geography, history, and foreign and ancient languages. There was no mention of manual training or vocational courses. Since the high school was thought of primarily as a necessary step leading to college, its course of study was subordinated to the demands of the universities.[35] In 1918, the select committee organized by the National Education Association defined more broadly the function of the high school. Arguing that "a comprehensive reorganization of secondary education is imperative at this time," they stressed the need to readjust the curriculum to what they perceived to be a new social order by providing explicit instruction for work, leisure, home life, and citizenship. The result was the "comprehensive high school," which included a "differentiated curriculum" that was a direct repudiation of Harris's model in the Report of the Committee of Ten.[36]

34. Wirth, *Education in the Technological Society*, pp. 33–42.

35. *Report of the Committee of Ten on Secondary School Studies*, Report of the Commissioner of Education for the Year 1892–93, 2, Pt. 3 (Washington, D.C.: Government Printing Office, 1895), 1457–64.

36. Commission on the Reorganization of Secondary Education, *Cardinal Principles of Secondary Education*, Bureau of Education Bul-

The most radical departures came as a result of a recognition that there was a public responsibility to offer training for special vocations because of the development of "a more complex economic order." The fundamental changes were "the substitution of the factory system for the domestic system of industry; the use of machinery in the place of manual labor; the high specialization of processes with a corresponding subdivision of labor; and the breakdown of the apprenticeship system." Harris, of course, had also perceived this, but because of his confidence in and commitment to the ideology of self-improvement, a common culture for all students, and the tradition of a literary education, he remained wedded to the older curriculum. Perhaps, too, his vision was focused on a society in which these changes were in a more rudimentary form. By 1918, after more than a generation of agitation for practical studies and the evidence of numerous analyses on the problems of youth, the committee was ready to recommend that, in addition to the usual college course, there should be agricultural, business, clerical, industrial, fine arts, and household arts curricula.[37]

These reforms went far beyond what Woodward initially envisaged or desired. Nevertheless, during his tenure as school director (1897–1911), he participated in bringing them about and pioneered in the development of the "comprehensive high school." Moreover, several of his former students at the St. Louis Manual Training School had major roles in advancing these innovations by serving as school directors and school officers, the most important of whom was Benjamin Blewett, Superintendent of Schools 1907–1917. That Woodward and his disciples should have presided over the transformation of the school was fitting, for Woodward's earlier work laid the base on which these changes would be made. He had insisted on the need for practical studies and had focused attention on the city's teenage population. Once it was clear that the schools must become a surrogate for apprenticeship by including in the work

letin, 1918, No. 35 (Washington, D. C.: Government Printing Office, 1918), p. 7.

37. Ibid., pp. 7–8, 22.

of the classroom that which was formerly acquired outside, there developed a powerful and irreversible movement to broaden the scope of the curriculum and extend the range of the student body. In order to support these activities, it became necessary to create auxiliary programs and a corps of officials to reach into homes, the courts, offices, and factories, and the city at large. By adding to the responsibilities of formal education, educators not only expanded the role and scope of their institutions; they moved beyond their walls.

9

The Strategies and Dimensions of Change

The return of Calvin Woodward to the board in 1897, after an absence of eighteen years, marked the beginning of a new orientation in school policy. Nevertheless, opposing voices could still be heard. The leading spokesman of the resistance was Superintendent Louis Soldan (1895–1907), a German-born immigrant who was attracted to the city's Hegelian group and became a disciple of Harris. Thus, in 1900, at the same time that Woodward was calling attention to the crisis in school attendance and presenting a case for practical studies, Soldan made one of the last but most vigorous apologies for the curriculum of the nineteenth century. Acknowledging that some changes were necessary to accommodate the system to the demands of industrial society, he nevertheless felt that they could be made within the framework of the "common-school training" that had remained substantially unchanged for about thirty years, or from the time that Harris became superintendent. Soldan admitted that arithmetic could be adapted to contemporary needs by emphasizing accounting procedures and mensuration. Geography and history, too, could be taught less as exercises in "word-study" and more to help students develop a sense of industrial society and its problems. Basically, however, Soldan echoed Harris's call for an "irreducible minimum" that comprehended reading, writing, and arithmetic with the goal that children should leave the school with the ability to read a newspaper "with its immense variety of political, economic, geographical, historic, and scientific information."[1] Maintaining the tradition of self-improvement, Soldan proposed a compression of the common school course into a six- rather than

1. *Annual Report, 1900*, pp. 151–53, 163.

an eight-year curriculum so that the city's youth would not be delayed from entering into the real world. In contrast to Woodward and other advocates of vocational education, Soldan saw an "inappropriate and sinister significance" to extending formal schooling, for in doing so "there was the danger that education, instead of being purely a preparation for life, will encroach on the time and functions of life itself."[2]

Soldan also pointed out that it was inefficient and unwise to offer practical courses because it was impossible to determine what a child would do when he grew up, and that since the system would not offer instruction in everything it would necessarily neglect some important areas by choosing to emphasize others. The only workable solution was to retain the common curriculum, which in any case "imparts such knowledge and power as is beneficial in each and every vocation." In addition, he feared that by shifting emphasis to practical studies "a thorough general education would be sacrificed," and the schools would compromise other fundamental purposes, especially their commitment to train a citizenry dedicated to democratic principles and their obligation to develop character. This was inadmissible, for "the great social mission of the public schools is to unite all classes of society in their rooms in the common educational preparation of life." Indeed, with Soldan the term "common school" passed from the vocabulary of St. Louis educators.[3]

The common curriculum began to fragment with the introduction of manual training. In 1898, a few private citizens donated funds to support manual training for boys and its equivalent, domestic science, for girls. Initially located in scattered schools and offered to children in the seventh and eighth grades, the board formally adopted the experiment as part of the curriculum in 1902, thereby following a precedent set by the acceptance of the kinder-

2. Louis Soldan, "Shortening the Years of Elementary Schooling," *The School Review*, 11 (January 1903), 4.
3. *Annual Report, 1900*, pp. 153–54.

gartens, which were also introduced through philanthropy and private initiative. Still, manual training accounted for only one to two hours of instruction per week so that the integrity of the traditional common curriculum was not seriously compromised. Woodward, too, considered this only a minor advance, for his real aim was the incorporation of manual training by the high schools, an objective for which he applied continual pressure.[4] In response to Woodward's urging, the board finally opened in 1904 two "cosmopolitan" or "comprehensive" high schools, as they were later called. These terms were used in recognition of the broadening definition for legitimate high school work and the willingness of the new institution to accommodate the untraditional. The terms were appropriate, for within a decade the high school had so diversified its offerings by moving in the direction of vocational studies that it had become a fundamentally different institution. As the high school changed, so did much of the remainder of the system. It can be claimed fairly that the transformation of the St. Louis schools began in 1904.[5]

From the 1850s through the 1890s the high school program had remained static, as had the rest of the curriculum. Then, in 1894, the high school course was altered to include five divisions: classical, English, scientific, business, and normal. This produced little real change, as only a limited number of electives were offered and then only during the last two years, when students could replace some language study with drawing, additional science, penmanship, business arithmetic, commercial law, and pedagogy. The pervasive commonality was further abetted by the network of small branch high schools, which served students through the tenth grade, and the presence of only one central high school that alone offered electives in the last two years. Thus, the high school remained, in the words

4. *Annual Report, 1899,* pp. 27–28; *Annual Report, 1902,* pp. 149–50.
5. Charles A. Bennet, "Manual Arts Instruction in the St. Louis High Schools," *Manual Training Magazine,* 18 (February 1917), 233–37; Calvin Woodward, "A New Era in the Public Schools of St. Louis," *School Review,* 11 (June 1903), 486–94.

of Superintendent Edward Long (1880–1895), "a finishing school, a fitting school for college, and a normal school."[6] Even with some further revisions in 1900 and the addition of art and commercial programs, the curriculum continued to consist of a common core of language, math, science, and limited electives in the eleventh and twelfth grades. The orientation still favored the college-bound or the future teacher. Only with the acceptance of the "cosmopolitan" high school did the system begin to address itself to the problem of the adolescent dropout by offering vocational preparation.[7]

The two new high schools that the board opened in 1904 reflected in their design the successful imposition of Woodward's ideas. The new buildings, which cost about half a million dollars each, included large shops complete with machinery and tools in addition to the conventional recitation rooms and laboratories. The visible emphasis on manual training reflected a concern with making "the student a strong, intelligent and industrious man able to adjust himself quickly and efficiently to the vocation which he will enter." The same was true of five other courses of study, for the construction of these new buildings inaugurated a new concept of secondary education. The new curriculum was a composite of nine courses in three major divisions, which unlike previous ones anticipated that students would follow different paths beginning in the ninth grade, or immediately upon completion of the district school course. The "college classical," "college scientific," and "teachers' college" were, as their titles indicate, for those who anticipated continuing on to college and the normal school. Of the remaining six, four were labelled "general education" and two were called "special courses." "General education" included general, art, noncollegiate scientific, and classical courses. "Special courses" provided commercial and manual training. While these six could also lead to college, and indeed, Washington University agreed in

6. *Annual Report*, 1895, p. 86.
7. For changes in the courses of study see, *Annual Report*, 1894, pp. xxvii–xxviii; *Annual Report*, 1900, pp. 93–109.

1911 to take graduates of any of them, it was also anticipated that these courses would be terminal for most students.[8]

While students were still required to take courses in English, algebra, geometry, botany, physiology, physics, and history, although in varying amounts, they were also able to choose from a far wider range of subjects as they entered different paths. Among the twenty-five new courses available were classes in bookkeeping, Shakespeare, commercial law, typewriting, stenography, art and drawing, Spanish, manual training or domestic science, music, chemistry, psychology, ethics, and commercial geography. During the next decade the high school added instruction in other areas including industrial history, salesmanship, advertising, printing, and auto mechanics. While the total number of paths tended to fluctuate between seven and nine, the proliferation of offerings ultimately eroded the common core. By 1917, the only courses that all high school students had in common were four years of singing and physical training, three years of English, one year of history, and one half-year semester each for community civics and vocational information. For St. Louis, the Cardinal Principles of 1918 were not a guide for future action but confirmed existing practices. The key element in this shift was the replacement of college entrance requirements with immediate vocational objectives as the dominant influence in shaping the high school. It took little more than a decade to destroy the uniformity of the classical curriculum that had characterized its program in the nineteenth century.[9]

These changes had an immediate impact on school attendance. In 1900, there were 2,349 enrolled in grades nine through twelve, but by 1910 there were 6,255 and by 1920, 11,393. While some growth was due to an expanding population, the real significance of these figures is that proportionately more students were continuing on in the higher

8. *Annual Report, 1905,* pp. 196–202. David Mahan, "The Influence of the Efficiency Movement on a Large Urban School System: A Case Study of the St. Louis Public Schools," (unpublished D.Ed. dissertation, Washington University, St. Louis, 1968), pp. 346–47.

9. *Annual Report, 1911,* p. 171; *Annual Report, 1917,* pp. 117–21.

grades. Only 2.96 per cent of the total day population went on to high school in 1900; 7.10 per cent were enrolled in 1910; and 10.65 per cent in 1920.[10] Further refinement of the school's statistics shows that there was an important shift in the distribution of the student body that was directly related to the new offerings. Analysis of the programs pursued by senior class students shows a decline in popularity of classical and scientific courses, the mainstay of the older curriculum, and increased enrollment in the new ones, particularly in general studies, and in manual training. In 1900, 14.5 per cent of the boys graduated in the classical, 67.7 per cent the scientific, and 17.7 per cent the relatively recent business course. In 1920, only 1.5 per cent finished classics and 21.3 per cent the scientific, while the vast majority chose the newer courses, especially the general, which attracted 51.3 per cent, manual training with 17.4 per cent, and commercial with 8.3 per cent. Moreover, the new courses substantially increased the relative number of male graduates, which climbed from 29.7 per cent in 1900 to 42.7 per cent in 1920. A similar pattern holds for girls; between 1900 and 1920 classics declined from 10.2 to 6.9 per cent and science from 38.8 to 2.9 per cent. Both commerce and domestic training were more popular, drawing 13.1 and 11.8 per cent respectively, while another 3.5 per cent studied art. As with boys, the general curriculum was the most popular, enrolling 61.7 per cent, although the attraction for girls undoubtedly stemmed from the fact that it was a step toward normal school. In sum, these figures show that the appeal of the general and vocational courses that were not necessarily related to college entrance was very great, and that the curriculum of the previous decades had lost the interest of all but a minority of students.

Despite the growing number of graduates, school authorities were dissatisfied. They aggressively sought to reduce the dropout rate even further and turned to vocational instruction as the instrument. Reasoning that four years of high school might demand too great a commitment from many teenagers, they introduced in 1910 one-year and two-

10. *Annual Report, 1920*, p. 288.

Table 10. Selection of Programs by High School Seniors, 1900–1920, by Percentage and Number of Students*

Four-year courses	1900 Boys	1900 Girls	1910 Boys	1910 Girls	1920 Boys	1920 Girls
College classical						
Percentage			1.8	.6		
Number			(4)	(2)		
Classical	14.5	10.2	4.1	3.3	1.5	6.9
	(9)	(15)	(9)	(11)	(5)	(38)
College scientific			4.1	1.2		
			(9)	(4)		
Scientific	67.7	38.8	12.3	3.9	21.3	2.9
	(42)	(57)	(27)	(13)	(87)	(16)
Art			2.3	20.6	.2	3.5
			(5)	(69)	(1)	(19)
Business	17.7	4.8				
	(11)	(7)				
Commercial			15.9	5.4	8.3	13.1
			(35)	(18)	(34)	(72)
General			31.8	34.6	51.3	61.7
			(70)	(116)	(210)	(339)
Manual training & domestic arts & science			27.7	14.6	17.4	11.8
			(61)	(49)	(71)	(65)
Normal course		46.3		15.8		
		(68)		(53)		
Distribution by sex:						
Number	(62)	(147)	(220)	(335)	(409)	(549)
Percentage	29.7	70.3	39.6	60.4	42.7	57.3
Total number	209		555		958	

* *Annual Report, 1900*, pp. 90–93; *Annual Report, 1910*, p. 292; *Annual Report, 1920*, pp. 284–86.

year vocational curricula for the ninth and tenth grades. Emphasizing very narrow fields of instruction, these courses offered youth an opportunity to learn a wide variety of crafts, including cabinetmaking, printing, automobile mechanics, machine work, a variety of office skills, and domestic arts. In striking contrast to their purposes in the nineteenth century, schools were now being transformed into the modern replacement for a decaying apprenticeship system.[11]

A parallel development was taking place in evening instruction. From the outset, the function of evening classes had been chiefly remedial and their curriculum modelled on the "irreducible minimum" of the district schools. As was discussed earlier, they typified the system's commitment to self-improvement. Their character and purpose remained unchanged until the first decade of the twentieth century. In 1900, Soldan characterized the student body as consisting of "young men and women who, through various circumstances, were deprived of an early education, or whose education is incomplete, and who feel the necessity of improvement, [and who] are offered, by the evening schools, an opportunity to obtain instruction in the common branches." Indeed, the *Annual Report* for 1900 listed the curriculum under the title, "Common Evening School Grades." During the next ten years change began modestly with the introduction of courses in shorthand, bookkeeping, and manual training. Approximately fifty new courses were added during the 1910s including practical electricity, architectural drawing, shop mathematics, cabinetmaking, automobile design, business correspondence, dressmaking, and millinery. These offerings reflect the new role of evening schools: "To give special training to those who desire to become more efficient wage earners." Letters sent to hundreds of employers by Superintendent Blewett to enlist their aid in encouraging students to participate in the new programs underscore the schools' objectives. In one such letter Blewett observed that "there can be no question of the fact that if a boy or a girl who lacks preliminary education will attend the evening schools for a few years he or she will render more service and more efficient service than if he had not attended." He promised, moreover, that "increased efficiency in the office, stockroom, or factory means economy

11. *Annual Report, 1910,* pp. 127–35.

to the employer and a better future for the employee."[12]

The new offerings were a great success. After a period of decline and stagnation from the highs of the 1870s, evening school enrollments rose sharply in the first decade of the twentieth century when they doubled the yearly averages of the 1880s and 1890s and doubled again during the 1910s, counting almost 23,000 pupils during the peak year of 1917. This growth is largely attributable to the expansion of the high school department of the evening schools, which included vocational courses, because the elementary section, which maintained the traditional common school subjects, showed more modest increases. The board records usually fail to give a breakdown between the evening elementary and high schools, but if the *Annual Report* for 1920 is typical, more than twice as many students took vocational training as the basic courses. It is likely, therefore, that the evening schools would have remained relatively unused without the attraction of vocational education.[13]

An important dimension of evening school growth was the vastly larger proportion of girls, whose entry coincided

Table 11. Average Yearly Enrollment in Evening Schools by Decades, 1860–1920, by Percentage and Number of Students*

Years	Boys	Girls	Total
1860–1870	88.1	11.9	
	(1,383)	(186)	(1,569)
1870–1880	85.8	14.2	
	(4,361)	(719)	(5,080)
1880–1890	89.2	10.8	
	(2,571)	(310)	(2,881)
1890–1900	86.4	13.6	
	(2,216)	(350)	(2,566)
1900–1910	76.7	23.3	
	(3,853)	(1,173)	(5,026)
1910–1920	58.5	41.5	
	(8,066)	(5,713)	(13,779)

* *Annual Report, 1920*, p. 306.

12. *Annual Report, 1900*, pp. 120–27; *Annual Report, 1910*, p. 154; *Annual Report, 1913*, p. 116; *Annual Report, 1917*, p. 377; *Annual Report, 1910*, pp. 153–54.

13. *Annual Report, 1920*, p. 305.

with the expansion of the high school department curriculum. During the 1890s 13.6 per cent of the students were female; in the 1910s their share grew three times to 41.5 per cent. While there are unfortunately no adequate statistics on enrollments in the various courses by sex, it is probable that girls, too, came to take advantage of the new offerings. This was certainly the intent of school officials who urged girls to prepare for the jobs available to them in the city through the schools. One survey undertaken by teachers in 1920 of possible vocations listed fifteen major occupational categories with forty-eight specialties in such areas as the sewing trades, the telephone industry, and office work. The schools did more than enumerate these possibilities; they advertised them and encouraged the girls to see in them a chance for personal fulfillment and an opportunity to contribute to the welfare of the community. "A Creed of Work for Women," which was developed for adolescent working girls, captures the spirit in which the schools attempted to foster what amounted to a revolutionary change in orientation—away from permanent domesticity toward a fuller participation in the life of the community. Included in the declaration of the Creed were:

> I believe that every woman needs a skilled occupation developed to the degree of possible support.
> She needs it commercially, for an insurance against reverses.
> She needs it socially, for a comprehending sympathy with the world's workers.
> She needs it intellectually, for a constructive habit of mind which makes knowledge usable.
> She needs it ethically, for a courageous willingness to do her share of the world's work.
> I believe that every woman should practice this skilled occupation up to the time of her marriage for gainful ends with deliberate intent to acquire therefrom the widest possible professional and financial experience.
> I believe that every woman should expect marriage to interrupt for some years the pursuit of any regular

gainful occupation . . . and that she should focus her chief thought during the early youth of her children upon the science and art of wise family life.

I believe that every woman should hope to return in the second leisure of middle age to some of her early skilled occupations,—either as an unsalaried worker in some one of its social phases, or, if income be an object, as a salaried worker. . . .

I believe that this general policy of economic service for American women would yield generous by-products of intelligence, responsibility, and contentment.[14]

The commitment to prepare youths for vocations found its most extreme application in the continuation schools, which provided daytime instruction in specific skills for four or more hours per week. These classes were introduced in September, 1919, as a result of a new state law that made such instruction compulsory for all youths between fourteen and sixteen years of age who had not completed the eighth grade and were voluntary for those between sixteen and eighteen who wished to learn new skills. The schools operated on a principle of released time, wherein students left their jobs in order to take the desired courses. During the first year, the courses were so popular that 5,000 enrolled out of a potential constituency of 7,000. Part of the reason for the success of the new classes was the cooperation of employers, who sometimes paid their workers for the time spent in school, donated equipment for classrooms, and provided teachers. The Postal Telegraph and Cable Company, for example, installed at its own expense twenty-four telegraphic machines and the necessary allied equipment in one school and recommended a teacher from among its own employees. In various other courses graduates of the normal school joined with sign painters, printers, salesmen, tailors, and machinists in educating the city's future workers. Moreover, the classes were scattered throughout the city both within school buildings and outside in factories and business establishments. In this concrete fashion,

14. *Annual Report, 1920*, pp. 114–16.

schools became intermediaries between youth and employers and thereby diminished the division between school and society.[15]

Since the process of sorting out pupils into probable careers began at ever-earlier ages and during rather than beyond schooling, vocational guidance became a natural and necessary concern of school officials. With the creation of so many new programs it was also essential to advertise the new options and explain their values. The initiation of informational services was, in addition, a logical response to Woodward's contention that a major factor in early withdrawal was the ignorance of pupils and parents of the kinds of skills necessary for success in an industrial community and how the schools could satisfy those requirements. The close relationship between vocational training and vocational guidance was also evident on the national level. Shortly after the establishment of the National Society for the Promotion of Industrial Training in 1907, members of that group called for a new association that resulted in 1913 in the organization of the National Vocational Guidance Association.[16]

The schools' guidance programs required the cultivation of new relationships with students and parents, and to achieve this officials experimented with a variety of techniques. In 1910, Blewett began sending out letters to eighth-grade pupils and their parents, since both were "frequently not well enough informed about the high school to make intelligent decisions in choosing courses, or to determine that it is best to give any time to the high school." The following year, the high schools sponsored receptions for this group, in addition to speeches and tours, during which principals and teachers privately consulted with parents concerning which courses might best suit their child. At the same time, Blewett initiated a series of conferences with eighth-grade teachers and elementary school principals in order to guide them in how better to direct and inform students on an ongoing and personal basis. In order to reach a

15. *Annual Report, 1920*, pp. 109–25; *Annual Report, 1919*, p. 13.
16. Wirth, *Education in the Technological Society*, pp. 98–119.

wider audience, the system began exhibiting in 1912 throughout the city a collection of large screens with photographs of high school classes and legends explaining the value of advanced schooling.[17]

A necessary adjunct to these activities was the use of class time to better acquaint the pupil with the world he was entering, so that he might appreciate the value of a more thorough preparation. For this purpose, an "educational museum" was established in 1905 that loaned illustrative materials and pictures to teachers of all the grades in order to present "more concretely the physical and social world." During the next two years, Blewett came to understand that such means "are not so impressive as the direct touch with the physical and social world itself." Consequently, in 1909, he originated a program of "excursions" into the city that brought students into different neighborhoods, business establishments, factories, government offices, and cultural and social institutions. Blewett explained that such a program would not be necessary for children growing up in the country, for they were better integrated into the life of the community. The city child, on the other hand, "does not really see the city because of the houses. He is distanced and lost in the rushing multitude of things, and in his confusion gets hold of very little outside of a very narrow circle of experiences." Blewett hoped that through these trips the schools could turn "the seeming prison house of the city into a world throbbing with human interest and full of opportunity for him who will open his eyes and heart."[18]

These programs, which spread from the elementary grades through the high school during the 1910s, came to serve a number of explicit educational goals. On the one hand, they provided the means for imparting some elementary notions of geography and economics. By comparing a shoemaker's shop with one of St. Louis's great shoe factories, for example, students learned about the transformation from handicraft labor to the modern factory system and developed

17. *Annual Report, 1910,* pp. 113–16; *Annual Report, 1911,* p. 70; *Annual Report, 1912,* pp. 198 ff.

18. *Annual Report, 1909,* pp. 145–47.

a sense for the existence of a national market. At the same time, teachers used these occasions for advocating the attainment of the highest possible skills, and by demonstrating the multitude of jobs and their interconnections they also "hoped to dignify the position of laborer in the eyes of the boys." As a further extension of this work, they adapted geography texts to teach about St. Louis industry and its place in the national market and introduced formal courses in "vocational information" for junior and high school pupils. It should be added that while these innovations are generally credited to an imitation of practices found in German schools, they had also been a part of Woodward's curriculum for the St. Louis Manual Training School since the 1880s, and Blewett was undoubtedly aware of them.[19]

The most extensive guidance programs were to be found at the continuation schools. First, all students filled out a "vocational guidance card" on which they registered their vocational preferences, those of their parents, and the explanation of these choices. Teachers also contributed information on scholastic aptitudes and behavior. The expectation was that these cards would serve as a basis for consultations between teachers, students, and parents. Moreover, students were encouraged to take "tryout courses" wherein they could experiment among the various offerings to discover in which areas they possessed native abilities and what kind of work they might enjoy pursuing. Finally, officials developed considerable knowledge of the job market as a result of the surveys conducted in the 1910s through interviews with employers and trade union officials, and disseminated these findings among students both in personal interviews and through such pamphlets as "Trades Open to Boys in St. Louis." This pamphlet, which listed more than twenty major vocational areas and more than a hundred specialties, revealed at once the difficulty of the decisions confronting youth as well as their opportunities. All the informational services, from trips to factories, consultations, and lists of jobs, provided the city's youth not only with a basis for making more intelligent choices as they selected

19. *Annual Report, 1911*, pp. 46–47, 181–86.

from the growing number of options within the system but educated them as to the nature of their community and thereby better prepared them to enter it.[20]

While the differentiated curriculum and its concomitant, vocational guidance, were primarily the consequence of adapting schools to changes in economic organization and technology, new attitudes toward the young also contributed to stimulate educators in these directions. Since the 1880s, both the child study movement and a scientific psychology concerned with child development led educators to an awareness of the differences among children and to recognize the various stages of individual growth. The result was a call for a more flexible curriculum that would be responsive to such variations. G. Stanley Hall, who profoundly influenced both pedagogues and psychologists, perhaps best expressed this change around the turn of the century in his concept of "individualization." Educational methods, Hall insisted, must be adjusted to differences of age, sex, ability, and vocational expectation. This would mean advocating a junior high school for the adolescent, special classes for the feeble-minded, acceleration of the talented through the schools, and the encouragement of some to prepare for the trades and others for college. Expressed institutionally, Hall's programs paralleled Woodward's. Thus, St. Louis schools moved away from the uniform, college-oriented curriculum in the context of better serving the needs both of their students and society.[21]

The conjuncture of both these objectives shaped the purpose and structure of Benjamin Blewett Junior High School which, established in 1917, was the last of the institutional innovations that altered the nineteenth-century curriculum.

20. *Annual Report, 1920*, pp. 109–25.

21. In two key addresses to the National Education Association, Hall set forth his ideas on how his studies on child development suggested a reordering of schooling: "The Ideal School as Based on Child Study," *Addresses and Proceedings of the National Educational Association, 1901*, pp. 474–88; "The High School as the People's College," *Addresses and Proceedings of the National Educational Association, 1902*, pp. 260–72. For a discussion of Hall's ideas see Ross, *G. Stanley Hall*, pp. 309–40.

Named for the recently deceased superintendent who had laid the groundwork for its acceptance, the junior high school carried to a further extreme the ideas that began with Woodward and were present in the new educational psychology. Following the lead of Boston, Cleveland, San Francisco, and other cities, the older structure of an eight-year elementary course followed by a four-year high school was replaced by a six-year elementary, three-year intermediate school, and three-year high school program. Superintendent John Withers, Blewett's successor, explained that the new plan made possible "a closer adjustment of the course of study both to the needs of individual children and groups of children and the needs of the community in which the school is located."[22] The junior high school was, in the first instance, another attack on the problem of early withdrawal, for Blewett and Withers expected that the rearrangement would enable St. Louis to replicate the experience of other cities which found that the new structure yielded increased attendance. This success was universally interpreted as the result of incorporating vocational studies in the seventh grade or immediately at the end of the new termination of the elementary course. With this adjustment, only the kindergarten and the first six years of the district school remained as the locus for common education. Characteristically, educators viewed this final departure from tradition as necessary for the proper preparation of youth for life in industrial centers.[23]

Giving a choice to seventh graders, who were generally thirteen and fourteen years old, was also consistent with the theories of adolescence that Hall had been the first to formulate. In addresses to the National Education Association in 1901 and 1902, Hall argued that since the early teens was a distinctive period in the development of the individual, distinctive institutions should be created for this stage of life. The segregation of seventh- through ninth-grade chil-

22. *Annual Report, 1917*, pp. 125–26.
23. *Elementary School Journal*, 18 (September 1917), 3–5. R. L. Lyman, "The Ben Blewett Junior High School of St. Louis," *School Review*, 28, Pt. 1 (January 1920), 26–40, and Pt. 2 (February 1920), 97–111.

dren was a concrete response to his theory of adolescence. Moreover, having undertaken extensive measurements among children, he urged that educators be more sensitive to differences in interests and abilities of students, particularly during this stage of their development. In 1920, the system acted on this recommendation by instituting achievement and intelligence tests that divided seventh graders into three groups—the most talented, the average, and the slow. Such "individualization" allowed for different rates of progress so that the brightest could finish the three-year program in two and the slowest, who were placed in smaller classes for greater individual attention, were allowed additional time. Withers considered this procedure not only psychologically sound but the ideal solution to a problem that had concerned Woodward and his followers for about forty years—how to keep children from being bored by schoolwork. Withers now believed that together with a system of electives that offered many practical courses these divisions would make advanced schooling a more attractive and valuable experience for all. Because of this attention to individual needs, both Blewett and Withers as well as most American educators considered the introduction of the junior high school a democratizing influence in public education.[24]

The provision of a greater variety of alternatives to meet the different needs of the city's teenage population contributed to a fundamental break with traditional patterns of school attendance. Table 12, which draws on the sample of the 1880 census and aggregate data from the censuses of 1910 through 1940, shows the dimension of change. As we have seen in Chapter 6, in 1880 and for the last part of the nineteenth century generally children attended school for about three or four years prior to age twelve. This fact was the point of departure for Woodward's agitation to reform the public school curriculum. By 1920, school attendance had been lengthened so that most children entered

24. Philip Cox, "The Ben Blewett Junior High School: An Experiment in Democracy," *School Review*, 28 (May 1919), 345–59; *Annual Report*, 1920, pp. 73–84.

at ages six and seven rather than seven and eight and began leaving at around fourteen rather than twelve. The net effect was to double the time children spent in school, from three and four to almost eight years. The completion of the elementary course was now normative, with a large number of students continuing through the junior to senior high schools and with still others taking advantage of the day and evening vocational programs. Unlike nineteenth-century St. Louisans, who began their careers with only a grounding in the three Rs, early twentieth-century youth had a more thorough training in fundamentals and, frequently, preparation in specific skills. This revolution in the relation of the young to formal schooling continued steadily so that by 1940 about half the children remained through age seventeen and completed the high school course.[25]

This change did not come about only through the attractiveness of the new programs and the system's efforts at persuasion; compulsion was also necessary. While Woodward believed that a major reason for early withdrawal was the irrelevancy of courses to the needs of children, he came to understand that curricular changes alone would not be sufficient. In 1904, at the same time that the system was introducing the "cosmopolitan high school," which was the forerunner of so many other innovations, Woodward advocated lobbying the governor and state legislature for effective truancy laws. The problem that prompted this approach was the same that had generated institutional reforms—how to deal with the thousands of children who were leaving after the fourth grade. Woodward's conversion to compulsory education, a proposal that is absent in earlier writings, was in keeping with a broad national movement concerned with child welfare that worked for child labor and compulsory education legislation. While the first compulsory attendance laws were enacted in Massachusetts

25. *Annual Report, 1920*, pp. 205, 304; *Annual Report, 1940*, pp. 30–33. In 1940, there were 8,876 fifteen-year-olds in school who came under compulsory education legislation. At the same time there were 4,037 seventeen-year-olds in high school and another 803 in vocational schools.

Table 12. School Attendance of All Children Ages 5–20, 1880, 1910, 1920, 1930, 1940, by Percentage*

	1880	1910	1920	1930	1940
Age					
5	19.0	...	45.7	...	59.7
6	54.9	55.5	82.9	...	91.5
7	79.4	83.3	91.6	97.7	96.8
8	87.0	88.8	93.3	97.7	97.5
9	88.7	91.2	94.3	97.7	97.6
10	91.2	95.0	96.1	97.7	97.7
11	88.6	95.1	96.4	97.7	97.8
12	82.3	94.8	96.3	97.7	97.5
13	72.3	93.4	95.7	97.7	97.1
14	52.3	74.1	82.8	84.8	95.5
15	36.9	49.0	60.3	84.8	88.7
16	20.3	31.1	34.5	42.0	72.3
17	13.1	19.2	21.9	42.0	53.4
18	6.5	11.7	13.8	15.1	29.5
19	4.3	8.0	9.7	15.1	16.2
20	1.6	4.9	6.5	15.1	9.7

* Source: For 1880, see Table 6. *Thirteenth Census of the United States: 1910*, 1, p. 157. *Fourteenth Census of the United States, 1920*, 2, p. 1136. *Fifteenth Census of the United States, 1930*, 2, p. 1146. *Sixteenth Census of the United States, 1940*, 4, pp. 360–61.

in 1852 and in many other states outside the South between the post-Civil War period, they were generally without enforcement provisions and tended to confirm already existing levels of attendance rather than bring in new students. Only at the turn of the century, with adequate enforcement, did attendance laws become in fact compulsory and a factor in raising the number and length of student enrollment.[26]

26. For reviews of the history and arguments in favor of compulsory education, see, Forest C. Ensign, *Compulsory School Attendance and Child Labor* (Iowa City: The Athens Press, 1921); Edith Abbott and Sophonisba Breckenridge, *Truancy and Non-Attendance in the Chicago Schools* (Chicago: University of Chicago Press, 1917). For discussions of the effect of compulsory education laws see William Landes and Lewis Solmon, "Compulsory Schooling Legislation: An Economic Analysis of Law and Social Change in the Nineteenth Century," *Journal of Economic History*, 32 (March 1972), 54–89; Moses Stambler, "The Effect of Compulsory Education and Child

Woodward succeeded in galvanizing support among his fellow directors, and together with some local citizens who organized into the Missouri Child Labor Committee he persuaded the legislature to enact a compulsory education law in 1905. This statute required that children between six and fourteen must attend school for at least half the school year and that children between fourteen and sixteen could be exempted if they demonstrated that they were gainfully employed. Exemptions could also be made for children of any age whose earnings were necessary for family support, the mentally and physically handicapped who could be required to attend special schools, which the city was empowered to make available, and "juvenile disorderly persons" who could be compelled to attend "truant or parental schools" if these, too, were established. Both parents and employers who disregarded the law were made guilty of a misdemeanor and were liable to fines. Further legislation in 1907 extended the required period of attendance from half to the entire year, attempted to eliminate loopholes through which children fourteen through sixteen circumvented the law, and rescinded exemptions for poor children under age fourteen. Finally, the statutes provided for truant officers who were charged with the responsibility of enforcing compliance and granting exemptions.[27]

As Table 12 demonstrates, the legislation was very effective. Due to vigorous enforcement, nearly all children were in school continuously from age six or seven until fourteen by the 1910s. In some years, officers investigated as many as 80,000 cases including sickness and legitimate employment as well as those involving irregular attendance, inveterate truancy, juvenile delinquency, and illegal child employment. The large majority of cases required only a visit of the attendance officer to establish the legitimacy of the absence, the prompt return of the child to school, or the issuance of the needed work certificate. In other instances,

Labor Laws on High School Attendance in New York City, 1898–1917," *History of Education Quarterly*, 8 (Summer 1968), 189–214. For Woodward's account of the movement toward legislation in St. Louis, see, *Annual Report, 1904*, pp. 17–21.

27. *Annual Report, 1907*, pp. 316–21; *Annual Report, 1920*, p. 192.

the attendance officer became an arm of the court system, serving legal papers or remanding children to the House of Detention, hospitals, or other institutions. For example, out of almost 78,000 investigations in 1915–1916, 1,805 "warning notices of proposed prosecution" were served on parents, but only 50 cases reached the courts. Apparently the energy with which attendance officers fulfilled their obligations was sufficient to ensure compliance without overburdening the court system.[28]

The high attendance rates were also a result of their toughness, for attendance officers granted very few exemptions based on poverty. In 1910–1911, for example, only 49 certificates of exemption were issued and these were for children thirteen years old for three-week periods, although they were renewable in some cases. On the other hand, 277 applications were rejected. It is probable that even more children would have applied, but the officers were undoubtedly known for their unwillingness to grant exemptions. Poverty was certainly more prevalent than the number of exemptions or applications indicate, for several studies undertaken by the chief attendance officer, John Quinn, estimated that poverty was the cause for about 70 per cent of the cases of children leaving after age fourteen. Apparently, the officers could recognize a poor home only if the child were above fourteen, but considered the same circumstances for those below this age as merely an "excuse" for nonattendance, as had Woodward much earlier. In the absence of an official definition of poverty, the attendance officers had considerable discretion and used it to maximize the fullest measure of attendance under the law.[29]

Although they were rigid in interpreting the law, the officers carried on their work with considerable compassion. In fact, they were less policemen than professional social workers who were chosen because they could relate well to children and parents. Every effort was made to create a competent and sensitive corps of officers by establishing

28. *Annual Report, 1916*, p. 372.
29. *Annual Report, 1911*, pp. 136, 279–80; *Annual Report, 1912*, p. 149; *Annual Report, 1916*, p. 258.

civil service examinations, paying salaries equal to those received by experienced teachers, and hiring blacks, whites, and those who spoke Italian, Yiddish, and other languages.[30] It was hoped that this select group could appeal to the child's honor and better nature in bringing about a reformation of habits rather than coercing him through the law. The desired relationship was not that of an antagonist but, as John Quinn wrote, "that of a friend who seeks to help him do right." Moreover, since the officers found that truancy and delinquency were related not only to poverty but were associated with homes broken by the death of a parent, divorce and separation, or by negligent and irresponsible parents, they were expected to attempt to resolve domestic problems so that the child would not be hindered from continuing his schooling. Here, too, sympathetic mediation was always considered preferable to confrontation in juvenile court. Indeed, Quinn measured the effectiveness of his department's work by the degree to which the courts could be avoided and problems settled amicably and informally.[31]

The largest sections of Quinn's reports contain case histories that document the wide variety of activities in which the officers engaged and, appropriately, came under the heading, "The Social Work of the Attendance Officer." They chased runaways; assisted parents with recalcitrant children; tried to settle family problems before the police were called; recommended medical attention; found jobs both for children and their parents; brought clothing and food not only for school-age children but for other members of the family; located wealthy individuals or charitable organizations that sponsored bright but poor children even through high school by subsidizing parents for wages lost through school attendance; dispatched some children to hospitals and others to institutions for delinquents; located jobs for street gang members who were beyond the school age; served as "drummers" for the schools by informing

30. *Annual Report, 1908*, pp. 253–54; *Annual Report, 1920*, p. 237. Attendance officers earned about $1,500 and the chief officer $3,500 or as much as the system's key supervisors.

31. *Annual Report, 1911*, pp. 136–39.

families of their location and what they offered; and functioned as vocational guidance counselors. In the course of these activities, they became a vital link between thousands of individuals and public dispensaries, free clinics, visiting nurses, employers, and various private philanthropists as well as charity groups. These included the St. Louis Provident Association, the St. Vincent De Paul Society, the United Jewish Charities, the Federation of Women's Clubs, the Child Conservation Scholarship Fund, and other interested groups, especially the Parent-Teachers' Association, the School Patron's Alliance, and the Mothers' Clubs.[32]

In addition, just as social settlement workers were agitating for institutional responses to problems of the urban child from their position outside the schools, the attendance officers became an important force for advocating reform from within. Their work with gangs, which impressed them with the need for expanded and improved facilities for delinquents, contributed to the establishment of industrial schools within the city as well as the Bellefontaine Farm, an institution composed of small family-type units outside St. Louis. Their intimate knowledge of life in the "congested districts" or slums led them to urge the development of school baths, swimming pools, and playgrounds, which were expected "to better the social environment of the children and minimize delinquency among them."[33] Since they had to deal directly with sick children, they supported the establishment of a department of hygiene, which was responsible for the physical well-being of school children, and held annual eye, ear, and dental examinations and gave blood tests and inoculations. As their duties also involved discriminating between those who were misbehaving because of mental defects rather than inherent or socially related deviancy, they became agents and advocates of special schools for abnormal children, which resulted in the establishment of the Psycho–Educational Clinic.

To be sure, it is likely that recreational facilities, indus-

---

32. *Annual Report, 1908*, pp. 258–59; *Annual Report, 1920*, pp. 206–7.
33. *Annual Report, 1907*, p. 331.

trial schools, rural reformatories, a department of hygiene, and schools for the retarded would have been created without the advocacy of the attendance officers, as a host of reformers, including settlement house workers, jurists, psychologists, physicians, and philanthropists generally were working toward the same ends throughout the nation well before the attendance division was created. Yet, the fact remains that these same laws, which provided for the attendance officer and made attendance compulsory for all the city's children for increasingly longer periods of time and with diminishing possibility for exemption, necessarily involved the schools with concerns that fell well beyond the traditional function of regular classroom instruction. Quinn's reports isolated and documented a host of problems that related to his basic responsibility of retrieving children for the schools, and thereby provided a sense of direction and the information that the superintendents and board needed for rationalizing these new endeavors. Finally, whatever weight is attached to the work and reports of the attendance officers, the inevitable consequence of laws that compelled all children to attend school for eight years, bridging the period of middle childhood through early adolescence, was to force the public schools to confront the problems of urban youth and become concerned with their welfare. Within the first decade of compulsory school legislation, the system maintained special schools for the deaf, retarded, and delinquent, as well as a host of health-related services that included lunch programs, physical examinations, baths, "open air" summer schools for the tubercular, and recreational programs outside of school hours and during vacation periods. With the provision of these social services and special courses, the problems of childhood and the concerns of mass public education became interconnected to an unparalleled extent.[34]

34. The connection between attendance laws and noninstructional programs was explicit. In explaining the establishment of schools for juvenile delinquents and abnormal children, Blewett stated: "The necessity for the establishment of these schools was emphasized in St. Louis as it had been in other places through the conditions forced by the adoption of a law compelling attendance." "Provision for

The enlargement of responsibilities both through curricular changes and the development of extracurricular programs had decisively transformed the schools. In meeting the challenge of a growing urban and industrial center, they interjected themselves into the lives of the young by demanding a greater commitment in time and into the affairs of the community by promising assistance in solving social and economic problems. As compared with the nineteenth-century system, these modern schools had a more complex interrelationship with the young, parents, and employers. In the struggle over the definition of purposes, the relatively limiting concept of common schooling that was championed by Harris had been defeated. Through the complementary strategies of a practical emphasis on instruction and effective but sensitive techniques of enforcing compulsory attendance, a far more broadly defined and engaged system had taken its place. As a result of these changes, "the sad state of things" that Woodward had described in 1900 was remedied, and his vision of a "public calamity" gave way to a restoration of confidence.[35]

Exceptional Children in the Public Schools of St. Louis," *Addresses and Proceedings of the National Educational Association, 1909*, p. 356.

35. For a particularly lucid statement on the alteration of the schools' relation to society, see Benjamin Blewett, "The School's Work," *Public School Messenger*, Department of Instruction, St. Louis Board of Public Education, 8 (November 1914), 3–8.

10

Bureaucracy and Politics

It was imperative to restructure school management if the system were to be able to proceed with the program of expansion it embarked on after the turn of the century. In order to do this it had first to be freed from the corrupting influence of local bosses, for like other municipal services the schools had long been subject to graft, both "honest" and "dishonest." Beginning in the 1880s, reformers campaigned to throw the rascals out and institute more efficient and corruption-resistant forms of governance. Their proposals were based on a model charter for schools that was similar to legislation developed at the same time for other branches of municipal government. This measure was calculated to reconstitute the schools in accordance with the organizational principles of public and private bureaucracies, which were becoming typical of modern capitalistic enterprises. The main features of the charter were identical to those that sociologist Max Weber described as characteristic of the new bureaucracies: the institution of rational and systematic procedures, and the transfer of power from elected officials or charismatic leaders to bureaucrats with expert training who performed specialized and well-defined functions.

Although changes in school management occurred at approximately the same time and were often initiated by the same people who were advocating changes in the curriculum, these were parallel movements and did not constitute a coordinated program of reform. Nevertheless, these developments were complementary and resulted from the same currents that were transforming the city. Even as the system was adopting new programs to train the young for life in a modern industrializing society, its own administrative machinery was being remodelled in accordance with the new principles of organization generated by that society.[1]

In the schools' early years, the most damaging abuse stemmed from board control over the extensive properties originally intended to subsidize free schools. The reorganized board of 1833 granted fifty-year leases on many public lands at 6 per cent of valuation. Considering the fantastic rise in real estate values in the course of the next several decades, this policy must be explained as the result of incredible shortsightedness or as wrongdoing.[2] When in 1858 the system was receiving only a 2 per cent return on the real worth of its properties, board President Edward Wyman offered a generous view of his predecessors' actions: "It would doubtless be unjust to characterize the early members of the Board as either unwise or recreant in these measures. It would perhaps be more correct, certainly more charitable, to regard their acts as misfortunes." Wyman was too tolerant, for during the 1840s there had been investigations, public accusations, and even preelection riots concerning these "misfortunes."[3] There may have been other areas of corruption, although the record is even less clear here. One tantalizing bit of evidence is preserved in Director William Garwood's comment in 1857 on the temptations that readily presented themselves to board members: "I am frequently offered a pair of boots, if I will get a measure passed by the Board—[while] another man will propose to

1. H. H. Gerth and C. Wright Mills, *From Max Weber: Essays in Sociology* (New York: Oxford University Press, 1958), pp. 196–266. For hostile analyses of the interrelationship between schools and corporate society, see, Joel Spring, *Education and the Rise of the Corporate State* (Boston: Beacon Press, 1972); Charles A. Tesconi and Van Cleve Morris, *The Anti-Man Culture; Bureautechnocracy and the Schools* (Urbana: University of Illinois Press, 1972). A valuable and more balanced treatment is David B. Tyack, *From Village School to Urban System: A Political and Social History* (United States Office of Education, Project No. 0–0809, 1972).

2. *Annual Report, 1855*, p. 3.

3. *Annual Report, 1858*, pp. iii ff. For examples of public protest see, *Daily Evening Gazette*, July 6, 1841; July 20, 1841; July 21, 1841; January 4, 1842; January 25, 1842. Also, *Annual Report, 1854*, pp. 49–50.

me another emolument in consideration of my anxious services." The solution he proposed to this situation, which was to compensate directors for their work, was not accepted.[4]

Despite such occasional indications of mismanagement, corruption did not become a persistent issue in School Board affairs until the 1880s. The questions that engaged St. Louisans before that time involved the sharing of funds with parochial schools, the place of blacks in the system, the question of the kindergarten, the high school, and German instruction. The politics of community conflict, not board reform, prevailed in midcentury St. Louis. The interest of citizens began to be redirected in the 1880s as reformers and a muckraking journalism, led by Joseph Pulitzer's *Post-Dispatch*, drew attention to the directors' misconduct. Linking school affairs with the same bossism that debased other areas of municipal government, John Snyder, a Unitarian minister, satirized the process by which directors were elected in one of the first calls for reform:

> A number of noisy, possibly half-drunken men form the "cell-germ" of our political system, the primary ward meeting. In the midst of this howling mob we see two or three men, who are struggling to bring their followers to the enthusiastic endorsement of a "slate" which they have arranged in the calm seclusion of their own dram shops. This is the Democratic primary. The Republican meeting is the twin-brother to it, possibly controlled in the secret councils of the bosses by precisely the same men. And then on election day we have the proud privilege of selecting by our votes the member of the board to which our ward is entitled, from the two gentlemen graciously presented by these howling mobs called party primaries.

Snyder faulted St. Louis's "gentlemen of property and education" for failing to provide the city with better alternatives. As a consequence of this neglect there was no pressure for reform, and the best that a voter could do was choose the "lesser evil." Since this was not an appealing

4. *Missouri Republican*, July 3, 1857.

prospect, only about a third of those citizens who normally cast ballots in municipal elections even bothered to vote for board members. The schools were an easy prey for the bosses.[5]

In 1887 reformers secured passage of the Drabelle Bill which attempted to substitute nonpartisan elections for the tyranny of ward politics. As we have seen in the discussion of the German question, the effort was frustrated as reformers were coopted by Democrats who used the opportunity to expunge German from the schools and gain control over the board. Even though there were some changes in party labels, the behavior of the directors remained the same. The board still had a preponderance of contractors and others who used their positions for furthering their party's and their own interests. In 1891, for example, eleven of the thirteen directors running for reelection were contractors, including carpenters, stove-dealers, painters, steam fitters, and blacksmiths.[6] Their victory resulted in continued mismanagement and the misuse of the board's resources. A few illustrations suggest the abuses that aroused criticism and gave impetus to the reform movement.

Alexander Cudmore, the representative of the fifteenth and seventeenth wards, had been part of the clique of directors serving on the Building Committee who were largely responsible for the pilfering of the school treasury before passage of the Drabelle Bill in 1887. Recognizing the change in public sentiment, Cudmore "joined the mob and yelled for reform as loud as any and catching the wave rolled in high and dry on the beach as a member of the 'reform' board." The veneer of integrity notwithstanding, his election was probably rigged, and the returns from his district disappeared soon after the ballots were counted. Moreover, under the new rules of 1887, seven of the electors were to be granted a four-year term while the remainder were to return to electorate in only another two years. By coincidence,

5. "Snyder Says, 'For Shame'," *St. Louis Republic*, November 7, 1881. This article and others are found in a collection of newspaper clippings relating to public schools in the 1870s and 1880s and are located in *Benedict's Notebook*, St. Louis Public Library.

6. "Why They Want It," *Post-Dispatch*, Ocotber 4, 1891.

Cudmore and some cronies, all of whom were contractors, drew lots for the four-year terms. Cudmore's return to the board was not altogether satisfactory, for he was at first relegated to the Library Committee and did not regain his place on the Building Committee, the most lucrative position possible, until 1890. An analysis of the contracts awarded to Cudmore's firm demonstrates the blow to his fortunes that overseeing the library entailed: In the three years and nine months of service on this committee, the Cudmore firm obtained only $18,821 in contracts; in only nine months following his return to the Building Committee his firm was awarded $19,129. It should be noted that payments were not made directly to Alexander Cudmore but to his brother John, since the reformed board had passed a rule that directors themselves could not perform contractual work for the schools. The pretense that Alexander had dissociated himself from the firm of J. Cudmore and Brothers was a fiction that everyone understood, and in fact theirs was only one of several brother or family acts that was enriched at the expense of the system.[7]

Directors often felt secure enough to ignore criticism even when confronted with public exposure of corruption. Edwin O'Connor, who like Cudmore was elected to office after he pretended to undergo a conversion in 1887, was openly contemptuous of the reformers' outrage. As a member of the Building Committee, or "Contractor's Roost" as it came to be known, he traded favors with other directors to obtain a monopoly on furnaces. On the surface everything was legitimate as there was supposed to be a system of secret bidding on all contracts. However, one company, Fuller and Warren of Chicago, consistently bid several dollars under the competition and was awarded all the jobs, with O'Connor's firm, as the St. Louis agent for the Chicago company, installing all the appliances. His monopoly caused one wag to celebrate O'Connor in a poem:

> Director O'Connor sat on a furnace
> Eating a School Board pie,

7. "Here's A Showing," *Post-Dispatch*, October 6, 1891; "All For John," October 11, 1891.

He stuck in his thumb and pulled out a plum
  And said, "What a great head have I!"

Said other stovemakers to Mr. O'Connor,
  "Pray give us a piece of your pie."
Said Mr. O'Connor, "Well, now, 'pon my honor,
  I can't, for a great Hog am I."

Confronted by a reporter with evidence of wrongdoing, O'Connor responded: "I don't give a ——— what people say." Similarly, other directors disregarded muckrakers who exposed scandals in the sale of books, furniture, insurance, and the provision of transportation for superintendents and directors and, indeed, all the diverse goods and services required by a system with about 70,000 students.[8]

The single most flagrant instance of fraud involved the sale of the Polytechnic Building for $120,000 in 1890 to a syndicate headed by Charles Miller, the School Board's president. Aside from Miller's connection with the purchasing group, the transaction was improper both with respect to price and the way in which it was consummated. The building, of the finest construction and located on one of the city's best downtown lots, should have sold for at least $250,000. In 1880, one syndicate of real estate promoters offered the board $180,000 and in 1888 another, headed by Miller, offered $210,000; but the board preferred to hold on to its property. In August, 1890, soon after Miller assumed the presidency, he used his position to obtain the building for less than half its real value. Knowing that there would be opposition when he suggested a resolution approving the sale, he saved that item of the agenda for the end of the meeting, hoping that dissident directors would have left and that those who remained would be too tired to fight. The dissidents did leave, not from fatigue, but in the expectation that their departure would result in the absence of a quorum, thus defeating Miller's plan. Undaunted, Miller offered his resolution just before adjournment "in a voice so low, it is alleged, that not all the members heard him," and accepted the illegal vote as binding. The next

8. "More Light," *Post-Dispatch*, October 18, 1891; "O'Connor's Conduct," October 19, 1891.

morning, President Miller received the deposit from his own syndicate, finalizing the sale and precluding a reversal of the decision by the board or action by the courts. The Polytechnic Building was razed soon after and replaced by one of the city's landmarks and a masterpiece of modern architecture, Louis Sullivan's Wainright Building.[9]

Directors also used their position to dispense patronage. Major opportunities were afforded by the hiring of janitors, whose total combined salaries amounted to about $72,000 in 1890. Janitors ultimately became important not only as cogs in local machines but in the management of contracts, for they could officially register workmen as having done repairs in a particular school while in fact they were doing work elsewhere.[10] The hiring of teachers provided yet another area of abuse and the most lurid materials for a series of scandals called the "petticoat pulls." One director was accused of cavorting with a woman who was charged with "too free use of beer"; another director, a married man, was seen taking "a certain young lady teacher in the public schools out driving and it was further alleged that they remain out until a most gossip-creating hour." There were reports of "bacchanalian visits to the home of a lady teacher" and directors conducting themselves with teachers "on terms of intimacy which could not stand any sort of investigation." Although certainly most teachers were appointed or received promotions without this sort of "pull," the exposés point out the enormous discretion of the directors in hiring, and suggest why next to the Building Committee the most sought-after posts were on committees regulating personnel.[11]

Despite these scandals, few directors were turned out of office. The fact that the board was responsible for appointing the judges to oversee its own election resulted in widespread fraud involving not only the miscounting of ballots but their theft and destruction. Dismayed reformers con-

9. "An Inexhaustible Mine," *Post-Dispatch*, October 26, 1891; "They Make Rich Reading," October 27, 1891.

10. "How It Is Done," *Post-Dispatch*, October 17, 1891.

11. The "Petticoat Pulls" were a daily feature in the *Post-Dispatch* from September 20, 1891, to September 28, 1891.

cluded that the board must be reconstructed along non-partisan lines by completely removing the election of directors from the ward system to an at-large basis.[12] During the next few years, as corruption continued and the calls for reform grew louder, a program for action was developed by the Civic Federation, an organization of business leaders and well-established citizens. In 1897, this group finally succeeded in having the state legislature pass a new charter for the schools. Based on a model charter developed in Cleveland and New York that attempted to do for public education what the National Municipal League's Model Charter of 1900 would propose for city government generally, the St. Louis reformed board became, in turn, a model for other city systems.[13]

Since the charter's major objective was more efficient and responsible administration, it adopted the pattern of contemporary corporate organization in its attempt to root out corrupt practices. It limited the directorate to assuring fiscal responsibility and deciding board policy issues but restrained it from intervening in the daily affairs of the system. Executive powers were concentrated in the hands of four highly specialized officers: the commissioner of buildings, secretary-treasurer, auditor, and superintendent of instruction. As a result, there was a division of responsibility, with the board's authority reduced to general supervisory functions, and the power of the experts who controlled operations was enhanced. In response to past experiences with corruption, and in keeping with notions of better management, the charter also called for civil service examinations for janitors and teachers, granting advancement solely on the basis of merit. It also established higher standards for directors and provided that they could now

12. "Will Keep Watch," *Post-Dispatch*, October 25, 1891; "He Was Hot," November 5, 1891; "The School Board Count," November 5, 1891; "Was It Fraud," November 8, 1891; "The School Election Lessons," November 6, 1891.

13. Elinor M. Gersman, "Progressive Reform of the St. Louis School Board, 1897," *History of Education Quarterly*, 10 (Spring 1970), 3–21. Tyack, pp. 100–48. Edward C. Eliot, "School Administration: The St. Louis Method," *Educational Review*, 26 (December 1903), 464–75.

hold no other office simultaneously and must run on a general rather than a party ticket. In order further to locate responsibility and ensure stability, the number of directors was reduced from twenty-one to twelve, and their term of office lengthened from two to six years.[14]

Although the charter envisaged that a nonpartisan board would root out corruption, this goal was unexpectedly achieved through a bipartisan arrangement. Reformers, by themselves, could not muster enough support to enact their proposals nor determine elections. As had occurred a decade earlier, Democrats, who controlled the state legislature but were in a minority in St. Louis, joined the reform effort in order to diminish the Republican hold in city affairs. This worked in 1887 when the two-thirds of the directorate that was not selected on an at-large basis was gerrymandered into Democratic districts. Since the 1897 charter provided only for at-large directorships, Democrats had to rely on a coalition with the Civic Federation to create a new city-wide majority. They were disappointed, however, when some members of the Civic Federation who were also active Republicans reneged on the bargain. This faction believed that, because Republican strength was so overwhelming, only through that party's backing could good men be placed in office. Led by Calvin Woodward, the dissidents arranged a deal with Chauncey Filley, the Republican boss, whereby the Republican central committee was given power to veto names suggested for the "nonpartisan" ticket but agreed in exchange to support a more respectable class of candidates than it had previously. Until straight-party tickets again emerged, the Republican bosses consulted with the Democratic city leadership and the Civic Federation to produce a board that was usually evenly divided between the two parties.[15]

14. *Annual Report*, 1898, pp. 367–77.

15. Between February and May, 1897, the *Post-Dispatch* was full of accounts of the byzantine politics of school reform. Key articles included "Rescinded Its Action," February 26, 1897; "Uncle Filley to Name the Ticket," April 12, 1897; "Beware of Filley's Tricks," April 23, 1897; "Statement from Professor Woodward," May 8, 1897; "Dr. Boyd on Prof. Woodward," May 9, 1897.

In effect, this agreement broke the hold of ward politicians by transferring the power of nomination to a relatively few brokers—politicians of city-wide importance and leading reformers. Their alliance replaced steam fitters, carpenters, and contractors with lawyers, physicians, educators, and important businessmen. This pattern became so entrenched that even with the return to party tickets in 1913 the board remained free of self-serving local politicans.[16] The result was that the system operated after 1897 almost without scandal. Indeed, when Lincoln Steffens and Claude Wetmore came to St. Louis in 1902 to collect materials for their exposé of municipal corruption, *Shame of the Cities*, the school board stood in singular isolation among the remainder of graft-ridden city institutions.[17]

With the reduction of waste through the accession of an honest directorate, the system was able to accelerate its building program and better serve the students' needs. Successive presidents congratulated themselves and board members for making St. Louis into a model of economy and operational efficiency. There was national recognition as well. President Charles Eliot of Harvard, for example, asserted that St. Louis' reformed administration "has attained something of celebrity throughout the United States for its exceptional merit," and stated that it provided the best example for reformers in other cities to follow.[18] What attracted Eliot and others was more than the ending of corruption. They were impressed with the ways in which the process of administration had been centralized, thereby

16. For analyses of the directors' occupations see Gersman; and Mahan, "The Influence of the Efficiency Movement on a Large Urban School System," pp. 123–34.

17. Claude H. Wetmore and Lincoln Steffens, "Tweed Days in St. Louis," *McClure's Magazine*, 19 (October 1902), 577–86. The difficulties of maintaining the charter during the 1910s are revealed in the large collection of clippings contained in the *Civic League Notebooks* (St. Louis Public Library). Despite some lapses into partisanship and corruption, the reforms of the charter were maintained. "House Cleaning in the St. Louis Schools," *School and Society*, 8 (April 23, 1921), 506–7.

18. Charles W. Eliot, "A Good Urban School Organization," an address delivered to the Public Education Association of Philadelphia, January 1904, reprinted in *Annual Report, 1904*, pp. 24–32.

bringing to a logical conclusion a movement to control public education that had been present since managers of urban
systems first wrestled with the task of running a growing
complex of schools. To a great extent, the 1897 charter did
for the administration of the system what the graded and
standardized curriculum and other innovations of the 1850s
had done for the control of students. Through the charter,
the "one best way" that Philbrick had espoused and which
had already been implemented in the internal regulation of
the classroom was now realized in the operation of the system as a whole.[19]

Control at the executive level was established through
the centralization of administrative functions in expert
officials, whose importance increased as that of directors
declined. In contrast to the extensive deliberations of sub-
committees and the full board, the reformed board's meetings lasted on average about an hour, and in some cases but
twenty minutes, as the directors merely approved reports
and recommendations that had been prepared and previously circulated by its officers. The new members preferred to
delegate responsibility for management to hired officials
because, as President Eliot observed, prevailing sentiment
held that directors were "not specially qualified in the various departments of educational work."[20]

Under the new arrangement the superintendent became
the most powerful individual in the system. He was en-
trusted with the appointment, transfer, and promotion of
teachers; the introduction and change of textbooks; the content of courses; and the maintenance of discipline in the
schools. In some cases the board had the power to confirm
or reject his decision, but the superintendent alone had the
authority to initiate action. Moreover, he was insulated
from criticism on specific measures by a four-year contract.

The great power and independence of the superintendency were not an unforeseen and accidental result of hap-
hazard legislation, but were deliberately planned and intended by the charter that Louis Soldan, then superintendent

19. Philbrick, *City School Systems in the United States*, p. 8.
20. Eliot, p. 28.

of schools, had an important role in framing. In analysing the effect of the new charter, the *Mirror* commented that "Professor Soldan is supreme. He is a pedagogic Pope, absolutely infallible, unamenable to anyone or anything."[21] The St. Louis case is not unique, for most of the new charters were written by superintendents in cooperation with reformist groups. This was natural, for there was a perfect marriage of interest between them. Superintendents were concerned with maximizing their influence, and the reformers desired a centralized, nonpolitical system, with locatable authority in the hands of experts.

The impetus for this transfer of power came as much from directors who continually deferred to the wisdom and responsibilities of the professionals as from the initiative of staff, particularly the superintendents. Soldan, Blewett, and Withers were all strong figures who aggressively maintained their autonomy and influence. The ever-increasing size of the system, the proliferation of programs, and the emergence of a profession of education based on the scholarship and new insights of pedagogues, sociologists, and psychologists all contributed to increased reliance on experts. Moreover, the efficiency movement, strongly informed by Frederick Jackson Taylor's studies in industrial engineering and by scientific techniques of business management, exerted a powerful influence over superintendents.

Superintendent Blewett utilized the new techniques in a number of ways. Beginning in 1910, he established a special conference of principals, high school teachers, and faculty members of the normal school, which met on Saturday mornings to consider methods for improving administration, supervision, and instruction. Participants prepared papers on a wide variety of topics, including "Experimental Studies in the Measurement of Children's Progress in Spelling," "Studies in Attendance and Progress of Pupils in the St. Louis Public Schools," and "Report on an Arithmetic Study in the Wyman School." Blewett introduced these innovations both in order to spare the schools the expense of a special "efficiency bureau," which other systems were es-

21. "Soldan's System," *Mirror*, May 13, 1897.

tablishing, and to keep his staff abreast of the latest techniques of analysis. The latter function was of particular importance, Blewett noted, because in the face of the growing responsibility of schools and the increasing complexity of the principals' work "it is practically impossible for any principal to measure fully up to the responsibilities of his office who is not a scientific student of present day problems of education." By the end of the 1910s, the regular teaching personnel were also required to attend special sessions during which the system's officials as well as outside experts expounded on the new technology of education. Thus from the top down the superintendent established a mechanism for the continued training and retraining of his staff in what he termed "the scientific study of education."[22]

In order to achieve "a better understanding of certain conditions that influence the efficiency of the schools," Blewett also opened the pages of the *Annual Report*s to extended analyses by outside educators as well as supervisors within the St. Louis system.[23] The result was a more sophisticated analysis, proceeding from increasingly specialized kinds of knowledge, which generally made more extensive use of measurements than before. A very simple indicator of the level of analysis is the growing emphasis on measurements. The 1900 *Annual Report* contained about 80 pages of tables; by 1920 this section included close to 500 pages. This development was not merely a reflection of the increased size of the system but was related to the kinds of information administrators came to feel they had to master in order to provide effective management. In addition to maintaining close watch over their revenues and expenditures, they cost-accounted nearly every educational program, investigated in great detail the progress of pupils in all departments, followed the course their graduates took once they left school, and recorded the health and physical characteristics of students. The scientific study of education had resulted in an explosion of information that in its

22. *Annual Report, 1914*, pp. 145–47.
23. *Annual Report, 1913*, pp. 96–107.

unceasing expansion demanded ever greater skills and expertise. If reformers appreciated the difficulty of supervising the affairs of the system in the 1890s, the kind of expertise and concentration required in the subsequent generation made the charter they had designed all the more necessary.

This dedication to the science of efficiency was foreshadowed by the pre-Civil War generation's concern with statistics, the standardization of instruction, and the acceptance of the idea of "the one best way." Harris had frequently pointed out that urban schools were superior to rural counterparts in their efficiency and machinelike character. Nevertheless, a change of great magnitude had taken place. It is still easier to imagine nineteenth-century educators as men of literature at ease with philosophic tracts, while their twentieth-century counterparts emerge as administrators imbued with techniques of scientific management with a slide-rule in one hand. Indeed, as Raymond Callahan has shown, the preparation of school officials became increasingly formalized in the universities and bore marked similarity to the kind of education business leaders received.[24] This change is also manifest in the schools' major documents. Nineteenth-century *Annual Reports* often had a literary flavor, since they were written for the general audience. In the twentieth century, the reports tended to dispense with words in favor of numbers, becoming progressively unreadable and uninteresting for nonspecialists.

As the operation of the schools became so sophisticated and specialized that even the directors separated themselves from their management, officials recognized that the system was in danger of becoming isolated from the public on which it ultimately depended for support. Blewett was the first to act on this understanding and encouraged the growth of new organizations and techniques that assured access to the people. A most significant measure was the cultivation of the school patrons' alliances, or what has come to be known as parent–teachers associations. Since the 1840s parents had organized to present complaints and sugges-

24. Callahan, *Education and the Cult of Efficiency*, pp. 179–220.

tions regarding local schools to the board. Not until Blewett's superintendency did such groups become formalized,
permanent, and gain official recognition. These groups were
not only important for voicing local interests but were an
instrument whereby superintendents could communicate
information and marshal support. Blewett reported to their
members the system's new programs, its financial problems,
and his aspirations for the future. He envisaged a political
role for the alliances. This view was shared by some of the
patrons who created a city-wide association that suggested
candidates for the directorship, including some of their own
number. Blewett reaped his greatest benefits in the campaign
to establish new financial resources from this approach for
the schools.[25]

As public education implemented new programs, its
costs rose commensurately. By 1909, a yearly deficit of
$70,000 was incurred despite the best efforts at efficient
management. Since the property tax reached its legal
limit in 1915, the board took up Blewett's suggestion that
it issue bonds, a technique employed by other municipal
departments and by business corporations. Hoping to enlist public support for this departure, Blewett invited a
team of educators of national reputation, headed by Dr.
Charles Judd of the University of Chicago, to conduct a
thorough investigation of the system from its finances,
teacher training, and classroom work, to the construction
of its buildings. He was certain that the survey would place
the schools in a favorable light, for he already had employed
the same kind of analysis and had proven that the system
was well run but was in need of more funds. Prior to the
actual work of his team, Judd offered the same view: "In an-
ticipation of the report which will give full details, it can
be stated on the basis of the results in hand that the work
in the classrooms and the general organization of the schools
are at a high level of efficiency. St. Louis has a successful

25. *Annual Report, 1917*, pp. 71–72. For examples of the political
activities of the school patrons, see, "Selecting the School Board,"
Star, December 28, 1914; "Patrons of 3 Schools Hold Meetings To-
night," January 28, 1915. Also, "School Patrons Fix Board Slates,"
St. Louis Republic, February 14, 1915.

system." Furthermore, he predicted that "the Survey will show that funds for the school buildings are absolutely necessary. There can be no question that the Survey will show that these funds cannot be legitimately taken from the work of present departments."[26]

Therefore, when the results were announced in September, 1916, it came as no surprise that Judd had concluded that St. Louis had one of the best-organized and most efficient systems in the country and merited additional support from the community. That this would be his judgment was also foreseen by national educational journals. *School and Society* and *The Survey*, for example, pointed out that no one doubted that the St. Louis schools were in any way deficient except with regard to revenues and that the survey grew out of "a natural demand for definite assurance of the need for a bond issue."[27] With this endorsement, Blewett sought support from the city's press, lay groups, and especially the patrons' alliances, whose assistance he judged to be of the greatest value. The response was enthusiastic and without reservation. In November a $3 million bond issue was overwhelmingly passed, and the system's instructional building programs proceeded with renewed vigor.

Blewett's initiative of enlisting popular support was appropriate to a new era in school politics. After the German question was resolved in the late 1880s, community hostilities subsided. An important factor in their demise was the decreased significance of the foreign-born in the city's population. Whereas in 1860 St. Louis had the highest proportion of foreign-born of any major American city, with 60 per cent of the population, their relative numbers had declined markedly by the end of the century. Unlike some cities, St. Louis's continued growth came not from the wave of "new immigrants," but from natural increase and internal migrations. Between 1890 and 1930, the proportion of St. Louis's foreign-born dropped from 25 to 9.9 per cent,

26. *Annual Report, 1916*, pp. 23–25.
27. "The St. Louis School Survey," *School and Society*, 4 (September 23, 1916), 482. Also see, "Further Referendum Election Results," *Survey*, 37 (November 11, 1916), 207; "The Future of the St. Louis Schools at Stake," 145.

while Boston's percentages were 34.7 and 29.9; Chicago's were 40.3 and 25.5; and New York's were 41.8 and 34 per cent. Moreover, a majority of St. Louis's foreign-born were still drawn from the older pattern of migration, particularly from Germany and Ireland. Thus, school elections were no longer concerned with the abrasive questions of who would be instructed and what they would learn as they had been in the nineteenth century.[28] In this respect St. Louis was spared the conflicts that exacerbated the politics of many eastern cities, which were undergoing basic changes in their demographic composition. Indeed, the St. Louis experience suggests that community conflict may have been given undue significance as a factor in understanding the reorganization of other systems and further emphasizes the importance of the rationalizing processes that characterized modernizing institutions.[29]

The success of reform in replacing grafting politicians with a tradition of comparatively disinterested stewardship diminished even further the presence of rancor in school

28. *Eleventh Census of the United States, 1890*, 1, Pt. 1, p. clxii; *Fifteenth Census of the United States, 1930*, 2, pp. 67–71. In 1910, for example, when the foreign-born population was reduced to 18 per cent of the total population, 46.7 per cent of this group were from Germany and Austria and 11.3 per cent from Ireland. The only other groups of some size were Russians, Hungarians, and Italians with 12.3, 6.9, and 6.0 per cent respectively. *Thirteenth Census of the United States, 1910*, 1, pp. 178, 828.

29. In not viewing the bureaucratic reforms as an attempt to seize the schools by upper-class groups, the interpretation presented here runs counter to much contemporary historiography. The social control model, which is largely based on studies of eastern cities, does not seem to apply to St. Louis. Elinor M. Gersman in "Progressive Reform of the St. Louis School Board, 1897" does attempt to make a case for the model in St. Louis. In my judgment the model is not convincing for three reasons: First, it is mere inference to assert that the presence of social-register types on the board represents a concerted attempt at social control; second, reform of the board does not appear to be part of a general plan by a cohesive group to control other areas of municipal affairs or redirect the board's educational policies; and third, it is difficult to maintain the idea of seizure if there is no opposition by other class or ethnic groups. School politics may have been different in St. Louis. For the best summary of the recent literature that also integrates the St. Louis experience, see, Tyack, pp. 100–147.

politics. Without the divisiveness of social antagonisms, charges of corruption, and partisan politics, the schools became relatively neutralized. Popular interest in education transcended communal fractionalism or partisan issues. In 1915, for example, when the selection of directors threatened to degenerate into partisanship, delegates from 230 organizations including 150 civic and community groups and 80 local parents and teachers' associations convened to protest successfully against a return to the old politics.[30] Major departures, even in such a radical area as compulsory education, aroused virtually no opposition.[31] Perhaps the most telling indicator of popular enthusiasm is the support St. Louisans gave for bond issues, which generally required a two-thirds majority. Between 1916 and 1947 the public never failed to endorse appeals for more revenues. Only since World War II, and particularly in the 1960s as the emergence of a large black population aroused the kind of communal discord that had obtained in the nineteenth century, have successive boards been increasingly frustrated by a lack of support. In contrast, educators in the first part of the twentieth century could count on an enormous amount of latent good will for public education.[32]

In the space of only a generation, public education had left behind a highly regimented and politicized system dedicated to training children in the basic skills of literacy and the special discipline required of urban citizens, and had replaced it with a largely apolitical, more highly organized

30. "230 Organizations to Suggest Men for School Board," *Post-Dispatch*, March 14, 1915.

31. The compulsory education bills of 1905 and 1907 passed the Missouri legislature by the votes of 129 to 13 and 117 to 5. In both instances, all the St. Louis delegates supported it. *Laws of Missouri* (Jefferson City, Mo.: Hugh Stephens Printing Co.), p. 512, p. 364. In addition, the ethnic, religious, labor and general press supported these measures. For an appreciation of the popular background of this legislation, I am indebted to a seminar paper by Richard Ives, "Compulsory Education and the St. Louis Public School System 1905–1907," July, 1972.

32. Gary Allan Tobin, *The St. Louis School Crisis: Population Shifts and Voting Patterns* (St. Louis: Washington University, 1970), pp. 88, 101. For the first time, a bond or tax issue failed to obtain a majority in 1959.

and efficient structure specifically designed to teach students the many specialized skills demanded in a modern, industrial society. In terms of programs this entailed the introduction of vocational instruction, a doubling of the period of schooling, and a broader concern for the welfare of urban youth. In terms of administration it meant creating a modern bureaucracy, modelled on the corporation, that was capable of dealing with these tasks. That administrators were careful to educate the public to the system's work and to seek mass support had made the transition relatively quick and free from conflict.

Unlike the nineteenth century, when expansion into such areas as German instruction, kindergartens, and high schools had aroused dissension, the institution of new programs was accomplished rapidly and was widely appreciated in the twentieth. Increased bureaucratization and professionalization did not result in the alienation of the public. Instead, the enlarged intersection of the schools with the lives of the young, parents, businesses, and the community engendered cooperation and hope rather than estrangement. The reorganized system, like the one it replaced, was a product of a discrete stage in the development of the city and was shaped by the society it was designed to serve. Further redefination of programs and structure would be necessary, and the trust reposed in this system could not endure indefinitely. For the moment, St. Louisans believed that the system was answering the needs of their children and fulfilling its mandate as a catalyst to the good and successful society.

Appendix A

Classification of Data from the Annual Reports

The tables in the following pages contain data drawn from the *Annual Reports* with which the definition of parental occupations and class mobility within the system were made. In the text, parental occupations were arranged in six classifications: unskilled labor; skilled labor; clerks and minor white collar; businessmen and managers; professionals; and unclassified. These were constructed by aggregating the data on specific occupations and were arranged as follows:

Unskilled Labor: "boatmen," "draymen and teamsters," "laborers," "laundresses," and "seamstresses."

Skilled Labor: "artists," "butchers," "confectioners," and "mechanics."

Clerks and Minor White Collar: "agents," "clerks," and "public officers."

Businessmen and Managers: "boarding house and hotel keepers," "bar keepers," "boarding house keepers and victualers," "saloon keepers," "farmers and gardeners," "manufacturers," and "merchants."

Professionals: "professionals."

Unclassified: "unclassified."

For the most part these classifications remain constant between 1860 and 1890. The only changes are (a) the addition of "confectioners" in 1880 and 1891; (b) "boarding house and hotel keepers," and "boarding house keepers and victualers" are interchangeable and added beginning in 1870; and (c) "saloon keepers" replaced "bar keepers" beginning in 1875.

Table 13. Fathers' Occupations of District, High, and Normal School Students, 1860*

Occupation	District school		High school		Normal school	
	Total	Per cent	Total	Per cent	Total	Per cent
Agents	194	1.86	14	3.62	3	2.78
Artists	78	0.75	0	0.0	1	0.93
Barkeepers	188	1.81	5	1.29	0	0.0
Boatmen	563	5.41	11	2.84	1	0.93
Butchers	190	1.82	5	1.29	0	0.0
Clerks	309	2.97	24	6.20	2	1.85
Draymen & teamsters	321	3.08	12	3.10	0	0.0
Farmers & gardeners	176	1.69	20	5.17	12	11.11
Laborers	1,138	10.93	24	6.20	0	0.0
Laundresses	195	1.87	2	0.52	0	0.0
Manufacturers	463	4.45	25	6.46	0	0.0
Mechanics	3,050	29.29	29	7.49	20	18.52
Merchants	1,214	11.66	89	22.99	13	12.04
Professions	446	4.28	23	5.94	14	12.96
Public officers	316	3.03	10	2.58	0	0.0
Seamstresses	177	1.70	2	0.52	0	0.0
Unclassified	1,395	13.40	92	23.77	42	38.89
Total number	10,413		387		108	

* *Annual Report, 1860*, p. 55.

Table 14. Fathers' Occupations of District, High, and Normal School Students, 1861*

Occupation	District school		High school		Normal school	
	Total	Per cent	Total	Per cent	Total	Per cent
Agents	222	1.88	14	4.40	3	3.75
Artists	91	0.77	4	1.26	0	0.0
Barkeepers	246	2.09	4	1.26	0	0.0
Boatmen	623	5.29	10	3.14	1	1.25
Butchers	205	1.74	1	0.31	0	0.0
Clerks	357	3.03	15	4.71	5	6.25
Draymen & teamsters	282	2.40	4	1.26	0	0.0
Farmers & gardeners	256	2.18	14	4.40	10	12.50
Laborers	1,389	11.80	12	3.77	0	0.0
Laundresses	188	1.60	2	0.63	0	0.0
Manufacturers	587	4.99	15	4.71	1	1.25
Mechanics	3,366	28.60	50	15.70	14	17.50
Merchants	1,519	12.90	75	23.53	5	6.25
Professions	401	3.41	26	8.16	10	12.50
Public officers	320	2.72	19	5.97	0	0.0
Seamstresses	325	2.76	6	1.88	0	0.0
Unclassified	1,391	11.82	47	14.77	31	38.75
Total number	11,768		318		80	

* *Annual Report, 1861,* p. 14.

Table 15. Fathers' Occupations of District, High, and Normal School Students, 1862*

Occupation	District school		High school		Normal school	
	Total	Per cent	Total	Per cent	Total	Per cent
Agents	147	2.66	9	3.92	0	0.0
Artists	44	0.80	3	1.31	0	0.0
Barkeepers	118	2.14	0	0.0	0	0.0
Boatmen	279	5.05	3	1.31	0	0.0
Butchers	72	1.30	0	0.0	0	0.0
Clerks	174	3.15	6	2.62	0	0.0
Draymen & teamsters	113	2.05	0	0.0	0	0.0
Farmers & gardeners	105	1.90	7	3.06	1	2.63
Laborers	305	5.52	4	1.75	0	0.0
Laundresses	91	1.65	0	0.0	0	0.0
Manufacturers	288	5.21	17	7.42	1	2.63
Mechanics	1,081	19.57	15	6.55	20	52.63
Merchants	961	17.39	67	29.25	9	23.68
Professions	262	4.74	24	10.08	3	7.89
Public officers	291	5.27	16	6.98	2	5.26
Seamstresses	156	2.82	4	1.75	0	0.0
Unclassified	1,036	18.75	54	23.57	2	5.26
Total number	5,523		229		38	

* *Annual Report, 1862,* p. 37.

Table 16. Fathers' Occupations of District, High, and Normal School Students, 1870*

Occupation	District school		High school		Normal school	
	Total	Per cent	Total	Per cent	Total	Per cent
Agents	622	2.61	23	5.88	6	4.32
Artists	111	0.47	0	0.0	0	0.0
Barkeepers	510	2.14	1	0.26	0	0.0
Boarding house keepers & victualers	312	1.31	3	0.77	2	1.44
Boatmen	758	3.18	9	2.30	0	0.0
Butchers	329	1.38	2	0.51	8	5.76
Clerks	768	3.22	20	5.11	0	0.0
Draymen & teamsters	965	4.05	1	0.26	4	2.88
Farmers & gardeners	462	1.94	17	4.35	0	0.0
Laborers	3,393	14.24	3	0.77	1	0.72
Laundresses	670	2.81	1	0.26	0	0.0
Manufacturers	2,015	8.45	9	2.30	8	5.76
Mechanics	5,268	22.12	69	17.65	21	15.11
Merchants	2,927	12.29	89	22.76	14	10.07
Professionals	784	3.29	49	12.53	11	7.91
Public officers	629	2.64	25	6.39	7	5.04
Seamstresses	660	2.77	6	1.53	5	3.60
Unclassified	2,634	11.06	64	16.36	52	37.41
Total number	23,817		391		139	

* *Annual Report, 1870*, pp. lxvii–lxxiii.

Table 17. Fathers' Occupations of District, High, and Normal School Students, 1880*

Occupation	District school		High school		Normal school	
	Total	Per cent	Total	Per cent	Total	Per cent
Agents	1,631	3.25	68	7.21	2	1.23
Artists	278	0.55	3	0.32	1	0.62
Boarding house & hotel keepers	528	1.05	3	0.32	1	0.62
Boatmen	715	1.43	8	0.85	2	1.23
Butchers	880	1.75	7	0.74	1	0.62
Clerks	2,486	4.96	66	6.99	15	9.26
Confectioners	292	0.58	2	0.21	0	0.0
Draymen & teamsters	1,984	3.96	4	0.42	2	1.23
Farmers & gardeners	1,065	2.12	23	2.44	2	1.23
Laborers	8,262	16.47	23	2.44	2	1.23
Laundresses	1,711	3.41	1	0.11	0	0.0
Manufacturers	3,645	7.27	36	3.82	4	2.47
Mechanics	11,513	22.96	134	14.20	16	9.88
Merchants	5,832	11.63	225	23.85	26	16.05
Professionals	1,866	3.72	113	11.97	9	5.55
Public officers	1,310	2.61	44	4.66	7	4.32
Saloon keepers	1,029	2.05	10	1.06	0	0.0
Seamstresses	1,065	2.12	13	1.38	5	3.08
Unclassified	4,054	8.08	160	16.96	67	41.35
Total number	50,146		943		162	

* *Annual Report, 1880,* p. cxii.

Table 18. Fathers' Occupations of Black Students, in District and High Schools, 1891*

Occupation	Total	Per cent
Agents	2	0.04
Artists	0	0.00
Barkeepers	25	0.51
Boatmen	79	1.62
Butchers	6	0.12
Clerks	12	0.25
Draymen & teamsters	427	8.78
Farmers & gardeners	114	2.34
Laborers	2,432	50.00
Laundresses	901	18.52
Manufacturers	0	0.00
Mechanics	73	1.50
Merchants	24	0.49
Professions	69	1.41
Public officers	11	0.23
Seamstresses	41	0.84
Unclassified	648	13.32
Total	4,864	99.97

* *Annual Report, 1891*, pp. xliv–xlv.

Appendix B

Classification of Data from the Manuscript Census

The collective biography is composed of 15,314 children drawn from twenty-six selected election precincts from the second enumeration of the St. Louis manuscript census of 1880. A child was defined as any person between one and twenty-one and any unmarried person over twenty-one who lived in his parents' household. The election precincts were chosen to provide a sampling of different economic, ethnic, and racial groups by analysing about one-eighth of the total population in sections of the city from the levee through Grand Avenue and the western suburbs. Within these election precincts, the entire population was examined to produce data on all children. The information on each child contains age, sex, color, civil condition, school attendance, child's occupation, number of siblings, position among siblings, relationship to head of household, total number in household, birthplace, birthplace of parents and grandparents, and ages and occupations of father and mother.

The occupational coding scheme is an adaptation of that employed by Stephan Thernstrom and Peter Knights in their studies of social mobility in Boston. See Peter Knights, *The Plain People of Boston, 1830–1860: A Study in City Growth* (New York: Oxford University Press), Appendix E. The only significant change involves accommodating categories for school attendance and female occupations. My tables correspond to Knights's classifications in the following way:

Knights's classifications	Tables in this study
1) Unskilled and Menial Service	Unskilled
2) Semiskilled and Service	Semiskilled
3) Petty Proprietors, Managers, and Officials	Petty Official or Businessman
4) Skilled	Skilled

5) Clerical and Sales; Semiprofessional   White Collar

6) Proprietors, Managers, and Officials   High Official or Businessman

7) Professional   Professional

By surveying the entire census, it also became a source for the collection of data on teachers. Public school teachers were identified by locating their names on school board rosters and in the census. Parochial school teachers were identified by their designation as "teachers" in residences recognizable as churches, convents, and parish schools.

Table 19. Education and Employment of Black Children Ages 5–20, by Percentage

Age	Attending school	Employed	Unknown	Total number
5	12.7	1.8	85.5	55
6	39.6	3.8	56.6	53
7	65.9	0.0	34.1	44
8	59.0	5.1	35.9	39
9	71.7	6.6	21.7	46
10	88.2	7.9	3.9	51
11	75.0	11.4	13.6	44
12	69.4	16.3	14.3	49
13	68.8	12.4	18.8	32
14	71.4	17.2	11.4	35
15	47.2	30.6	22.2	36
16	20.4	63.3	16.3	49
17	22.4	57.2	20.4	49
18	5.6	77.7	16.7	72
19	5.9	73.5	20.6	68
20	1.0	82.8	16.2	99

Table 20. Occupations of Black Males and Females, Ages 10–20, by Percentage

	Attending school	Higher occupations	White collar	Skilled workers	Semiskilled workers	Unskilled workers	Unknown	Total number
Age 10								
M	92.9	0.0	0.0	0.0	0.0	7.1	0.0	14
F	86.5	0.0	0.0	0.0	0.0	8.1	5.4	37
Age 12								
M	75.0	0.0	0.0	0.0	3.6	10.7	10.7	28
F	61.9	0.0	0.0	0.0	0.0	19.1	19.0	21
Age 14								
M	50.0	0.0	0.0	0.0	21.4	14.3	14.3	14
F	85.7	0.0	0.0	0.0	0.0	4.8	9.5	21
Age 16								
M	14.3	4.8	0.0	0.0	14.3	66.7	0.0	21
F	25.0	3.6	0.0	0.0	0.0	42.9	28.6	28
Age 18								
M	6.7	0.0	3.3	0.0	33.3	50.0	6.7	30
F	4.8	2.4	0.0	0.0	0.0	69.1	23.8	42
Age 20								
M	0.0	2.4	0.0	0.0	39.0	51.2	7.3	41
F	1.7	3.4	0.0	0.0	1.7	70.6	22.4	58

Table 21. Crosstabulation of School Attendance of White and Black Children Ages 13–16 with Fathers' Occupations

Fathers' occupations	Percentage at school	
	white	black
White collar and higher*	67.2 (395)	33.3 (1)
Blue collar*	38.4 (330)	62.3 (43)
Unknown	35.4 (289)	40.0 (32)
Total number of children	994	152

* White collar and higher includes professionals, high officials and businessmen, white collar, and petty officials and businessmen. Blue collar includes skilled, semiskilled, and unskilled.

Table 22. Household Relationships of White and Black Children, Ages 6–12, 13–16, by Percentage

Relationship	6–12		13–16	
	white	black	white	black
With mother and father	84.3	55.5	64.4	44.1
Without father	8.5	24.2	11.4	25.0
Without mother	1.9	1.2	2.5	2.6
Other (cousin, nephew, grandchild, etc.)	3.0	12.9	5.3	11.8
Boarder	1.0	2.1	3.9	6.6
In institution	0.7	0.0	4.8	0.0
Unknown	0.6	4.0	7.8	9.9
Total number	3,208	326	994	152

Bibliographical Note

During the last decade, historians of American education have attempted to construct a new historiography
based on the accomplishments of schooling rather than on
the promises. This movement has been based on the assumption that there was a distinction between the rhetoric
and the reality of education. Originally conceived as a
contribution to this movement, the tone and findings of this
book are less negative and pessimistic than is usually found
in the recent literature. Lawrence Cremin provides an excellent review of the celebrationist tradition in *The Wonderful World of Ellwood Patterson Cubberly: An Essay on
the Historiography of American Education* (New York:
Bureau of Publications, Teachers College, Columbia University, 1965). Recent studies that focus on the workings
and politics of major eastern systems for the first part of
the nineteenth century are Carl F. Kaestle, *The Evolution of
an Urban School System: New York City, 1750–1850* (Cambridge: Harvard University Press, 1973); Michael B. Katz,
*The Irony of Early School Reform: Educational Innovation
in Mid-Nineteenth Century Massachusetts* (Cambridge:
Harvard University Press, 1968) and *Class, Bureaucracy and
Schools: The Illusion of Educational Change in America*
(New York: Praeger, 1972); and Stanley K. Schultz, *The
Culture Factory: Boston Public Schools, 1789–1860* (New
York: Oxford University Press, 1973). The best of the
studies for the latter part of the nineteenth and early part
of the twentieth century are Marvin Lazerson, *Origins of
the Urban School: Public Education in Massachusetts, 1870–
1915* (Cambridge: Harvard University Press, 1971); Joel
H. Spring, *Education and the Rise of the Corporate State*
(Boston: Beacon Press, 1972); and Arthur Wirth, *Education
in the Technological Society: The Vocational-Liberal Studies
Controversy in the Early Twentieth Century* (San Francisco:
Intext Educational Publishers, 1972). For an excellent over-
all synthesis with broad chronological and geographic com-
pass see David B. Tyack, *The One Best System* (Cambridge:
Harvard University Press, 1974).

The decision to focus on St. Louis derived from the rich-
ness of the system's *Annual Report*s beginning particularly
in the Harris superintendency (1868–1880). Unfortunately,

there is a serious hiatus between 1833, when the board was reconstituted, and 1854, when the first bound volume of the *Annual Reports* was issued. The newspapers, city directories, and the board's history of itself in *First Annual Report* provide the best sources for the early years. Also missing is a continuous record of the board's minutes, entitled "Proceedings of the Board of Public Schools," which were first published in pamphlet form beginning in 1871. For the previous years, a patient turning of the pages in the city's newspapers, in which they were usually reported, provided the only avenue for reconstructing this vital area of the schools' history. Together, however, the minutes and *Annual Reports* comprise the single most important body of documents for revealing the nature and direction of the system's growth.

Of primary importance are the *Annual Reports*. Written at a time when educators were pleading the cause of public education, these volumes contain more explanations of programs than statistical reports. Reflecting this need to broadcast their message, the board published between 4,000 to 7,000 copies in English and German with an average of 250 to 300 pages during the second part of the nineteenth century. In addition to explanations and justifications of the schools' work, they contain essential information on a wide variety of matters including curriculum, architecture, duties of directors and teachers, histories of the different departments, and laws relating to education. Statistics come to play an increasingly important role by the turn of the century, although the *Annual Reports* throughout provide a wealth of information on students, parents, teachers, buildings, and the operations and development of the system.

Manuscript sources were useful primarily for understanding the role of key individuals. The most important collection for William Harris, Susan Blow, and other early leaders is the *William Torrey Harris MSS* in the Missouri Historical Society in St. Louis. The other major collection of Harris materials is located in the Library of Congress, but this had limited value since it largely consists in essays which are found elsewhere. In addition, much of what Harris had to say was formulated early in his career and is printed in the *Annual Reports*. The *William Torrey Harris, Miscellaneous Papers*, which are in the Education Department of the St. Louis Public Library, had several useful items. Other valuable materials at the Missouri Historical Society include the *Hamilton R. Gamble Papers, Stephen Hempstead Papers, St. Louis Miscellaneous Envelope,* and the *Schools Collection, 1817 through 1875.* The *William G. Eliot MSS* at Washington University contain much information on education and social reform for mid-nineteenth century St. Louis. Some rare and diverse materials are found in *Various Uncatalogued Pamphlets of the Public Schools of St. Louis,* State Historical Society (Columbia, Mo.).

The other key sources for understanding Harris and the schools are Kurt F. Leidecker, *Yankee Teacher: The Life of William Torrey Harris* (New York: Philosophical Library, 1946), Merle Curti, *The Social Ideas of American Educators: With New Chapter on the Last Twenty-Five Years* (Paterson, N.J.: Littlefield, Adams and Co., 1959), Chapter 9; Charles M. Perry, *The St. Louis Movement in Philosophy: Some Source Material* (Norman, Okla.: University of Oklahoma Press, 1930), and Francis B. Harmon, *The Social Philosophy of the St. Louis Hegelians* (New York: By the author, 1943). A list of Harris's works is found in Kurt F. Leidecker, *Bibliography: William Torrey Harris in Literature* (n.d.: n.p., University of Missouri Library, Columbia, Mo.).

Calvin Woodward played a role comparable to Harris's during the post-1880 period. The volume of literature on Woodward is unfortunately far less complete. A major source for establishing his role and understanding his ideas is the *Annual Reports* from 1897 to 1904. Essential reading includes Calvin M. Woodward, *Manual Training in Education* (New York: Scribner and Welford, 1890), "Manual, Industrial, and Technical Education in the United States," *Report of the Commissioner of Education for the Year 1903* (Washington, D.C.: Government Printing Office, 1905), and Charles Penney Coates, *History of the Manual Training School of Washington University,* Bureau of Education, Bulletin, 1923, No. 3 (Washington, D.C.: Government Printing Office, 1923). Also valuable are Berenice M. Fisher, *Industrial Education: American Ideals and Institutions* (Madison: University of Wisconsin Press, 1967) and Paul H. Douglas, *American Apprenticeship and Industrial Education,* Columbia University Studies in Economics, History and Law, 95, No. 2 (New York: Longmans, Green and Co., 1921).

Newspapers were not only important for filling in the official record, they were necessary for establishing the context in which the system developed. Letters to the editor, occasional special features, election editorials in the spring and fall, reports of the annual examinations in May and June, and advertisements and comments on the reopening of school at the end of the summer were invaluable for measuring the impact of the schools and defining the nature of the controversies which their growth engendered. In order to provide continuity, the *Missouri Republican* was read until 1880 and the *St. Louis Post-Dispatch* from 1880 until 1920. At critical periods, other papers were consulted, particularly the *Missouri Democrat*, which became the *St. Louis Globe-Democrat* in 1875; the *Western Watchman*; *Anzeiger des Westens*; *Westliche Post*; *New Era*; and *Daily Union*. In addition, the St. Louis Public Library has two collections of clippings that are very useful for educational and political issues: *Benedicts Notebooks* for the 1870s and 1880s and *Civic League Notebooks* for 1905–1920. A compilation of available newspaper resources is found in William H. Taft, *Missouri Newspapers: When and Where 1803–1963* (Columbia: State Historical Society of Missouri, 1964).

There are numerous dissertations on public and parochial schools. Most, however, are reportorial, relying only on official records. Notable exceptions are Elinor M. Gersman, "Education in St. Louis, 1880–1900; A Case Study of Schools in Society" (Unpublished Ph.D. dissertation, Washington University, St. Louis, 1969), David J. Mahan, "The Influence of the Efficiency Movement on a Large Urban School System: A Case Study of the St. Louis Public Schools," (Unpublished D. Ed. dissertation, Washington University, St. Louis, 1968), and James D. Logsdon, "The Development of Public School Administration in St. Louis, Missouri," (Unpublished Ph.D. dissertation, University of Chicago, 1946). There are no comparable studies on parochial schools. This is an area that needs attention not only in St. Louis but in other cities. A useful start can be made with parish histories. The best collection on St. Louis is found in the library of Notre Dame University. In addition, there are several standard histories: John Rothensteiner, *History* of the Archdiocese of St. Louis in Its Various Stages of Development from A.D. 1673 to A.D. 1928 (St. Louis: Blackwell and Wielandy, 1928); J. A. Burns, The Catholic School System in the United States: Its Principles, Origin, and Establishment (New York: Benziger, 1908); and Walter H. Bek, Lutheran Elementary Schools in the United States: A Historical Development of Parochial Schools and Synodical Educational Policies and Programs (St. Louis: Concordia Publishing House, 1939).

There is a considerable body of useful secondary sources both scholarly and popular, although there are few recent monographs that touch on significant themes in the city's political, social, or economic history. Consequently, a necessary starting point for historical reconstruction is a review of city directories, which often contain important descriptive introductions. Related to this genre are Joseph A. Dacus and James Buel, A Tour of St. Louis; or, The Inside Life of a Great City (St. Louis: Western Publishing, 1878); J. O. Yeakle, The City of St. Louis Today: Its Progress and Prospects (St. Louis: M. M. Yeakle, 1889); and E. D. Kargau, Mercantile and Professional St. Louis (St. Louis: Nixon–Jones, 1902). A basic study of mid-century economic development is Wyatt W. Belcher, The Economic Rivalry between St. Louis and Chicago 1850–1880 (New York: Columbia University Press, 1947). An introduction to St. Louis politics may begin with Charles H. Cornwell, St. Louis Mayors: Brief Biographies (St. Louis: St. Louis Public Library, 1965); Thomas S. Barclay, "The Liberal Republican Movement in Missouri," Missouri Historical Review, 20, No. 2 (January 1926), and 21, No. 1 (October 1926); Louis Geiger, Joseph Folk of Missouri (Columbia: University of Missouri Press, 1953), and William E. Parrish, Turbulent Partnership: Missouri and the Union, 1861–1865 (Columbia, University of Missouri Press, 1963); and Missouri Under Radical Rule, 1865–1870 (Columbia: University of Missouri Press, 1965). Still important for a host of subjects are the largely turn-of-the-century urban biographies, especially Walter B. Stevens, St. Louis: The Fourth City, 1764–1909 (St. Louis: S. J. Clarke Publishing Co., 1909), 3 vols.; William Hyde and Howard Conrad, eds., Encyclopedia of the History of St. Louis (St. Louis: Southern History Company, 1889), 4 vols.; John Thomas Scharf, History of St. Louis City and County (Philadelphia: Lewis H. Everts, 1883), 2 vols.;

and Floyd Calvin Shoemaker, *Missouri and Missourians: Land of Contrasts and People of Achievements*, 5 vols. (Chicago: Lewis Publishing Co., 1943). For additional sources, consult Selwyn K. Troen, *A Guide to Resources on the History of Saint Louis* (St. Louis: Institute for Urban and Regional Studies, Washington University, 1971). Compiled as part of the research that was entailed in this study, it is a comprehensive bibliography on the city's history containing more than 2,000 items with a chronological and thematic index.

Index